THE EXTRAORDINARY LIFE OF
Rebecca West

Also by Lorna Gibb
LADY HESTER

THE EXTRAORDINARY LIFE OF

Rebecca
WEST

LORNA GIBB

COUNTERPOINT
BERKELEY

First published in Great Britain in 2013 by Macmillan
Typeset by SetSystems Ltd, Saffron Walden, Essex

Library of Congress Cataloging-in-Publication Data is available
ISBN 978-1-61902-306-2

COUNTERPOINT
1919 Fifth Street
Berkeley, CA 94710
www.counterpointpress.com

Printed in the United States of America
Distributed by Publishers Group West

10 9 8 7 6 5 4 3 2 1

In memory of my beloved dad,
IAN GIBB
1937–2011

And for our dearest friend,
PAUL COOMBS
1953–2007

Contents

PROLOGUE

꿍

A woman of surprising contradictions, socialist and Thatcherite, a defender of women's suffrage, a disciple of St Augustine and lover of H.G. Wells, successful novelist and astute, prophetic chronicler of the Near East: Dame Rebecca West was all of these, and more, much more. She engaged passionately with the events of almost a century. A uniquely talented personality, West was showered with rewards and tributes for her novels and journalism during her lifetime. Sadly her eclecticism was her undoing; her writing could not be categorized into those pigeon holes so beloved of the literati and her literary status was never as secure as that of contemporaries like Virginia Woolf.

Her success also brought domestic disharmony. Her son, the writer Anthony West, thought her a terrible mother, and the kind of familial disagreements normally played out within the family became a very public and acrimonious row, observed by hundreds, a kind of reality TV acted out by correspondence, the effects continuing even after Rebecca's death.

West's troubles were universal and timeless. The conflicting demands of motherhood and career, the longing for love and companionship tempered by the need for independence, were spelled out in letters and diaries, articles and books, while the world changed, bringing new dilemmas and consequences. Her struggles are as pertinent now as they have always been. West's private life was entwined with political events, the unfolding history of a century symbiotically related to the mundane and the personal, the minutiae of her life. Her diary entries and notebooks present something more than pictures from a lost age; they form a map showing the places we have come from.

When travelling in a region I always ask friends who have been there before me for advice on a book to take that will aptly capture or add to my experience. During such a trip in Eastern Europe *Black Lamb and Grey Falcon* was my introduction to Rebecca West. The friend who recommended it was a diplomat. He had been told to read this very large tome for a prior posting and had begun to do so somewhat reluctantly. It was the 1980s. Following Tito's death, Yugoslavia was faced with an economic crisis; Serbian nationalism, with Kosovo as its symbol, was growing rapidly. Some way into West's book, my friend, caught up in the local unrest, was hooked, finding answers to, and questions about, the things he was witnessing some fifty years after she had written it.

My own experience was the same, except my friend, like so many men enchanted by Rebecca's words, fell a little in love with the author too. This is part of West's skill, an ability to act as a social commentator on a period that was yet to come, and, while doing so, to beguile and enchant her reader.

Looking at my book collection, it seems that, of those books by West that I have acquired over the years, a disproportionate number were gifts. Three of her novels as well as *The Meaning of Treason, Henry James* and *St Augustine* were all delightful presents. For me, as for so many of my peers, West is a shared pleasure, passed on, read, then later discussed in dingy student Soho coffee shops in the eighties, or more recently, over wine at a picnic in a garden. Perhaps the most wonderful thing of all is that, because of the eclectic nature of West's writing, these exchanges could be on so many topics: literature, espionage, travel, the role of women, all originating from a book or article by a single author. West dealt with big topics, many of which still reverberate today, such as the integration of Eastern and Western religious faiths, the contradictions of femininity and power, the causes and effects of wars. Yet, in her consider-ations, she did not lose sight of the domestic concerns, those personal and intimate stories taking place against the backdrop of social change and unrest. As she once stated in an article for *The New Yorker*, she did not wish to write history as Gibbon liked to record it, but a history of the endless troubles of every-day life.

In a letter to V.S. Pritchett, written in July 1941, West lamented 'our curious national habit of writing monographs in one subject without looking into its context'. In West's own biographies she was careful not to make this mistake. Bernard Levin, in a 1981 Radio broadcast for the BBC, praised the 'astonishing world view' of her writing. The extraordinarily rapid developments of the twentieth century were a mirror to West's remarkable life. They were also the cause of many of that life's difficulties.

Rebecca West was a pseudonym, a moniker chosen hastily from an Ibsen play, because Rebecca didn't want her mother to see the family name displayed on a poster about an article she had written in support of women's suffrage. West was born Cicely Isabel Fairfield, in 1892; it was, she said, a 'Mary Pickford' of a name for someone blonde and pretty and wouldn't have suited a professional writer through life at all.[1] For Wells and for her son, she was Panther; for one of her lovers, Tommy, she was a firefly; and to her husband, Henry Andrews, she was both Cicely Andrews and Rebecca.

These many names came to represent different aspects of her personality. Rebecca West was a successful, feted writer and a shining success, loved by her friends and admirers. Rebecca once wrote to one of her closest confidantes, Emanie Arling, that she loved her most, of all her friends, because she called her Rebecca and never anything else. But Cicely Andrews was a lonely wife who felt that many of her friends pitied her for Henry's infidelities and laughed at her behind her back.

Her home in her last decade reflected this dualism. The front room was likened to a stage set by the people who worked for her. There, Rebecca, bewigged, with her hearing aid, glasses and exquisitely cut gowns, would greet visitors regally, like an actress in a play. The back part of the flat was where she cried out in the night for the dead husband who had betrayed her, where she piled her chaotic papers, and wept over her failing health.

When she was born, Queen Victoria was on the throne, Einstein had not written the theory of relativity, Tolstoy, Brahms and Oscar Wilde were still alive.* Her childhood years were spent at the end of a century that was imbued with the social mores and expectations of the fifty previous years. But from the beginning she embraced change. A keen suffragette, the teenage West volunteered for the Women's Social and Political Union and wrote engagingly on the position and plight of women.

The passionate political involvement of her youth enlivens her early journalism. Housework was 'domestic slavery to be shunned like rat poison',[2] and 'Never will woman be saved until she realizes it is a far, far better thing to keep a jolly public-house really well, than to produce a cathedral full of beautiful thoughts'.[3] Fearless and opinionated, she did not hesitate to take on some of the more established women of her day.

She championed the rights of women with illegitimate children (before she herself became one) and dismissed women's relegation to a domestic role. However, West remained steadfast in her belief that marriage was necessary, not only for a woman's emotional fulfilment, but, more surprisingly, for her artistic development. Explicitly, she felt that spinsterhood with its restrictive experience made women unable to understand, and therefore to depict, the character of half the population who were male: 'Spinsterhood is not necessarily a female quality. It is simply the limitation of experience to one's own sex, and consequently the regard of the other sex from an idealist point of view ...

----

* In his address at her memorial service on 21 April 1983, Bernard Levin reflected on this, as well as on the fact that many everyday objects, such as matches, razor blades, aspirins and zips, had not yet been invented.

The spinster is ridiculous because she is limited (I write as a most typical spinster).'[4]

◦◦◦

For most of her life, West struggled between these two opposing ideals. She had as little interest in the strident feminism of the seventies as in the puritanical feminism of the Pankhursts. Indeed it was because of the latter that she ultimately distanced herself from the WSPU (Women's Social and Political Union) and thus renounced an active part in the suffrage campaign. West's understanding of the female position was much softer, much more familiar and understandable to contemporary readers. Yes, she wrote angrily about the necessity of better working conditions for women and dismissed the 'playing at wage earning' which she observed to be fashionable by encouraging women to genteel activities whilst so many other women worked in terrible conditions to make a meagre living, their plight overlooked. But there is far more of a thirty-something lonely heart than of a radical feminist in her plaintive letters to her favourite sister about her lack of success in finding a 'boof', their slang for a beautiful boy. More than once she remarked to friends that there was nothing as sad and lonely as the lot of a woman who did not have a man.

While her youthful relationships with much older men were unremarkable for someone of her generation, her long marriage to a younger man was far less usual for a woman born in the nineteenth century than it would be for one in her thirties today.

In her writing on the domestic side of two world wars, we are given an intimate glimpse of the home front. From her personal correspondence during the 1910s, we see how her own position as mistress of H.G. Wells, and ultimately mother of his illegitimate son, clashed with the accepted behaviour of the era. For almost a decade the illicit relationship between Wells and West was carried on like a script for a B-movie. Their carefully constructed alter egos (after all, both participants were writers) plotted subterfuges and arranged clandestine trips. Yet, most bizarrely, this was not in order to keep the affair private from Wells' wife, who knew and accepted the situation, but rather to avoid the public censure that might seriously affect Wells' successful career if it became known.

～∽◦∽～

West's son by Wells, Anthony, was born on the eve of Britain's entry to the First World War. But while Wells saw his journalism and writing reach an ever larger readership as he charted and predicted the course of the war, West felt that any joy in motherhood was subsumed by fear of the international situation. Later, that apprehension became frustration at being trapped at home with the small tediums of wartime restriction when she too could have been writing about the turmoil. The writing she did produce at this time records beautifully the difficulties and aggravations of the home front, but also the pain and longing of an impossible relationship against a backdrop of war.

Her great work on Yugoslavia, *Black Lamb and Grey Falcon*, took five years to complete and was to establish West as a brilliant non-fiction writer. Read today, it is an astonishingly predictive work. Weaving hard facts with West's own impressions and the fictitious characters she used as a means of transmitting ideas, it presents a country on the brink of dissolution and is still regarded by many experts as the best account we have. Yet West's astute and, at times, harsh deliberations are tempered by continually gentle and admiring references to her husband of thirty years, Henry Andrews. Writing was the thread that bound together West's public and personal worlds, her political judgements and her private tenderness.

Through West's journalism we can see the unfolding of an age. We share her observations of Fabian socialism, the birth of Fascism, espionage, McCarthyism, apartheid and Thatcherism. From her personal correspondence we see the parallel, private worlds of the Roaring Twenties, the parties with Scott and Zelda Fitzgerald, friendships including those with Shaw and Chaplin, and more difficult associations with Virginia Woolf and Max

Beaverbrook. Her judgement of people, situations and literature was generally extreme: F.R. Leavis used 'fastidiousness like a *nouveau riche* who buys asparagus tongs for eating asparagus'.[5] T.S. Eliot was responsible for the 'sustained grizzle' of modern literature, the notion that 'the only respectable status is discontent'.[6]

Inevitably, because her work was public, her private life became so too. The difficulties that she faced with motherhood, her gentle concern for her son, Anthony West's welfare, and the carefully constructed deceits to protect him from any awareness of the difficulties of his own situation, returned to her with a spectacular and understandable vengeance.

Rebecca, who once wrote to Oscar Wilde's son that she was glad that a volume of his father's letters moved the focus away from his homosexuality towards his writing, was forever burdened by her notoriety as the mistress of H.G. Wells. Just as sometimes her reputation seemed overshadowed by her former association, so did her personal life become tormented and unhappy, largely as a result of her heartbreaking relationship with her son. Anthony, unable to communicate with his mother any other way, wrote *Heritage*, a pastiche of his troubled childhood, his very public retaliation against his 'mother's passionate desire to do me harm'.[7]

West's bewilderment about this account is by turns touching and strangely imperceptive. It seems that the meticulous and brilliant observations that West made of the world did little to help her comprehend the changes happening much closer to her home.

In another illustration of her imperceptiveness in personal matters, we see the tragedy of West's later years, when, after her husband's death, she found a stash of letters, photos and cards that revealed the extent of his many infidelities, hidden from her throughout their long marriage. She acknowledged that the marriage had not been as she had tried to believe it was: 'I pretend to have been happily married to Henry, whereas I was wretched with him'.[8]

She was married to Henry Maxwell Andrews for thirty-eight years, but he stopped making love to her within a couple of years of their marriage. Despite the accolades brought by success, a DBE, a *Légion D'honneur*, a Yugoslavian Sava, she never regained her confidence in her sexuality, or even in her attractiveness to the opposite sex. Her brief affairs both before and after her marriage were unsatisfactory and seemed only to highlight her own fears. When news of Henry's indiscretions with a range of women from all social spheres reached her, she blamed the sexlessness of their marriage and her own unattractiveness as often as she blamed Henry's poor mental health, caused by the cerebral arteriosclerosis that she thought might have gnawed away at his sense of right and wrong.

She was the chronicler of her time, revelling in momentous global events, yet somehow, like so many of us, never quite getting the hang of how to live. Happiness eluded her. Often she despaired of her own passions and her ability to hold back. The outspoken opinions that made much of her writing so compelling were her own undoing. She lamented, 'It seems that, on reflection, I do not behave as I would have liked to. Why do I spoil things by noisiness and impulsiveness?'[9]

She proudly referred to herself as a 'news hen' and often bemoaned the difficulties for women of the time in that profession. In post-war London, she hung around anti-Semitic demonstrations, in dimly lit, vaguely dangerous districts of North London, and reported on them. Her journalism had captured the uneasy peace, the nervousness that followed the Second World War, yet also gave a clue to her own contradictory nature. At the country home she shared with Henry at Ibstone in Buckinghamshire, she took walks with her dog Albert, basked in her surroundings, but then despaired of the isolation and loneliness that long winters brought.

∽≈∾

In September 2010, when I was approaching the end of the years I had spent researching and writing this book, I had lunch with a former employee of Rebecca West. Liz Leyshon was Rebecca's secretary in the late seventies. Originally we had met up some years back so I could listen to Liz's memories of her time with Rebecca. However, we soon found out we had a lot in common and became friends, affording a late-afternoon, postprandial stroll the combined pleasure of the comfort of friendship and the anticipation of a new glimpse of the woman I was trying so hard to capture.

We walked through Hyde Park to Princes Gate, and the apartment where Rebecca lived until she died, after Ibstone, with its memories of her husband and the life they had shared. We spoke to the doorman and walked through the hallway, carpeted in red – it had been green in Rebecca's time – to the garden. This was the place Rebecca had called 'the recreation ground for the dead', where she had imagined a kind of ghost of Henry standing below the trees, 'his spectacled face turned upwards'.[10] But it was also the apartment where she had written the long rambling journal in which she described the pain of Henry's infidelity with a beautiful ballet dancer, and where she had learned of the horrible death of her beloved great-grandchild.

I stood in the garden and looked up at the narrow balcony, where I was told Rebecca loved to sit on clement days, and thought of those last years of hers. So little had been written about them and yet they were filled with as much spirit and sadness and conflict as all the decades that had gone before. But it wasn't Rebecca's vision of Henry I saw beneath the shady alder tree whose leaves made dappled light patterns all over her living room, or even the grand old lady herself, Dame Rebecca West, familiar from so many television interviews, not a woman in her eighties, but rather a young, giggling Cissie Fairfield. I thought of the Cissie who ran around Max Beaverbrook's garden in the old black-and-white film clip I'd seen in a British Library cubicle. There she was, laughing by the rose bushes, flirting madly with a handsome young man, running down the path, then turning to shout back at her beau in that lovely actressy rich voice. Not a beautiful girl in the classical sense, but someone you were compelled to watch, someone who lit up the garden and commanded it. Then she was gone: the long white frock, the piled auburn hair, faded from my mind, leaving the garden and, more importantly, her words, millions upon millions of them, the only things that might help me conjure her again.

Chapter One

SCHUMANN AND THE
SHABBY PROSPERO

It was the first family home she could recollect. Sixty-six years after the Fairfield family moved out, Rebecca West still recalled the address: 21 Streatham Place, by Brixton Hill. Over time, her memories of the semi-detached, slightly dowdy Regency villa in South London became increasingly idyllic. The overgrown garden with its green woodpecker, and the magical, voluminous elder tree and grove of graceful chestnuts stayed in Rebecca's imagination. Generous high-ceilinged rooms, filled with fine, antique furniture worn beyond its best, and settled into shabby gentility, became the background of the first remembered years of a haphazard, but happy childhood. And, even in later years, the legacy of the ramshackle garden would remain: the scent of the elder tree would fill her with 'mystery and joy'.[1]

In 1894, when the family settled there, Rebecca, then Cicely Isabel Fairfield, was just two years old, the youngest of three girls. Letitia, the eldest, was seven, while Winifred was five. Their parents, Charles and Isabella Fairfield, had chosen the area largely for practical reasons. Streatham was the only London suburb with all-night trams, convenient for Charles, who worked, albeit intermittently, as a journalist.

In those days, Streatham had an added advantage for the little girls. As part of the celebrations for Queen Victoria's Diamond Jubilee in 1897, many of her Indian troops were brought to London and billeted there for up to two years. These lavishly dressed, turbaned men loved nothing better than fussing over children in their baby carriages as they passed in the park. Cicely, known to her family as Cissie, was a dark child, and later she wondered if this was what had made her particularly appealing to the homesick soldiers. They would lean over her carriage, gesture to see if they might stroke the child within and watch delightedly as Cissie grabbed out to reach the hilt of a dagger whose precious stones and gleaming metal glittered in the sunlight. Occasionally these visitors even came to the house, presenting small gifts and sweets for the children and delighting in Charles' few words of Hindustani, learned by the side of his older brother, Digby, while the latter was preparing for a commission in India. Charles relished these encounters, impressing upon the children that they had to treat the Asiatic visitors with respect at all times, to compensate for the ignorance of other, stupid people in the country who would undoubtedly insult them. Isabella was by turns amused and wary.

The house, it seemed, was always filled with sound. Isabella was from a musical family; she played the piano expertly and at times used her skill to earn a living for herself and her family. Beethoven sonatas and Schumann's 'Carnaval' echoed through the rooms and out onto the street, causing passersby to stand at the Fairfield door to listen, and imbuing a lifelong love of music in each of the girls. Political discussions and arguments were audible from Charles' study. Stories were told by both Isabella and Charles, in the evenings after dinner. The house had an air that was 'thick with conversation'.[2] But the liveliness of this home atmosphere, the longing of the neighbours, straining to hear the music from the Fairfield drawing room, belied the truth of the family's situation. The Fairfields were a family steadfastly aiming for respectability but constantly pulled back by debts and money difficulties, mainly attributable to Charles' irresponsibility.

Charles Fairfield had achieved some success as a writer and caricaturist for the *Glasgow Herald* and the *Melbourne Argus*; his political beliefs tended towards the right and he was a key member of the anti-socialist society the Liberty and Property Defence League. Charles and Isabella had spent the earliest years of their relationship in Australia and Charles wrote disapprovingly of the state socialism he observed there, claiming that it preached 'to willing disciples the despicable gospel of shirking, laziness, mendicancy, and moral cowardice'.[3] Charles believed in educating his daughters, thinking that they could better raise children and run a house if they were educated, but opposed women's suffrage, writing articles for the *Argus* which criticized suffragettes and labelled them as 'strange shipwrecked, lost souls'.[4]

He did not drink but his abstemiousness regarding alcohol contrasted with his sexual licentiousness. Not only was he promiscuous, but he had a marked predilection for women employed by Isabella as governesses and servants, as well as for prostitutes he picked up on the street.[5] Isabella was aware of his affairs and would challenge him, asking if he meant to leave the family and marry whatever woman he was dallying with at the time. His reply was always the same: 'Good gracious no, I certainly don't intend to marry them!'[6] Additionally he had a 'stock gambling mania' that meant the few things of value the family did have were sold or pawned in the pursuit of promised riches that never materialized.[7] While they were living in Streatham one of the last heirlooms, a family portrait, was sold to provide food and rent, and Cissie regarded it as miraculous that the painting had managed to escape his speculations for so long.

The sisters grew up believing that Charles' family background was Irish and aristocratic. Property in Ireland, although mortgaged more than once and in a state of disrepair, supplemented the family's meagre resources with rental income throughout the girls' childhood. Despite Charles' womanizing and gambling, his undeniable charm meant that he retained a kind of romantic veneer for his youngest daughter; he would be portrayed as the 'shabby Prospero' in her novel *The Fountain Overflows*. Charles was the magical father in hand-me-down clothes, a brooding figure who looked 'exotic, romantic, and a zealot'.[8] She proudly observed the farm girls flirting with him when they went together to buy milk and was captivated by his 'physical maleness'.[9] She loved his 'extraordinary intellectual liveliness'.[10] It was an idealized perception, a child's adoration of her father, but, in time, it would shadow every serious romantic relationship that Cissie ever had.

Charles was a skilled horseman and a gifted orator, family stories abounded about his brilliance. In one frequently recounted tale he was said to have held his own in a debate against George Bernard Shaw. Charles and the younger Irish immigrant Shaw debated all night in the Conway Hall until a weary caretaker came and turned out the lights. While she was growing up, Cissie was quick to draw comparisons between her father's personality and her own. She loved the fact that he kept late hours, just as she loved and took great delight in his approbation. She enjoyed recalling a time in Streatham when Charles found her playing in the garden soil. He asked her what she was doing and she explained that she was digging up conkers she had buried earlier. When he asked why, she replied, 'I am God and they are people, and I made them die and now I am resurrecting them.' Puzzled, but obviously impressed, Charles sat beside her and continued, 'But why did you make the people die if you meant to dig them up again? Why didn't you just leave them alone?' Cissie replied, 'Well that would have been all right for them. But it would have been no fun for me.'[11] His amusement and admiration were obvious even to a toddler, and she ran to him and was swung up into his arms. When Charles related the conversation to his wife, he said that his daughter 'had blown the whole gaffe', and he saw an exciting future for her 'on the lines of the atheist popes of the middle ages'.[12]

Charles took his impoverished family to Regents Park and Hyde Park to teach them the 'points of the horse', even though the family's social position was not one where such knowledge was useful or relevant.[13] His was the air of a chaotically driven man, compelled to try to be the best at everything that mattered to him, and even more importantly to be seen to be better than any of his peers. Beyond that, even the doting Cissie conceded 'he had not a moral idea in the world'. Isabella attributed the downturn in family fortunes to Charles' recklessness, but his personal history was far more sinister than either his wife or daughters knew.[14*†]

Charles Fairfield was born in County Kerry to an army officer who was a minor landowner, and his second wife.[15] He was one of five children, with three brothers, Digby, Arthur and Edward, and a sister, Lettie. Digby went to India with the Royal Artillery and was dead of cholera by the age of only twenty-five. Arthur went on to marry a woman called Sophie Blew Jones. Her tales of her brother-in-law's early life were dismissed as fantasy by Cissie, who loathed her dreaded Aunt Sophie. At just over seventeen, Charles enlisted as an ensign in the Rifle Brigade, and was subsequently promoted to lieutenant. Based in his company's depot, he made the most of London, joining a club and the Royal United Service Institute. The Institute occupied several buildings between Whitehall Yard and New Scotland Yard and included a museum which was open to the public, and a library exclusively for the members' use.

The library and the museum housed a very impressive collection of books, coins, medals and regimental badges and were designed to be of interest to the intellectual officer looking for a good place to relax in a convenient location. Charles enjoyed these but also sought entertainment befitting an officer, in hunting and steeplechasing, becoming a moderately successful rider. Putting horses into races cost money and so he subsidized his activities on the turf by gambling – for quite considerable sums of money. His army career was short-lived and he resigned

---

* It is possible that Isabella or the eldest child, Lettie, knew more than they ever told the others. Alison Selford, Winnie's daughter (one of Cissie's sisters), told me in an interview that she thought only Lettie of the girls might have had even an inkling about Charles' early disgrace. However, the revelations about Charles came as a complete surprise to everyone in the family now living.

† Memoirs D, 2/51/7: 'A long time before he married my father had realized and spent [what] he had inherited from his parents, and my mother saw this as the cause of our poverty', Tulsa.

his commission only three years after becoming a lieutenant. He had served for just seven years and five months; four years had been spent at the depot and more than two years on leave, at a time when almost all of his contemporaries were on active service overseas.

Charles moved back with his mother and brothers and briefly took up a career on the stage, joining a company that specialized in burlesques of popular plays. Then, at the age of twenty-seven, Charles left London and his family, boarding the *City of Baltimore* and arriving in New York on 24 March 1868.[16] But he no sooner set foot in America than he booked another passage and mysteriously sailed straight back to London. He applied for a post as Secretary at the Soldiers' Daughters' Home soon after his arrival. The charity had an office in Whitehall and ran a hostel at Rosslyn Hill in Hampstead. While waiting to hear about his application, penurious after his American trip, Charles visited his club and the Institute Library. The cabinets filled with coins, medals and badges proved too much of a temptation and, over the following two months, Charles stole more than four hundred specimens, making a half-hearted attempt to cover his theft by cutting out pages from the manuscript catalogue that related to some of the items he had taken.

He traded in the valuables he had hoarded, selling them at gold- and silversmiths in Soho, Covent Garden and the City, and less flamboyantly, at pawnbrokers, including one in St Martin's Lane. With the jewellers he used his own name, but with the pawnbrokers, he was more discreet. His final visit to the library was to lift a two-volume edition of Coleridge's letters. The goods found their way back to someone who recognized them and, a week later, when Charles returned to the library, he was detained. He was wearing one of the stolen gold coins, as if it were a medal, attached to his jacket.

He was quickly identified by a wholesaler from Garrick Street as the man who had sold him the stolen goods; Charles confessed, going so far as to volunteer the information that he had been cutting pages out of the catalogues to obscure how much he had actually stolen. Charles' mother, Arabella, and his brothers, Arthur and Edmund, were stunned and began their own search of the house in Pimlico as soon as news of his arrest reached them.

∽∾∽

On 1 October 1868, Charles was brought before Bow Street magistrates' court. Charles' former rank and good family meant that the case garnered a huge amount of publicity. The trial was covered in the London papers and the story was syndicated across the country; Charles was identified by name and by his battalion in the Rifle Brigade.[17] Some headlines hinted darkly at the possibility of insanity. The second hearing came two weeks later and one of his brothers obligingly produced the pages from the coin catalogue which he had found stuffed and hidden in a drawer in Charles' bedroom. Additionally, there were sixteen gold and thirty-seven silver coins at home, which Charles had not had time to sell. Charles pleaded guilty and his barrister pleaded mitigation on the grounds of unsound mind. It was the only option; theft of such a magnitude could carry a prison sentence of up to twenty years. His actions did not seem entirely rational; his failure even to try to hide his crime, once it had been discovered, and the brazen way in which he had conducted it did not seem reasonable in the light of his evident intelligence. The court concluded that Charles did understand the nature of his crime, but made no explicit judgement as to whether he was sane or not.

Charles was sentenced to five years' penal servitude, an exceptionally light sentence given the gravity of his offence, and his family were left to decide whether to appeal to the Home Secretary for leniency. They did not. He was taken to Pentonville and immediately assessed as 'delicate' and 'thin', weighing just a little over ten stone, despite being five foot nine in height.[18] The weeks in custody had taken their toll on his officer's physique. There was an added surprise; at some point he had been infected with syphilis.[19] This was a secret, like his criminality, that

Charles would keep throughout his life. Charles' family continued to visit him, despite the shame of his imprisonment, and when he was finally released, it was on licence to his old home address in St George's Square.

When Arabella died, less than two years after Charles' release, she left the St George's Square house to Arthur and Edward as well as equal shares in the Irish property. To Charles, a testament to his disgrace, she left only £600, less £50 she had already loaned him on his release from prison. When Edward died childless, he too did not include his black-sheep brother as an heir, instead dividing his inheritance between Arthur and Isabella. [20]

A decade after Charles left prison he sailed to Australia aboard the *John Elder*. In Melbourne he met Isabella Campbell Mackenzie, thirteen years his junior. They married in 1883 and settled in St Kilda, a suburb of the city, to have a family. The missing years before his voyage, Cissie came to believe, were spent in America. She later told her sisters that their mother was Charles' second wife, and that he had been married to a woman called Allison, and given her a little boy. Cissie claimed to have found and met her half-brother, but the rest of the family, who were never introduced, remained sceptical as to whether he existed or not.

Isabella Campbell Mackenzie was a Scotswoman. Her immediate family included a brother, Sir Alexander Mackenzie, who was the principal of the Royal Academy of Music. Isabella had made her own living, prior to her marriage, by working as a musical governess to a wealthy family in London. Her employees, the Heinemanns, were a cosmopolitan couple, a Jewish businessman from Hanover, naturalized as British, and his American wife; they had eight children. Isabella taught the two daughters, Emily and Clara, and the family were so taken with her that after she left she received a small pension from the mother, who had become as much of a friend as an employer. The relationship between Isabella and her former pupils also endured and the eldest daughter, Emily Bolland, became Cissie's godmother.

Acutely aware of the importance of appearances, Isabella worked hard to give her children some of the trappings of a middle-class life. But the concerts and theatre and clothes she saw as essential dwindled further and further away from financial reality each year. The time she had spent in St Kilda, just after her marriage to Charles, became imbued with nostalgia. When she spoke of their house near the beach, of swimming in the sea with her eldest children, her voice filled with longing.

In Britain, she searched tirelessly for scholarships and awards that might give her daughters the education she could otherwise not afford. Yet education was more than good schooling, and she allowed Cissie to play truant so she could see Sarah Bernhardt in a matinee. Isabella was ingenious at finding new ways to rescue the family from poverty. Typewriting was a new skill, much in demand, so she took classes, briefly supporting her daughters by typing for a couple of American evangelists, Torry and Alexander. When they learned of her musical abilities, she took charge of that side of their sermons too, whacking 'the Glory song out on the grand piano on the platform'.[21] Her daughter thought it 'a very noble thing to do'.[22]

By the time the family settled in Streatham, Charles' womanizing and squandering had led to a breakdown in the relationship between him and his wife. It was no longer a happy marriage. Cissie had been the result of an unsuccessful attempt at reconciliation between her parents and after her birth they slept in separate rooms.[23] For Cissie, her parents' relationship would always be 'the marriage of loneliness to loneliness'.[24]

Just two years after the family settled in their South London house, the Dreyfus case dominated the press and Charles quickly took it up as a terrible miscarriage of justice, championing Dreyfus. In 1894, a small counter-intelligence unit of the French army, the Statistical Section, received word that information about the French army was being passed on to the enemy – a discarded memorandum had been found in a waste-paper basket in the German Embassy in Paris. On inspection, the French General Staff concluded that this information was important and secret and furthermore could only have been passed on by an artilleryman. Captain Alfred Dreyfus was suspected, for no better reason than his handwriting was deemed to have some similarity to that of the memorandum. This was scant evidence, and – added to the fact that there were no clearly defined consequences of the purported crime – the whole thing should have been dropped. But Dreyfus was Jewish and anti-Semitism was rife. Just two weeks after his arrest, the press named Dreyfus, and the anti-Semitic daily *La Libre Parole* capitalized on the opportunity. Dreyfus was court-martialled and sentenced to life imprisonment on Devil's Island, a former leper colony. Charles' stance was unusual for the time; Letitia remembered the frequent debates in the house, later pointing out that 'from the English point of view there wasn't much concern at that time about anti-Semitism'.[25]

Just one year later, in 1895, in a tragic echo of the much-more-publicized event, Charles' brother Edward Fairfield, then Assistant Undersecretary at the Colonial Office, found himself cast as the victim in another miscarriage of justice. The Jameson Raid, as it was known, was supported by the Colonial Secretary, Joseph Chamberlain. Volunteers, supporting a rebellion of pre-dominantly British settlers who hoped to create a united South Africa, led by Sir Leander Starr Jameson, attempted to raid the Boer colony of the Transvaal. The foray was opposed by Edward, who was convinced that it would replace the anti-African Boer government with something still more dangerous. His position was in direct opposition to that of his superior, Chamberlain.

In July, Edward Fairfield seemed to be vindicated when the raiders, who had, after all, launched an attack on a friendly state without any declaration of war, were put on trial in England and convicted. Four were condemned to death, although not actually killed, others were sent to prison.[26] But Edward, who had so vehemently argued against the action, found himself a scapegoat for Chamberlain, and was charged with sending approval for the raid to go ahead.

Broken by the stress and the public shame, Edward died in 1897, still waiting for the hearing that might have cleared his name. When Charles heard, he went into Cissie's bedroom and opened her curtains wide to the night-time. He lay down on the bed beside his nine-year-old daughter and she heard him humming softly to her. His soft music gave way at first to sobs, and then to quiet tears as they rested together, watching the branches of a tree swaying in the starlight.

Edward's legacy was to leave his nieces with 'a very acute sense of what the real meaning of empire was – if you got people who were killing each other and slaughtering each other and putting out their children to be eaten by jackals and lived under terror of ghosts – you brought what you thought was civilization to them'.[27] One of Cissie's earliest published articles would begin: 'There are two kinds of imperialists – imperialists and bloody imperialists.'[28] Still later, the Dreyfus case would represent for her an early form of Fascism: 'The crux of the case was that it didn't matter whether Dreyfus was guilty or not, you mustn't spoil the image of the army. That was more or less Fascist.'[29]

Her sister Lettie acknowledged the significance more explicitly. It was one of the most formative events of their life, because it showed the children how important politics could be, 'that they couldn't be kept remote from one's personal life'.[30]

For Cissie, Streatham was 'a dark place with something like light pouring out through the windows, but it was not light, it was the force pulsing out of our family'.[31] But her elder sister, Lettie, had a less romantic view of it. As an adult she remembered it as that 'dreadful little hovel'.[32] It was not the only matter on which the two disagreed. Lettie was the bane of Cissie's childhood. She believed that her elder sister resented her, regarding her as 'a revolting intruder in her home'. Lettie's capacity for unprovoked 'sullen anger' and her jibes at Cissie that she was 'a destructive child' frightened her younger sister and coloured their relationship throughout their lives.[33] When Lettie did deign to speak to her, Cissie thought it was always with 'rage in her voice' and a constant aim to humiliate her.[34]

This was in complete contrast to the middle sister, Winnie. Rebecca thought Winnie lovely, in later life even saying she had

been 'the most beautiful child' she had ever seen.[35] Always
perceived by Cissie as kind and gentle, Winnie read poetry to
her younger sister and went walking with her, hand in hand. In
1897, when both Lettie and Winnie contracted meningitis and
were close to death, it was Winnie's recovery that Cissie awaited
and rejoiced in, because she would again have someone 'to walk
with me who would pick me up if I fell and pluck me back if I
started to cross the road without making sure it was clear'.[36] The
sisters had a series of nicknames for each other, some of which
lasted over the years. Cissie was 'Anne', a name derived in fun
from her childhood pronunciation of Antelope, and her insistence that 'Anne Telloppy' was the way it should be said. The
name stuck, so that for years afterwards she still signed letters to
her sisters as 'Anne'. Winnie and Lettie were known as Podge or
Cow and Frisk.

Charles' arrangement with the *Melbourne Argus* came to an
end in 1897, and the change in economic circumstances necessitated another house-move. Their new home, in Richmond, was
unanimously disliked by the three sisters, but its cost was far
more suited to the family's meagre budget. It was a run-down
eight-bedroomed place with a small garden, on Hathersage Road.
Isabella's Scottish relatives still thought this 'extravagant madness' at £60 per year, but it was cheap by London standards at
the time.[37]

Charles stayed with his family for only three more years.
While he admired his wife and was proud of his daughters, Cissie
realized 'he felt no desire to keep or assist us in any way'. In 1900
Charles left London, and his family, for Sierra Leone, where he
hoped to launch a pharmaceuticals factory. Charles wrote to
Lettie, now sixteen years old, from Kensington before his departure: 'This is a venture on which I go.'[38] He was sixty years old
and seemed to Lettie to have no more sense of responsibility
than his youngest child.

The family was divided still further when Lettie was accepted
at the Medical School of Edinburgh University. She had won a
grant from the Carnegie Trust to help with the fees. Isabella's

aging mother was in poor health and so Isabella travelled to Edinburgh with her eldest daughter, to look for a home so that the family might relocate there. In the meantime, Cissie would go as a boarder to a school in Bournemouth, where Jessie Watson Campbell, one of her cousins, taught music and French.

Charles' venture in Sierra Leone failed. Unsurprisingly, given his age and lack of relevant experience. He only managed to scrape the return fare home as far as the Elder Dempster Docks in Liverpool. There he stayed for five years, living just a mile from the docks, in Toxteth, eking out an existence in the back room of a boarding house by copying documents. Destitute as he was, he did not return to his wife and children, believing he would bring them more hardship than comfort in his reduced circumstances. When he died, in that same dingy room, his wife was sent to collect his body. It lay in a narrow cot bed. All of his possessions, even his studs and cufflinks and the battered old dressing case he'd first set out with, were gone, presumably sold or pawned. Beside his corpse the doctor who attended him had found scrawled messages on scraps of paper, declaring his love for his wife and his daughters.[39] It was one of these notes, with the words 'Bad News. Come immediately' written on the back, that had summoned his widow.[40] Isabella alone attended and arranged the simple burial. The grave remained bare until Lettie arranged for a kerb and inscription in 1927. Afterwards, Isabella went to Liverpool cathedral, where, tears streaming down her cheeks, she listened to a choirboy with a pure and sweet voice, singing 'I know that my Redeemer liveth'.[41] Before travelling home, she visited the boarding house a final time. There, she had a chance meeting with a young clerk, a fellow boarder of her late husband's, whom Charles seemed to have befriended in his last two years. Charles had been a competent Spanish speaker and helped the young man prepare for an exam. The clerk said to her, 'At first we didn't believe all his stories of great men, he talked as if he had known them, and then I went to the Public Library and checked up on some stories, and of course, they were all true.'[42] The stories were all that remained. Cissie wrote, 'If he had been found dead in a hedgerow he could not have been more picked bare of possessions.'[43]

A regimental badge, left behind when Charles departed for Africa, was the only memento Cissie had of the father she adored. She kept it with her, displaying it in flats and houses, in the middle of the mantelpiece, the only item she had that 'he could ever have held in his hand'.[44]

Chapter Two

DISTURBING SPIRITS

The family settled in Edinburgh. Isabella found them a house that was both convenient for Lettie's studies and large enough for them to be comfortable. Their new home was in the Meadows, at 2 Hope Park Square, on the corner of a run-down area but overlooking the Park on one side and the backs of houses of George Square on the other. It had three bedrooms, a dining room and a drawing room but no garden, and at just £16 per year meant they could all survive on the allowance Isabella still received in conjunction with her earnings. Isabella realized on her husband's departure that she was going to have to find some way of supporting her family. Her odd typing jobs had grown into a small business and, assisted by her youngest daughter, she regularly typed manuscripts for several clients, including the music faculty of Edinburgh University.

Finances were still precarious and the family was thrown into further apprehension when Isabella's benefactress, Mrs Heinneman, passed away. But fortunately Mrs Heinneman's eldest daughter, Cissie's godmother, Emily Bolland, despite money problems of her own, continued to honour her mother's gift. For Isabella, Edinburgh meant a quieter life than she had enjoyed in London, limited by working, caring for her mother and by the fact that her thirty-year absence meant that she had lost most of the friends she had ever had in the area.

Arthur Fairfield's widow, Sophie, came to visit and the twelve-year-old Cissie was appalled by her attitude to her and

Winnie. Aunt Sophie insisted they were a burden on their mother, a fact that Cissie found absurd given that both she and Winnie had scholarships by this time; only Lettie escaped her censure. In fact it was a gift of £100 from Aunt Sophie that enabled Lettie to take up her medical award. Aunt Sophie also told critical stories of their late father, tales that were dismissed by Cissie as malicious and untrue, but were less of an invention than the girls suspected. Aunt Sophie was 'the terror of my childhood, a coarse-featured and coarse-voiced harridan, who always seemed drunk though sober'.[1] Cissie also felt that her attitude further consolidated Lettie's sense of superiority to her sisters, increasing the tension that already existed between them. Lettie's age may have contributed to her less-defensive attitude towards their father; she remembered more of what had gone on. For her, he would always have a 'sense of degradation about him'.[2] Decades later, in 1956, Rebecca was still writing to a friend lamenting about the malicious story about her father that had been repeated by a hated relative over the years, a story that she was sure was a lie.[3]

When money was very short, Isabella fed her children and starved herself so that she seemed almost skeletally thin and haggard to her daughters.[4] Cissie remembered family meals as a 'dreary diet of bread and butter, porridge and eggs and milk'.[5] But despite the difficulties, Cissie always said that her greatest defence against the sorrows of her life, in her later years, was the heritage from both of her parents. They both had a tremendous capacity for joy, which could override even the most meagre of surroundings: her father, concentrating on his delicate watercolours, and glowing as he discussed a political idea; her mother playing Schumann or teaching her daughters to admire the splendour and grace of Hampton Court.

The girls tried to make the best of their new situation. Winnie left Edinburgh to return south, in order to take up a scholarship at Cheltenham Ladies College, the famous boarding school. And when the family moved again, to a flat at 24 Buccleuch Place, Cissie gained a bursary to nearby George

Watson's Ladies College. Cissie was well educated there; her subjects included Latin, Greek and music. Beyond school, and in spite of their economic struggles, Isabella continued to try to sustain the girls' cultural education, managing to take her daughters to classical concerts so that they saw both Debussy and Saints-Saëns perform.

Yet, in spite of their good upbringing and education, the girls remained painfully aware of what they saw as their inability to fit in. Edwardian social life was defined by class, and the girls' lack of money and run-down lodgings were not compatible with the expectations of their schoolmates. They did not belong to either the working or the middle class and found friendships and social opportunities difficult as a result.

The matter was brought home to them when Lettie and Cissie were invited to visit Emily Bolland, at her home in the Midlands. They travelled together, worrying about the shoddiness of their clothes, hoping that their hosts would be 'too kind to mind', but looking forward to evenings of music and intellectual conversation. Instead they found themselves made fully aware of the lowliness of their social position in comparison with that of Emily and reminded that they were, after all, just 'the former governess's children'.[6]

Cissie's health was shaky and a tubercular infection of the left lung caused her schooling to end prematurely in 1907, although not before she had won the best-essay prize. Her illness necessitated long periods of rest and the convalescence thus enforced on the young girl seemed to make her reflective; she read voraciously, passing hours in the Carnegie Library, and wrote notebooks and diaries. Eventually these gave way to an unfinished autobiographical novel, The Sentinel.[7]

As her health improved, she began to take advantage of Edinburgh's proximity to the countryside and wrote to Lettie, now working at a Jewish hospital in Manchester, of her invigorating hikes around the Pentlands. However, far from behaving with the decorum that would have been expected on these walks, Cissie was already beginning to rebel against the expectations of society. She reported proudly to her sister that she alone of the small party of women dared to climb up Habbie's Howe, and went on to explain that it was made all the easier because she'd taken her shoes and stockings off and run along the heather barefoot. Her descent was carefully observed, much to her amusement, by three pairs of opera glasses, behind which stood a rather conservative American woman dressed in rich black silk and large hat, her very henpecked-looking husband, and their subdued son. When Cissie reached the bottom they had disappeared, but after paddling in the river, she turned a corner to find them picnicking together. It was too much for them, and unable to hide their horror at her impropriety, they stood suddenly, dropping their lunch and shouting, 'Why! She hasn't got her shoes and stockings on yet!'[8]

Despite the family's pleasure in the outings and little joys that Edinburgh offered them, money was still a constant concern. When Isabella became ill with diphtheria and was taken into hospital, the rent fell into arrears. A cheque arrived from Ireland too late and could not be endorsed by the seriously ailing woman. Recently vaccinated against diphtheria, and consequently feeling ill, as well as sick with worry for her mother, Cissie had to go to the landlord alone and beg for more time to pay. He acquiesced, but not before shouting at the pathetic figure in front of him.

Edinburgh, as well as London and Manchester, had been a centre for women's suffrage since the movement's inception in 1867. The original groups were small but vocal, with committed, campaigning members who had managed to grow the number of active organizations to over seventy by the time Cissie was fifteen. Charles had always been passionately opposed to the idea of the female vote, partly because of its link to the socialist movement. It was not until he left for Africa that two of his daughters, Lettie and Cissie, quickly became enthusiastic supporters of the cause. Cissie joined the Edinburgh 'Votes For Women' club, a sort of 'secret militant society'. Lettie, in Manchester, became a vanguard member of the Women's Social and Political Union. The WSPU and its sister organizations were vibrant groups made up of women united by idealism, who, uniquely for the time, came from all classes of society. For the first time, the two girls, who had spent their lives worrying about their relative social position, had found a group where it was of little, or no, concern. They made firm friends and rallied to defend their compatriots. Although both of her daughters were involved in the cause, Isabella was less enthusiastic, having already been called to question by Cissie's headmistress for her daughter's difficult and radical views.

George Watson's Ladies College, while providing an excellent education, was not a place for young women who did 'extraordinary things'. As a scholarship student, Cissie was warned that she should subdue her will to those who supported her or lose their backing. One cause of her headmistress's anger was that Cissie's opinions had been published; her first, passionate letter to the Scotsman appeared on the Editor's letters page on 16 October 1907. This had been a spirited defence of Suffrage for Women, drawing particular attention to the tragic plight of working-class women in leadworks, and was a counterattack to a letter written by a reader calling herself 'Mater'.

The sisters' shared commitment and enthusiasm seemed to alleviate the difficulties that had plagued their childhood relationship. After Lettie finished working in Manchester, she went to take up a post as a clinical assistant in London and she and Cissie exchanged frequent, lengthy letters telling one another of their respective suffragette activity. They attended local demonstrations, handing out leaflets and chronicling events in their letters and in the news pamphlets of their organizations.

When Sir Edward Grey, Secretary of State for Foreign Affairs, proposed a visit to speak at Leith Gaiety Theatre on 4 December 1909, he prompted an unprecedented degree of security in the area. He was an unpopular figure with supporters of the suffrage campaign. Unusually for the Liberal cabinet, he was a staunch supporter of the prime minister, Asquith. To the dismay of suffragettes across the country, Asquith, who was open in his contempt for the movement, had replaced the ailing Campbell-Bannerman as leader of the country in 1908. While Asquith's stance was opposed by many of his own ministers, Grey was a loyal adherent. Following a public meeting of his in 1905, suffragette demonstrators were imprisoned for the first time, expressly at his insistence, because they protested during his speech. He was passionate and dogmatic in his support for the status quo with regard to voting legislation.

On the Monday after Grey's visit to Leith, the *Scotsman* reported that in order to keep the 'disturbing spirits' at bay 'all the approaches [to the theatre] were vigilantly guarded by stewards, and all the streets were patrolled by numbers of policemen in plain clothes and uniform'. Cissie pointed out to her sister that in fact the majority of the police presence had been around the Waverley Theatre and the platform where Grey was going to speak. Knowing this, the suffragettes had concentrated their attention on his visit to the Gaiety.

Streets in Leith were, and are, narrow and confusing. The accumulation of protestors and crowds led to inevitable congestion and confusion in the maze of wynds and paths around the theatre.[9] Fixing her hair up in a bun, Cissie, just weeks short of her seventeenth birthday, tried to make herself look older so she might be taken more seriously. Armed with piles of the Society's handbills, she headed for Leith where her fellow members were already congregated. The wording of the papers that she handed out to the growing crowds was explicit: 'Men and Women of Leith – Come and teach Sir Edward Grey and his Liberal Cabinet that they must reckon with me when they oppress women.'

Cissie was caught up in the excitement of the day. Wayward and defiant, she mimicked the dress and mannerisms of her newfound group of friends. The large crowd of WSPU and National Union of Women's Suffrage Society members were mainly gathered around a rather tatty wagonette at the foot of Leith Walk. On this wagonette, a series of women gave speeches on their aims and determination. Edith Hudson was a familiar figure to those on the suffrage scene. A hospital nurse of forty, with a strong physique, she was an important activist in the

Edinburgh branch of the WSPU, and a neighbour to the Fair-fields. The information we have of her is scant and contradictory. In a skirmish two years after the Leith protest, she was held in Holloway Prison where she was reported as having knocked out six of the attending wardens who were attempting to force feed her, yet a friend referred to her as 'about the most gentle person I knew'. Cissie thought she was magnificent.

Clutching the purple, white and green flag that represented the cause, Edith climbed down from the wagonette, with the crowd, including Cissie, in hot pursuit.[10] Running to the theatre, Miss Hudson tried to storm the doors, but the police managed to divert her up a narrow close. Here she was temporarily imprisoned by the crowd who had rushed to offer their support. As they continued to push towards her, she found the only exit from the narrow passage blocked by the jostling hordes.

But in a second it was over. Miss Hudson was carried aloft over the crowd, back to the theatre doors, by a well-built man dressed in working clothes. Cissie looked on, breathless and excited. This time the police did not try to corral Miss Hudson away from the building but instead beat her repeatedly. Cissie's exhilaration turned to dismay, then horror, as she watched the woman she regarded as a heroine hit repeatedly on the windpipe, and finally retaliate by grabbing the offending officer by the throat.[11] The ensuing melee affected many of the spectators, who howled in outrage as policemen beat them down with truncheons. Cissie wrote 'It was a disgusting sight – one man had his head cut open ear to ear, and several people were covered with blood.'[12]

Cissie's description captured something of the feeling and the horror of this first-hand experience of violence, but also set down a heroic image, one which captivated her sister. Miss Hudson, bruised 'from the elbow to the shoulder', clutching her throat with one hand, was led away. Cissie was captivated by her bravery and determination, admiring how she 'held the purple, white and green flag above her head the whole time', even as she was finally taken into custody.[13]

Her campaigning for the WSPU necessitated trips around the

country and Cissie travelled to Harrogate in Yorkshire and was adopted by one of the leaders there, Mary Gawthorpe. She was a 'merry, militant saint'.[14] Cissie observed 'she had wit and common sense and courage, each to the point of genius' and named her 'Lovey Mary'.[15] Both sisters became friends with her, as well as admirers of her 'great charm' and ability to enthral an audience. Cissie's adulation of Mary is most apparent in *The Sentinel*, her first, incomplete attempt at a novel.[16] Its heroine, sixteen-year-old Adele Furnivall, is a committed suffragette and there are striking similarities between the narrative of *The Sentinel* and Mary Gawthorpe's life story.[17]

Descriptions of suffrage meetings feature also in a second novel, *The Judge*, written a few years later. From these it is clear that the young author was captivated by the dramatic looks and manner of many of the women.

> Mrs Ormiston, the mother of the famous rebels Brynhild, Melissa, and Guendolen, and herself a heroine, lifted a pale face where defiance dwelt among the remains of dark loveliness like a beacon lit on a grey castle keep; and Mrs Mark Lyle, a white and golden wonder in a beautiful bright dress, moved swimmingly about and placed herself on a chair like a fastidioxus lily choosing its vase. Oh! it was going to be lovely![18]

If the drama of the suffragette movement had captured Cissie's imagination, the drama of the stage attracted her ambition, mirroring the theatricality she revelled in, but seeming to offer a career. Letters about suffrage activity became regularly punctuated by others filled with commentary and criticism of the productions she attended. Captivated by, and at times critical of, the performances of great actresses – not only Sarah Bernhardt, but Ellen Terry and Mrs Patrick Campbell – Cissie joined an amateur drama group. The group was disappointing. She regarded its organizer, Graeme Goring, as 'a perfect and Entire Ass with an absorbing reverence for the romantic drama' and thought his only redeeming feature was that he was a good voice coach.[19]

When Cissie was finally given a part she was mortified. She had to enter a room tap dancing, her hands behind her back, singing:

> Handy Spandy Spicketty Spo!
> Which will you have, high top or low?[20]

And this to 'an elderly gentleman in a perfectly cut grey suit'; it was 'a severe trial'.[21] Then, in 1908, Cissie was invited as a backstage guest of the Kings Theatre in Edinburgh. She found it lovely, admired the beautiful dresses, and stressed to Lettie in a letter how highly respectable it really was. But, she said, the company was very *bushossy* – a made-up word the sisters used to describe someone overworked and underfed, like a bus horse or 'bushos', a horse that pulled the buses. This did not deter her. On the contrary, buoyed up by the experience, she wrote to Lettie that she and her companion Nellie 'were about the best looking there'. She was now determined to pursue a career on the stage.[22] Her sisters were less enthusiastic. Winnie was wary of some aspects of the profession and had refused to take Cissie to see Vesta Tilley, whose cross-dressing she regarded as shocking. Furthermore Cissie's temperament did not seem ideally suited to the stage. She tended to faint when she was upset and Winnie worried that this, coupled with a very slight involuntary facial tick, which manifested when Cissie was stressed, would make a theatrical career impossible.

Her sisters' misgivings proved to be unfounded when, during a charity performance in a local theatre, Rosina Filippi, a teacher at the Academy of Dramatic Art (ADA), noticed Cissie and invited her to audition for the ADA. Filippi felt that Cissie's character and mannerisms were ideally suited to comedy and assured her that she would not only graduate well from drama school but be able to find work.

A year after her backstage visit, Cissie travelled to London, and wrote to Lettie of her melodramatic first day. She fainted on the stairs at Baker Street tube station, on the way to her audition, and three women rushed to attend to her, concerned that she was alone in the city. She explained weakly that a theatrical manager would be coming for her and the women responded, 'Poor child – an actress! I'll pay for the brandy'.[23] The judging panel was apprized of her illness and stopped her audition because she 'looked so bad', but nevertheless offered her a place.

Afterwards, Cissie went to York Road in Lambeth to meet a friend of Lettie's. Again, the excitement of the day proved too much and she collapsed on the doorstep, only to be taken in by Chris Hartley. In time, Chris and Cissie became friends, and on this first occasion Chris welcomed her in and, when the younger girl had recovered, chatted with her about mutual friends and some scandalous gossip concerning the well-known writer H.G. Wells and his new book, *Ann Veronica*.

Following the success of her ADA audition, seventeen-year-old Cissie and her family moved back to London. The hiatus in the feuding between the eldest and youngest sister continued, although Cissie ceased to be an active suffragette after her arrival at drama school. Cissie's letters to her sister showed her excitement and happiness that they were at last to be closer. She joked 'it will be good to be nearer you so we can inspect you at more frequent intervals' and went on to write delightedly of their plans for the garden that surrounded their new home. Winnie was drawing up the plans, but while Isabella stipulated wallflowers, Cissie insisted on a lilac bush and an almond tree. They named the semi-detached cottage, at 5 Chatham Close in Hampstead Garden Suburb, Fairliehope Cottage, after a farmhouse in the Pentland Hills with a beautiful view of the Forth.

Cissie's term dates meant she had to travel to London before the family could move into their new home. She was disappointed to be made to stay with the hated Aunt Sophie rather than with her mother's relatives, the Mackenzies. They were regarded by the Fairfield family as 'vulgar' but Cissie infinitely preferred them because of their musical abilities and bohemian ways. Cissie found the stress of her stay unbearable, and was frequently bursting into tears because of real or imagined slights from her relative.

Lettie was already established in London and, like her friend

Chris Hartley, had joined the Fabian Society, a popular socialist organization made more attractive by famous members such as George Bernard Shaw and Sidney Webb. She introduced her sister, who became part of the circle while still a student at drama school. However, Cissie's theatrical education was not a success. Filippi rowed with the head of the school, Kenneth Barnes, and had left by the time Cissie became a student. The principal proved to be none too fond of his former employee's protégée. Arrogant and insecure, Cissie became dispirited as she was given only male parts, even harbouring beliefs that Barnes was out to get her.[24] She retaliated by analysing every proposed play from a literary point of view and questioning the value of performing it at all, a trait which understandably made her unpopular with the teachers. Lacking the conventional beauty of her peers and plagued by the nervous twitch that had given Winnie such misgivings over her choice of career, she failed even to complete the course.

At the end of three terms she left, feeling beaten by the school, but nevertheless still resolved to follow her chosen career. But work was sporadic; a small part in the summer season on Brighton Pier and the role of Regine in Ibsen's *Ghosts* did not lead to any more permanent or exciting runs. Lettie wasted no time in making a dig at Cissie: 'Don't you think, dear, that you'd better realise your looks are against you, and try to get into the Post Office?'[25]

The sisters' old enmity was instantly rekindled. Cissie never forgave Letitia's reaction and, almost fifty years later, she still recalled with bitterness how 'my sister Letitia's unkindness was very great when I failed as a student at the Royal Academy of Dramatic Art'.[26]

Chapter Three

AN IMPOSSIBLE NAME

Cissie's association with the Fabians was to prove more enduring and more influential than that she shared with the Academy of Dramatic Art. The Fabians aimed to create a socialist society, but realized that in order to do so people had to be raised out of existing poverty and malnourishment. Although generally united in its idealism at the time Cissie joined, the group was fractured within, with two of its most prominent members engaged in a very public dispute.

Sidney and Beatrice Webb were among the very first Fabians. The Webbs were left-wing idealists of contrasting personalities. Sidney was warm and kind, while his wife was intense and introverted. Together, they and their fellow Fabians envisioned a future with a 'just co-operative state'.[1] The Webbs believed that human beings who were well nourished and happy could not fail to be good. In the first decades of the twentieth century, their most important political achievement was the acceptance by a majority of trade unions of the notion of a national minimum wage, an idea they had originally posited. But the 'state social-ism' they espoused was gradually giving way to syndicalism. In addition to arguing for a national minimum wage, syndicalists believed that public services should be nationalized, as did the Webbs. However, for Beatrice Webb, syndicalists were guilty of a kind of idealism that made them ineffectual when confronted with the powerful political force of trade unionism at the time. It was an ideal for the 'inexperienced middle-class idealist' not for the working man or woman; a theoretical construct without any real application.[2] She thought an exploiting state could be as dangerous as an exploiting capitalist and could not agree with this break from the traditional Fabian position that endorsed a balance between public ownership and bureaucratic collectivism.[3]

By 1912, Herbert George Wells, formerly a prominent Fabian, who had been introduced to the group by George Bernard Shaw, had resigned from the society, partly because of political differences and partly because of the scandal caused by his personal relationships within the group. The disparity in ideas originated from 1906 when Wells had written a report which, amongst other changes, recommended that the society reappraise its relationship with the Labour Party and its position within the socialist movement. Shaw resented what he saw as his friend's bid to take over the organization, remarking that Wells 'is a spoiled child. His life has been one long promotion.'[4] Wells reacted in a typically forthright way and called Shaw an ass. Shaw went on to ridicule Wells' manners, and wrote to him:

> There is an art of public life which you have not mastered, expert as you are in the art of private life. The fine art of private life consists almost wholly of taking liberties; the art of public life consists fundamentally in respecting political rights. Intimate as I am with Webb, I should no more dream of treating him as you have treated him than of walking into the House of Lords and pulling the Lord Chancellor's nose.[5]

However, it was Wells' private life, or more precisely his aptitude at seduction, that was the second catalyst in his break from the group. Despite being married to fellow Fabian Amy Catherine Robbins, he had an affair with the twenty-year-old Amber Pember Reeves. Reeves was the daughter of a New Zealand government agent whose wife was on the executive committee of the society. Infatuated with the charming Wells, who was almost twice her age, she pursued him for more than a year. When the affair blossomed, Reeves and Wells moved to Le Touquet in France to escape her parents' shock and dismay. He alternated between Reeves and his wife, who had long grown accustomed to his dalliances and tolerated them. But when Reeves fell pregnant the situation in Le Touquet became intolerable for her. She felt lonely and bored when Wells was back in England, but they quarrelled whenever they were reunited. Both the travelling from France and the general inconvenience of a double life wore Wells down. Shockingly, he suggested that Reeves marry a former boyfriend and bring up the child with him. Short of another alternative, and relieved to find that the young man in question was prepared to accept this rather absurd arrangement, she duly did so. Wells provided financially for the new family he had engineered and went on to write *Ann Veronica*, a barely disguised fictional account of his affair with Reeves. It became a topic of much gossip in the circles that Cissie frequented.

This affair was quickly followed by another, with the daughter of another fellow Fabian, Hubert Bland. This latter liaison was particularly scandalous as Wells persuaded her to elope with him even though she was engaged to Clifford Sharp, yet another society member. Mrs Reeves and Hubert Bland joined indignant forces and, rather bizarrely, banned Wells' wife from attending the executive meetings. In 1908, Wells resigned but retained his hatred for Shaw, even writing a vitriolic, condemnatory obituary while Shaw was still alive, to be published, unadulterated, after his death.

The restructured group, headed by Shaw and Sidney Webb, invited Lettie to become a member. There was a family connection with the Fairfields in so far as Sidney had known Edward Fairfield during his time in the Colonial Office, and thought highly of him. Immediately on joining, Lettie was approached by Sidney, who wanted to confirm that she was the niece of Edward Fairfield. He went on to enthuse, 'I can't tell you what I owe him; he was extraordinarily good in showing me the ropes.'[6] Female medics were a rare and invaluable resource and almost immediately Lettie was elected to the executive committee because of what she called her 'scarcity value as a woman doctor'.[7] She had discussions with George Bernard Shaw on several issues related to school hygiene and working-class children and frequently lectured for the society.

When she suggested bringing her sister to a meeting, Sidney was delighted to have yet another of Edward's relatives on board and made Cissie welcome. But Cissie still needed to find work. Her precipitous departure from ADA had not led to much theatrical work. As Cissie had come from a home 'where we all wrote and thought nothing of it', some sort of journalism or reviewing presented an obvious alternative to acting.[8] She began reworking *The Sentinel* and the heroine's name, Adele, became the name of the revised book. However, this was not paid employment and occasional reviews were not enough to make a living. But a new paper, the *Freewoman*, seemed to offer a solution.

The *Freewoman* was the creation of Dora Marsden, a suffragette who had been imprisoned for her activities. Marsden was a tiny woman whose delicate appearance belied her strength of character and passion. She saw the paper as a means of widening the scope of the suffragist movement beyond the issue of political enfranchisement. She was joined in her enterprise by Mary Gawthorpe, Cissie's 'Lovey Mary' from the WSPU, and now also a Fabian. Repeated imprisonment, force-feeding and brutality had invalided Mary to the point where she could no longer actively campaign with the WSPU, but in spite of her illness she welcomed the chance to be part of the publication.

On 30 November 1911, when it was only a week old, Cissie wrote her first piece for the paper using her own name. It was a scathing criticism of a book entitled *The Position of Women in Indian Life*. Cissie deplored the authors, the Maharani of Baroda and S.M. Mitra, for championing what she called 'playing at wage-earning, this pathetic skulking on the outskirts of industry, brought to us during the Victorian era'.[9]

During its lifetime, the fledgling journal was attacked by the censors, criticized by the mainstream newspapers, and eventually banned altogether from W.H. Smith's outlets when Mrs

Humphrey Ward wrote to *The Times* claiming that the paper represented 'the dark and dangerous side of the women's movement'.[10] W.H. Smith withdrew all copies from their shops, stating: 'The nature of certain articles which have been appearing lately are such as to render the paper unsuitable to be exposed on the bookstalls for general sale.'[11]

The journal dealt with women's sexuality in a far more explicit way than had ever been done previously. H.G. Wells had famously described it as existing 'chiefly to mention everything a young lady should never dream of mentioning'.[12] Cissie, in later years, wrote that 'the greatest service that the paper did its country was through its unblushingness.'[13] Intrinsically, the paper spoke out against the romantic idea of women. Women who were single and childless might indeed resent their state, but so might women who were married with children. Women were not simply content with whatever might befall them and they needed to have the power to change their own situation so that they might become so. Cissie believed this to be the most important aspect of the growing feminist movement. Her reviews combined socialism and feminism, linking the two inextricably, as when she urged women to become publicans, saying: 'The various duties of that profession, such as wringing a licence out of a bench of insolent country gentlemen, paying the rent regularly on quarter days, and chucking out the drunkards on Saturday night, might foster the qualities of independence, thrift and firmness of character, so sadly lacking among upper-class women today.'[14]

Cissie's mother was aggrieved at her daughter's affiliation and consequently Cissie decided to adopt a pen name. The name she chose was taken from Ibsen's play *Rosmersholm*. In the play, Rebecca West is the mistress of a married man; it proved to be a prophetic choice. Less appropriate for someone of Cissie's strength of character was that Ibsen's Rebecca ended her life in a pact with her lover. The name stuck, although later Rebecca would say that she had chosen it in haste just as the paper was about to go to press and that she hated both the play and the character. As to discarding her own name, when she was seventy-nine years old West confessed, 'I had an impossible name. I don't think anybody could really be taken seriously as a writer under the name of Cicily Isabel Fairfield. It sounds like something blonde and pretty, like Mary Pickford.'[15] The name was much more than a writer's pseudonym: new friends, colleagues, even her husband at times, would call her Rebecca; only her sisters and her mother did not.

Even Rebecca's work for the *Freewoman* was insufficient to provide a living in itself. But, after reading her attack on Sir Almoth Wright, a notorious anti-feminist, Robert Blatchford invited her to write for his socialist newspaper, the *Clarion*. Blatchford was one of the founders of the Manchester Fabian Society in 1890. A passionate critic of capitalism, he was eager to include Rebecca West's acerbic attacks on society. From 1912, when her first articles appeared, she presented a glimpse of a new kind of feminism, markedly different from the austerity of the Pankhursts, and much more familiar to a twenty-first-century reader. She expressed dismay that women could be expected to 'regulate their dress according to men's lack of self control rather than their own comfort'.[16] Delighted by a visit to the music hall, she rejoiced in the dancer's ability to provide escapism to a world of 'May mornings and ices and money enough to go where you like' but was dismayed that the Bishop of Kensington was concerned with her scanty clothes. Surely, the Bishop had much more pressing concerns, such as poverty and starvation, than criticizing a healthy, joyous young woman who was 'tingling with life'.[17] Feminism for the young, passionate Rebecca was not about denial; it was about fighting, while at the same time celebrating the joys of womanhood. She wrote of the joys of Christmas shopping and the fact that poor women need the beauty of nice things as much as the wealthy. She sees defiance in a working-class girl wearing an extravagant hat because 'she is a better rebel than the girl who accepts her poverty as a matter of fate and wears its more durable badge of drab garments'.[18]

Of course, early twentieth-century concerns such as votes for women and equal pay for equal work are a constant refrain, but Rebecca, delighted by possibility, refused to embrace the sobriety that usually accompanied them. This was a feminism way beyond its time. She could write of the ever-present horror of contemporary events, the 'Cat and Mouse Act',* the appalling treatment of suffragettes. Recounting the tragedy of Emily Davison, her mistreatment in prison and dramatic suicide when she threw herself in front of the King's horse at the Derby, she was 'choked with rage'. Yet still amidst the anger, the pain of injustice, she found reason to rejoice in womanhood. Rather than old-fashioned socialism, she saw syndicalism as the way forward for women as well as men. A central governing bureaucracy could have little or no understanding of the workers it sought to defend, whereas syndicalism recognized 'the natural bond between the worker and his work'.[19] Working women could argue far more effectively and pointedly for better conditions than a detached body trying to represent them. It was a position that took her further and further from her earlier association with the WSPU. Adela Pankhurst, argued Rebecca, would have done far more for women had she remained a teacher and argued against the grievances suffered by her profession, than she had done as a WSPU organizer, of delicate health, unable to withstand the physical ordeals of protesting.

In contrast to Webb's view that syndicalism was a middle-class ideal, for Rebecca it was a populist one that gave power to the worker rather than controlling them from a central position in a representative body. This was an important distinction and a formative one; Rebecca's later staunch anti-communism surprised many critics who had not fully understood her 'new socialist' beliefs.

---

* The popular nickname for the 1913 Prisoners Temporary Discharge for Health Act, which allowed suffragettes on hunger strike to be released from prison if they became too weak or ill, but reimprisoned as soon as they recovered – this cycle of release and reimprisonment was viewed in poor taste by the public, hence the idea of a cat playing with a mouse.

The articles brought both criticism and approbation. Vera Brittain, who later became famous for her book *Testament of Youth*, as well as a good friend, thought Cissie was a twentieth-century Mary Wollstonecraft.[20] However, Mrs Humphrey Ward, the Mary Whitehouse of her day, was far from approbatory and found the topics and manner of Rebecca's writing shocking.

In the autumn of 1912, two reviews resulted in meetings that would have lasting consequences for Rebecca. The first review was of a novel entitled *The New Humpty Dumpty* by Daniel Chaucer. Rebecca was well aware that this was actually a pseudonym for Ford Madox Hueffer (later Ford Madox Ford). The book was a fictionalized account of the breakdown of his marriage and his subsequent love affair with the writer Violet Hunt. In fact, the primary reason for the pseudonym was so that Ford could avoid paying a percentage of the royalties to his estranged wife. Rebecca did not like the book, regarding it as a sort of poorer version of H.G. Wells' *The New Machiavelli*. However, the review was witty enough to attract the attention of Hunt and Ford and they invited her to tea.

South Lodge, or 80 Campden Hill Road, was a well-known address in literary London. Its semi-detached conventional facade belied the richness of its interior, a Pre-Raphaelite delight with William Morris wallpaper and one of Wyndham Lewis' first abstracts, a huge work that dominated the study, a space that was highlighted by red skirting boards and red doors. Violet was the niece of Holman Hunt and his family portraits hung in most of the rooms. The atmosphere at soirees and lunches, however, was more formal than one might have expected from a couple known for their unorthodox living arrangements. Hunt strictly observed the proprieties of dress and visitors were expected to arrive with top hats and 'London clothes', to wear gloves and carry canes.

It had been Hunt's home since she was three years old, and was the centre of a literary circle that included visitors such as Somerset Maugham, May Sinclair and H.G. Wells. The young American poet Ezra Pound became so frequent a guest that Hunt's parrot would loudly greet visitors with repeated cries of

'Ezra! Ezra!' Hunt and Ford shared a Pre-Raphaelite background: Ford was the grandson of the artist Ford Madox Brown and nephew of William Michael Rossetti, a founding member of the Pre-Raphaelite brotherhood. Neither Ford nor Hunt was conventionally good-looking; Rebecca described the former as 'stout, gangling, albinoish'.[21] Hunt had been regarded as a beauty; as a young girl she had most famously modelled for the lovely, confused virgin in Burne Jones' *King Cophetua and the Beggar Maid*. But, at fifty, she was eleven years Ford's senior and, furthermore, suffered from syphilis, a legacy from a previous affair, which left her face and wrists marked with spots whenever it flared up.[*]

An air of scandal surrounded their situation, as well as one of celebrity, and Rebecca was thrilled to be invited to meet them. For their part, Ford and Hunt were surprised that their very cutting reviewer was so young and so pretty. Hunt described her: 'She came. She had a pink dress on and a large, wide-brimmed, country-girlish straw hat that hid her splendid liquid eyes, which, however no brim of any kind could hinder one from apprehending.'[22]

For Hunt, Rebecca's youth was a wonderful thing: she was 'ostentatiously young', with a power over those around her. Hunt mused, 'if she wants to hurt you she will; if she wants to be kind to you, well and very good.'[23] Rebecca was only eighteen but already she 'ruled Fleet Street'.[24]

Ford had only recently stepped down as editor of the *English Review*, the same publication in which Rebecca's review of his book had appeared. Talk that day was of the *Review* and of the cameo portraits barely concealed in the book. Hunt admired Rebecca's talent as a listener and her mellifluous voice, 'compounded of milk and honey'.[25] The visit was an unmitigated success and heralded a long-lasting friendship between Hunt and Rebecca, a less-robust one between Ford and Rebecca, although

---

[*] Rollyson, *The Saga of the Century*, (p. 33), gives Violet's age as forty-six in 1912, the same as H.G. Wells, when in fact she was born in September 1862.

she retained a great admiration for his editorial skill, and a plethora of important introductions in subsequent evenings and afternoons at South Lodge. Violet thought Rebecca able to combine seemingly contradictory characteristics in a beguiling way. She was 'guileless' but discreet, and 'deep as the sea yet adorably frivolous', capable of gossiping but not maliciously.[26]

Another review that Rebecca wrote in the same period was to be of far greater import to her life. The article appeared in the *Freewoman* on 19 September 1912 and attacked one of the most successful and famous writers of the day. It was a short and damning piece about H.G. Wells' book *Marriage*.

Chapter Four

'YOU ALSO WRITE'

Rebecca's review of *Marriage* was blistering. She described Wells' mannerisms as 'more infuriating than ever' and deplored his generalizations of the roles of the sexes as exemplified by the novel's characters. The sex obsession that lay 'clotted' on Wells' books 'like cold white sauce was merely old maids' mania'.[1]

At the time her criticism appeared, Wells was living with his wife, Amy Catherine, whom he called 'Jane'. Rebecca had heard gossip about his various extramarital dalliances but had not actually met Wells, even though he too was a frequent visitor to South Lodge. Wells was forty-six, short and portly with piercing blue eyes and an undeniable charm that had brought him numerous sexual encounters, including an affair with Violet Hunt six years previously;[2] Amber Reeves was only one of his more recent conquests. Jane was actually his second wife, and his elopement with her, and consequent abandonment of his first wife, had outraged Jane's family. Following his divorce they were married and had two sons, George (Gip) in 1901 and Frank in 1903, but afterwards his philandering nature showed itself again. Wells acknowledged his need of Jane and the stabilizing influence she brought to his life. She was, for him, 'the resolute little person' who sustained her 'belief that I was worth living for' and 'who stuck to me so sturdily that in the end I stuck to myself'.[3] But nevertheless he did not see his need of her as limiting his sexual adventures in any way. Jane seemed resigned to his extramarital relationships but eager to preserve outward appearances and avoid social scandal. To this effect the couple had an agreement: Wells could take lovers, Jane would turn a blind eye, but he needed to be discreet and he should only sleep with women that Jane actually liked.[4] Over the years, Rebecca became convinced that there was a sinister reason for Jane's acceptance, that she took a kind of sadistic pleasure in the way the other women were treated. For Rebecca, Jane was a malicious woman who only pretended to tolerate Wells' affairs because she could not do otherwise and secretly delighted in the humiliation of his mistresses. However, to those in their immediate social circle the Wells presented a happy front. Their children's governess describes long winter evenings when groups of friends amused themselves with games of charades and dressing-up parties, carefully organized by Jane.[5] From time to time, she organized fancy-dress dances for much larger groups of people at the Drill Hall, close to their Hampstead house.

In September 1912, Wells was having a passionate love affair with Elizabeth von Arnhim, the aristocratic novelist, cousin of Katharine Mansfield. Elizabeth was a widow. She had arrived in England with her two children, German citizens by virtue of Elizabeth's marriage. Concerned by what she saw as a serious Prussian threat, in these years before the Great War, she had also sold the family estate in Germany and was in the process of building a huge chalet in Jura, Switzerland.

As a mistress, she suited both Wells and Jane. Elizabeth was of an age with Wells and accepted his marital status while nurturing ideas that she might one day rescue him from its dreariness. Jane found their *ménage à trois* easier to handle than the drama of his two previous affairs and acquiesced quietly to Elizabeth's position. Dinner was occasionally taken together at Elizabeth's home in St James's Court. Indeed, the two women developed a relationship amicable enough that Jane, on occasion, late in the affair, visited Elizabeth's Swiss home.*

---

* That Jane was Elizabeth's guest in Switzerland was later denied by Gip. However, Rebecca insisted that both Wells and Jane had told her personally

However, Wells was curious about the young woman who had so savaged his latest book and responded by inviting her to tea with himself and Jane, at Easton Glebe, the Wells' country home. Wells' governess described her arrival at the residence on 27 September 1912: 'Miss Rebecca West arrived today. She looks about twenty-two years of age, and is very vivacious.'[6] For his part Wells was taken with her 'curious mixture of maturity and infantilism', reckoning 'I had never met anything like her before and doubt if there was anything like her before'. He admired her 'dark expressive troubled eyes' and her 'big soft mouth' as much as he admired her prodigious intellect and memory and was impressed by the way she stood up to him in an argument.[7]

Rebecca described Wells as 'one of the most interesting men I have ever met'.[8] In later years she reminisced that 'it wasn't an immediate meeting of body. He wasn't really an Adonis by any means and he had a little high voice.'[9] She even went so far as to say he 'was one of the ugliest men in England' but that with 'half an hour start' he could quickly knock out the best-looking men in the vicinity because of his 'endless charm and lightness and humour and wit'.[10] They spoke excitedly of books and ideas for more than five hours, 'with immense vitality'.[11] Jane charmed her new guest but remained in the background, probably all too sensitive to the growing attraction between the two. After the initial meeting, Wells and Rebecca were regularly in contact. Just two weeks later Rebecca wrote to Charles Sarolea, editor of the *Everyman*, asking if she might write for him. With her letter she enclosed a reference in support of her appeal. It was from her new friend, H.G. Wells.[12]

When she came to see him again in his small Hampstead home on Church Row, close to the nineteenth-century church of St John, the relationship took its next step. Wells was hesitant, out of some loyalty to Elizabeth rather than Jane, and did not

about a visit Jane had made to Elizabeth and her chalet. See RW to Gip Wells, 29 July 1974, Tulsa.

immediately try to seduce Rebecca, despite the obvious mutual attraction. He described those first few hours in Church Row as being 'bookish and journalistic'. Yet, standing before his book-shelves, discussing literary style, an atmosphere grew between them so that 'apropos of nothing', they paused, catching each others' eyes, and kissed.[13]

It was what Rebecca had been waiting for. She declared a burning passion for Wells and entreated him to take her as a lover. Wells, suddenly coy, perhaps all too aware that he was yet again on the brink of a 'difficult' liaison, protested, saying he had given no indication that this was a possible course. Rebecca insisted, understandably seeing the kiss as the beginning of a seduction. Wells tried hard to justify himself: 'She demanded to be my lover and made an accusation of my kiss. It was a promise, she said. I too was by way of thinking that a kiss ought to be a promise. But it was a very unexpected kiss.'[14]

Rebecca was infatuated, Wells rather more controlled; he refused to have sex with her. The set-up with Elizabeth and Jane was comfortable and Rebecca might prove to be a bit too disruptive. Obviously Elizabeth did not welcome the idea of adding a fourth to their arrangement and pointedly suggested he go to Italy with her for a month's holiday. Jane too preferred the discretion and convenience of his current mistress and did not relish the thought of a return to the hysteria of the Amber Reeves experience. Wells broke off contact with Rebecca. Years later Rebecca learned he had actually first tried to break with Elizabeth but had been persuaded to end the flirtation with her instead.[15] It seems an arrangement for four was more than even Wells could contemplate.

∽◦∾

Rebecca was distraught and her subsequent depression shocked both her sisters and her mother. Isabella decided to try to abate her daughter's melancholy with a change of scenery and took Rebecca off to Spain for a month. Her mother's strategy had some success. While travelling, Rebecca returned to writing and the passion and the disappointment of the previous weeks poured out in her subsequent pieces.

The *Freewoman* ceased publication just a month after Rebecca visited Easton Glebe. There was almost no money and W.H. Smith's boycott meant there was little hope of making any.

The failure of the paper was distressing for Rebecca, who was determined to raise funds and relaunch it. And, by June 1913, she had succeeded, thanks in part to backing from the unmarried, and very rich, Harriet Weaver.

The new paper was far from what Rebecca had envisaged. On her return from Spain, Rebecca took up her new post as assistant editor for the now-renamed *New Freewoman* and set about finding contributors who might provide the literary content she had always felt was lacking from the original paper. One writer she pursued was Ezra Pound, who was then based in London and working to promote a small group of struggling young poets. Pound's initial contact with Rebecca was promising. However he had very fixed ideas about the amount of control he wanted over the literary content, which made Dora Marsden, the paper's founder, wary. It was agreed that he would have a completely free hand for a trial run of six issues, at which point the situation would be reviewed.

Wells, hearing of Rebecca's renewed professional activities, obviously hoped the trip to Spain had had a cathartic effect on what he regarded as her hysteria, and sent her a note to invite her to his new flat, at 52 St James's Court. Unfortunately for Rebecca it did not seem to resolve anything. The offer of friendship to replace what, for her, had been the grandest kind of passion was almost insulting. She wrote to Dora Marsden, saying, 'I don't think we shall speak or write again! I'm longing to slaughter him!'[16] The next letter she wrote to Wells was similarly dramatic and uncompromising. Only the draft remains: 'During the next few days I shall either put a bullet through my head or commit something more shattering to myself than death.'[17]

She claimed he had ruined her, that she was 'burned down to her foundations'. He had obviously worried over her obsessive passion for him and urged that it could, like a sickness, be cured. She retaliated now, in melodramatic fashion, by saying that for her, there could only be passion and now there was nothing. She despaired that he had once found her love for him 'beautiful and courageous' but now found it simply 'indecent'. She ended, proclaiming 'I would give my whole life to feel your arms round me again'.

Wells showed the letter to both Jane and Elizabeth. Both women urged him to stay well away from what was showing all the signs of becoming a public melodrama. When Wells did write back to Rebecca his reply was cold and matter-of-fact: 'How can I be your friend to this accompaniment? I don't see that I can be of any use or help to you at all. You have my entire sympathy — but until we can meet on a reasonable basis, goodbye.'[18]

Rebecca's articles from her Spanish trip, charged with her emotional distress, appeared in the New Freewoman. The first, entitled 'Trees Of Gold', spoke of how she felt overwhelmed by her emotions:

> By the heat of its desires and adorations the mind may become like hot wax: incapable of receiving the sharp impressions which are all it lives for. The fire by whose blaze the soul meant to lighten the world may burn it down to its foundations and leave it a smoking ruin, as unlovely as any factory or building designed from the first for base uses.[19]

A short story called 'At Valladolid', which appeared two months later, is a heavily autobiographical account of a trip from England to Spain, where the distraught heroine tries to commit suicide twice. In echoes of Rebecca's pursuit of Wells, the heroine cries: 'For though my lover had left my body chaste he had seduced my soul: He mingled himself with me till he was more myself than I am, and then left me.'[20]

A third piece, 'Nana', recalled a singer in Seville whose spirit and flesh seemed to echo that of the music-hall dancer who had so captivated her in earlier years. Nana had a 'dazzling body', which cried out 'Here am I, nothing but flesh and blood. When your toys of the mind and the spirit are all broken, come back to my refreshing flesh and blood.'[21]

For Wells, this may have hinted at a more positive outlook and he wrote to Rebecca: 'You are writing gorgeously again. Please resume being friends.'[22] Rebecca, wary of their last meeting, did not reply, but went on to review Wells' new novel *The Passionate Friends* for the *New Freewoman* of 1 October.

It was a mixed notice. While acknowledging that 'the first thirteen pages of *The Passionate Friends* stand among the most beautiful achievements of elucidating emotion', she was troubled by what she saw as the book's lack of any real substance. She admired its depiction and understanding of fatherhood. Most importantly, for Wells at least, Rebecca seemed to be advocating the possibility of sex without emotional attachment: 'Surely the only way to medicine the ravages of this fever of life is to treat sex lightly, to recognize that in this as in philosophy the one is not more excellent than the many, to think no more hardly of two lovers who part soon than we do of spring for leaving the earth at the coming of June.'[23]

Rebecca had one misgiving though, she felt that the atmosphere Wells depicted was conducive to jealousy, the very thing he saw as so destructive in relationships.

Despite this, and perhaps enticed by the insinuation that a less-intense relationship might be on offer, Wells once again approached her. His personal circumstances had changed for the worse. Jealous of the daily letters that he still wrote to Jane, worn down by the new threat of Rebecca, Elizabeth had left Wells in Italy and gone alone to her recently finished Swiss chalet. The abandoned Wells sent her a stream of pleading letters. 'You are the whole universe to me,' he declared. Jane had 'every virtue, every charm' but was 'as dead as herring to him'.[24]

Rebecca was young, brilliant and adoring, and Wells' battered ego needed attention. When he returned from his Italian trip with Elizabeth in November, they were reunited. This time there was no hesitation; they became lovers soon after. Wells told Jane and, once again, she accepted the situation – with the caveat that he and Rebecca acted discreetly. Rebecca gave herself and Wells pet names; she loved cats – now she was 'Panther', he was 'Jaguar'. At other times they were the 'Pussteads', two animals in cosy domesticity. Rebecca confided in Violet Hunt about her affair. Violet Hunt's own domestic arrangements were highly unconventional; Ford's first wife still refused to divorce him. She was the only friend that Rebecca told and proved to be both sympathetic and protective. However, in spite of his initial desire for carefree sex, it was clear that Wells too was finding that the relationship was having a significant impact on his life. She had 'taken the ugly creases out of my mind'.[25] Rebecca's professional life was also in a state of flux. Writing for the *New Freewoman* was one thing, but she found herself increasingly caught up in the politics between Ezra Pound and Dora Marsden. Rebecca was torn between loyalty to Dora, who felt that Pound was taking over the paper, and her belief that Pound was also exceptionally gifted as an editor. In October, she resigned. Harriet Weaver offered her a month's salary but she refused it, saying: 'As Miss Marsden has let me go, I think the least I can do is to go without looting the till.'[26]

Wells might have been happy with the arrangement he had with Rebecca, but he was wary of her family. He felt that her mother had a 'violent anti-sexual bias' and wanted to keep her daughters single and successful.[27] In fact, her mother was far more concerned with the fact that Wells, a well-known womanizer, and father of two sons, was keeping her hitherto virginal daughter as a mistress. Wells had visited the family at Fairliehope early in the relationship and professed paternalistic concern for Rebecca. Isabella was wary even then, and now felt that all her concerns had been brought to pass.[28]

Wells and Rebecca met secretively, in part because of Rebecca's family, as Wells later claimed, but also, no doubt, out of deference to his wife. They met in Wells' St James's Court flat one afternoon. It was only the second time they had made love but, anxious that they might be interrupted by a valet, they were careless and Rebecca fell pregnant. Later Wells accepted that, as the more experienced partner, he should have been more careful: 'It should not have happened, and since I was the experienced person, the blame is wholly mine.'[29]

Rebecca's recollection of events also blamed Wells but in a much more direct way: 'One day he said to me he had taken no precautions, I might have a child . . . I felt I loved you so much and hated you so much I had to stab you with this child.'[30]

At Wells' suggestion, Rebecca went to Violet Hunt's country cottage in Sussex for a break. She spent a sombre twenty-first birthday there, a pale and miserable guest who could not confide in her hosts. She pondered the possibility of an abortion but decided it was immoral, preferring instead to think of adoption. When she left the Hunts, she was taken to a nursing hospital in London because her childhood lung inflammation returned. Wells, escaping from these complications, went to Switzerland to see Elizabeth and tell her his news. But if he expected her to be sympathetic he was sorely mistaken and they slept in separate beds for the whole week he was there. Disappointed and rejected, on his departure, egotistical and insecure as ever, Wells demanded: 'It's because I'm common, isn't it?'[31] As he left, Elizabeth wrote in her memoirs, 'There I stood on the terrace, having duly waved him good bye and I felt like a convalescent, like one whose fever had left him, and who is filled with great peace.'[32]

For Rebecca, however, the fever was just beginning. It was 1914, a year that would bring many more horrors, far beyond any domestic tragedy. An illegitimate pregnancy was a shocking thing for society and difficult even for someone as apparently daring as Rebecca. She had championed unmarried mothers in an article just a year earlier and pitied the difficulties of their plight, as well as the treatment dished out to their offspring. And now, here she was in that very same position. Wells announced the fact of Rebecca's pregnancy to Jane over a dinner, at which various guests were in attendance. With characteristic forbearance, Jane replied that Rebecca would need a great deal of help to manage alone with a baby.

Undeterred either by Rebecca's condition or her recent illness, Wells set off on a planned trip to St Petersburg. From there he wrote both to Jane: 'Dear Mummy, Russia is most amoosing' and to Rebecca: 'St Petersburg is more like Rebecca than any capital I have seen, alive and dark and untidy (but trying to be better) and mysteriously beautiful.'[33]

He urged Rebecca to move away from their social circle, suggesting Llandudno in Wales, but entreated her not to give out her new address. He reasoned that it would 'leave us far freer with each other and it will save Jane enormous embarrassment if our secret is kept'.[34] He made intricate plans for a facade that would help Rebecca keep the semblance of respectability. They would be Mr and Mrs West: 'Mr West is in the cinematograph business and he has to write things. He wants a quiet room to work in and he has to have a separate bedroom (though he proposes to spend much time in your delicious bed). You also write. Make this clear and get everything comfortably arranged.'[35]

His plans for Rebecca were explicit. She had to 'take care of me and have me fed and have me peaceful and comfortable'.[36]

Wells expected Rebecca to be discreet even with her own family, and she only confided in her sisters after Wells had given her permission to do so. Predictably, Rebecca spoke first to Winnie, her favourite, and then, when she proved sympathetic and supportive, went on to explain her predicament to Lettie who, much to her surprise, was equally kind. Isabella, when she was told, was furious, feeling manipulated by Wells and convinced that her daughter's shame would make a good marriage nigh on impossible for her sisters. For his part, Wells felt that Isabella was a man-hater driven by blind opposition, and that her disapproval spoiled any arrangement they might have come to for Rebecca.

On his return from Russia, Wells found a new home for Rebecca. It was in Hunstanton, Norfolk, a small and unshowy seaside resort which was conveniently unfashionable, and therefore remote from the London scene.[37] The house was a small late-Victorian villa, on a cliff beside an old but functioning lighthouse, set above the esplanade looking out to the sea and the wintry beach. Hunstanton was, for Rebecca, 'a wholly tedious East Coast' town.[38] Trains travelled directly there from Bishop's Stortford, the closest station to Easton Glebe, allowing Wells to move between his women without the inconvenience of having to change in London.

The owners, Mr and Mrs Murray, let out furnished rooms and did so happily to 'Mr and Mrs West'. The journey to the new lodgings was also shrouded in secrecy. Rebecca and Wells travelled on separate trains from London, Wells deeming that separate carriages on the same train would be too risky. Reunited at the Hunstanton railway station, Wells spent a week with Rebecca before returning to Jane and his sons. It was a pattern that continued throughout Rebecca's pregnancy. Wells stayed with her when he could, usually for a couple of days at a time, spending the rest of the week with his wife or in London. They did not entertain guests, perpetuating the idea that Rebecca was still convalescing from lung disease. She kept the truth even from Violet Hunt; Wells, who still regularly saw both Violet and Ford at Easton Glebe, commented that Violet thought Rebecca to be close to death's door. He wrote to Rebecca 'V.H. hasn't an idea of your baby. She said "Poor little girl she can't last long."'[39]

In wintertime they wrapped up in thick wool and tramped through the surrounding woodland. Later on, during the warmer weather of May and June, they spent days in the beach hut that they had hired with the house, bathing and walking along the coastline. In this seclusion, Rebecca made some changes to her professional life. She was growing dissatisfied with journalism and left the *Clarion*, choosing to concentrate instead on a book, a study of Henry James. Wells began work on *The Research Magnificent*, a barely fictionalized account of his love affair with Rebecca. When the couple were apart, they wrote intimate notes and letters. 'Jaguar' missed 'Panther', life was boring without her:

> Dear little mate
> Fing I like talking to
> Fing I like to sit about with not talking

Person that it's pleasant to be against
. . . The world bores me to death
(or rather my world does)
It bores me and irritates me
When I am away from you.[40]

Wells remained adamant that Rebecca should keep their whereabouts secret from her friends, but with his own friends, Wells
himself was not always so circumspect. In the summer of 1914,
Wells wrote to Robert Ross, inviting him to stay with himself
and Rebecca. Ross had been Oscar Wilde's first male lover, and
together with Reggie Turner, another friend of both Wells and
Rebecca, had accompanied Wilde to Paris on his release from
prison. Using their assumed names, Wells wrote that 'Mr and
Mrs West' would welcome him. 'Mrs West is brown and now
dreadfully big with young, she has a dear ugliness that grows
upon the affection. Mr West adores her. They go down on to the
beach where they have a hut and he bathes and then one sits
about in a dry bathing suit gossiping. That is all.'[41]

But events escalating around them broke into their retreat
and the topic of conversation, in the sunny afternoons, turned
to the ever-increasing likelihood of conflict in Europe. Wells
had long predicted war on a large scale. As early as 1908 he had
written a piece for the New York World, warning America that
Europe was preparing for war, and his futuristic novel, The War
in the Air, published the same year, considered a civilization
destroyed by aerial bombardment. In 1914, he published The
World Set Free, which forecast a world war fought with nuclear
weapons.[42] When Archduke Franz Ferdinand was assassinated on
28 June, Wells became immediately convinced that the resulting
war 'would set the world alight'.[43] He began dividing his time
between his latest book and articles about the impending war
and its consequences.

On Monday, 4 August 1914, there was a fair at Easton Glebe.
Jane and Wells attended with their weekend guests, who included
George Bernard Shaw, and the subject of war was constantly in

the air. Wells and Shaw resumed their old hostilities during a debate, Shaw holding back, while Wells (perhaps mindful of the warning of his former lover, Elizabeth) shouted, 'The Germans are frightfully efficient and will invade us too . . . We must get out our shotguns and man the hedges and ditches, but it will be the end of civilization.'[44]

That evening Wells wrote an article that would come to represent the conflict in the dreadful years to come: 'The War That Will End All Wars'. The rekindled enmity led to the Irishman launching a response with a piece entitled 'Common Sense about the War', in the *New Statesman*, explicitly denying that the Allies had the moral high ground.

While Wells admired the gardens at the fair, strolled with his wife or bickered with his erstwhile friend, Rebecca went into labour. In the early hours of 5 August, just a few hours after Britain had formally declared war on Germany, a little boy was born. His middle name was a testament to the affair that had made him; the pet name Wells had given his mother. He was called Anthony Panther West.

Chapter Five

HARRY LAUDER AND WAGNER

It had not been an easy birth. Rebecca was attended during labour by her doctor sister, Lettie, and also by Carrie Townshend, a friend of Wells, who had often allowed her house to be used as a trysting place. Wells, contacted in London and told that there were dangerous complications, rushed to Rebecca's side, having first told his wife of the circumstances. With her habitual tolerance of her husband's philandering, Jane's reply was concerned and kindly: 'I am full of misery at your telegram. It isn't Rebecca herself who is in danger. I try to think the message might mean the child – not her. Will you wire to me if there is any better news to send? This is horrible. Give her my dear love if you can.'[1]

After the birth, however, Wells did not remain with Rebecca and instead hurried back to his wife. From his marital home at Little Easton Rectory, he wrote to Rebecca that he 'was radiant' and 'so delighted that I have a manchild in the world'. Overcome with paternal feeling, he pledged 'to get the world tidy for him'.[2]

The international events that coincided with the birth affected the new mother too and she wrote: 'This was motherhood with a difference. When the mists of chloroform cleared away and they held out her squealing son, she looked at him, not with the passive contentment of the mother in peacetime, but with the active and passionate intention: "I must keep this thing safe".'[3]

Wells continued to visit mother and son every few days, in

between writing about what he referred to as 'national catastrophes'. Rebecca's mother, although still unhappy about her
relationship with Wells, visited her new grandson. Although the
idea of adoption had been briefly considered during the pregnancy, faced with the bond of motherhood, Rebecca could no
longer even contemplate separation from Anthony. Carrie
Townshend wrote to Wells, very shrewdly judging that in spite
of Rebecca's apparently independent nature, 'a lover at discreet
intervals isn't enough for her: she needs a baby and a home as
well'. Townshend ridiculed Wells' suggestion that Rebecca
needed 'a young man's life', pointing out that she was simply
incapable of compartmentalizing sex in the way that he himself
did.[4]

The outbreak of war had shattered any hopes of a domestic
idyll but it inspired Wells to produce a flurry of articles. He
continued to write to Rebecca, painting himself as a protector,
dealing with 'national catastrophes', leaving her to 'lie and purr'.
Wells took a strong position, and one that was at odds with
many socialists who had hitherto shared his opinions and ideas.
Horrified by the war, he nevertheless thought Britain was right
to take part in it.

While the war marked the beginning of one of Wells' most
prolific periods, Rebecca, with a newborn baby, was to find her
situation 'not good for work'.[5] Lonely and bored, she decided to
break the silence and deception that had surrounded her pregnancy and wrote to Violet Hunt, telling her the real reason for
her seclusion. She began by justifying her affair with Wells.
Because she was not a practising Roman Catholic, she reasoned,
the sanctity of marriage was not something she felt she had to
respect. She loved Wells and in honest and open response to
those feelings she took him as a lover. Consequently, she fell
pregnant but was warned by the doctor that there were complications and the child might not be born. The reason she had not
explained her true situation before was just this, and furthermore,
a real fear that 'There was a sporting chance I would become a
heroine. Pale Fabians would say I was the Free Woman and I had

wanted to be the Mother of the Superman, and the old school left over from the nineties might say I was his wife in the sight of God and similar clichés.'[6]

∽◦◦◦∽

Echoing Mrs Townshend's sentiments, Rebecca went on: 'I am really orthodox in the extreme and think unchastity is sexual slatternliness and polygamy always tragic even when quite happy and an advantage to no one except the Railway Companies, and arguing these points would be difficult.'[7]

Yet, the visits, which seemed so infrequent to Rebecca, were putting a strain on the usually acquiescent Jane. In an attempt to reassure her, Wells wrote from Hunstanton that his 'abundant absences' were not about any hostility towards his wife but were because he was needed by Rebecca and the new baby. Furthermore, Easton Glebe was being renovated and he found the disruption to his writing caused by builders and plumbers intolerable. Home was a 'noisy, unsympathetic, uninteresting muddle'.[8]

'I hate things unfinished and out of place,' he grumbled. He was irritable because of 'sexual exasperation'. This would improve later, presumably when Rebecca had recovered sufficiently from childbirth, but for now the situation was impossible for him. 'I love you very warmly, you are in so many things, love of my love and flesh of my flesh,' he urged Jane, 'but the other thing is a physical necessity.'[9]

A month after the birth, Wells helped Rebecca to move a little closer to London. Both were tired of the temporary nature of boarding-house life, and Rebecca longed for a proper home for Anthony. She was also glad to be away from a town she later referred to as 'the deadliest place on earth'.[10]

Wells was as usual governed by his twin needs, to be near Easton Glebe and to be discreet. He found them a large rented farmhouse, Quinbury, in the tiny Hertfordshire village of Braughing, and sketched a new assumed identity. Rebecca would be Mrs West, married to a newspaper man who travelled frequently.

From Wells' point of view it was perfect. From Quinbury to Easton Glebe was a journey of no more than ten miles on mostly unused country lanes. However, the house itself was gloomy, set down a dirt road, a quarter of a mile from the only other feature of the hamlet, a small public house. The train to Liverpool Street left from Standen, two and a half miles away, and the journey there meant hiring the horse and trap kept by the landlord of the public house. It was September when Rebecca moved in, and a sudden onslaught of bad weather made the practical problems of the place more and more apparent. Some supplies could be bought from the door-to-door tradesmen who visited once or twice a week, but all other shopping was reliant on the limited supplies of the small village one and a half miles away, or a five-mile trip, again by horse and trap, to the nearest market of any size. Now that the repairs at Easton Glebe were complete, Wells was enjoying his home environment once more and was caught up in writing about the war, as well as finishing a novel, Mr Britling Sees It Through. As autumn gave way to winter, Wells visited Rebecca and Anthony far less often. Rebecca displaced her resentment of Wells into hatred of Jane who she thought was making more and more demands on his time. A row with her mother, who insisted that she should move back to her house with Anthony, rather than bring him up on her own, further heightened Rebecca's isolation; her mother was now so furious with Wells that she stopped visiting lest she see him while she was there.

But then Lord Kitchener, the Secretary of State for War, intervened. In the autumn of 1915, he requisitioned Rebecca to cook for eleven soldiers billeted in an empty house nearby. Grateful for the food and no doubt for the company of the attractive young mother, the men became a fixture around the cottage and seemed to lift her out of the moroseness that had followed Anthony's birth.

Her letters became peopled with amusing anecdotes of their antics and of a squabble involving a neighbour, and she described her current state to her friend, the writer Sylvia Lynd, as 'living in such amazing atmospheres'.[11] In spite of her occasional complaints that the men were a distraction, Rebecca began writing again: articles for the *Daily News* and *New Republic* as well as working on her biography of Henry James. Wells was less happy with the visitors and, with characteristic egocentricity, wrote to Rebecca that the 'visitor business has to be got straight'. He elaborated that it was essential that he should be 'free to come when I like' and, almost as an afterthought, added that 'a lot of shady visitors will be bad for servants and disturbing for you'.[12]

The demands of running the household also interfered with Rebecca's work. A particularly harsh winter left her debilitated, then she discovered that her housekeeper was stealing from her. When Rebecca, ill and coughing, confronted the woman, she brazened it out, demanding that Rebecca give her the money she was trying to take. If she did not, the housekeeper warned, she would expose her as an unmarried mother, both locally and to Wells' wife Jane. This latter was a somewhat empty threat. The two women lived in an uneasy state, but were nevertheless fully aware of one another. Rebecca refused to back down and the housekeeper left. But she made good her threat and, on her way to London, she told local residents the truth about Rebecca's situation. It was obvious that yet another move would be necessary and Wells, shaken by a confrontation with the woman, who had indeed gone straight to his home to denounce him to his wife, set about looking for a new home for Rebecca and his son. Rebecca, missing her London social life, suggested that she and Anthony move in with Violet Hunt, who had happily offered them a home.

Wells was opposed, perhaps wary of the close friendship that seemed to be growing between an ex-lover and a current one. He told Rebecca that he was convinced Violet would gossip, and that such an arrangement would make it far less convenient for him to visit whenever he liked. While an alternative was sought, during July and August, Rebecca took Anthony to a hotel by the Thames, in Maidenhead. But she hated the town, thinking that its faded gilt and grimy plush made it look like a cluster of brothels. Meanwhile, during the autumn of 1915, Wells eventually settled on a new home for his alternate family in Hatch End, Pinner.

Pinner was not as it is now. Rather, it was an isolated suburb with no shops less than two miles distant and no public transport at all. The house itself was large, an Edwardian terraced villa with a huge garden. This in itself proved problematic, as the size of the house meant it was impossible to fully equip it with the little that Rebecca and Anthony, used to rented rooms, possessed. Rebecca described her days there as being 'a pinched life', as she desperately tried to economize by learning basic carpentry and plumbing. This time Rebecca was Miss West and Anthony was her nephew. Mr Wells, their frequent visitor, was a dear family friend of long standing. And lest there be any careless slip, Anthony was taught to call Rebecca 'Auntie Panther'. Winnie and Lettie helped Rebecca settle in and her mother once again resumed contact, enjoying visits from her daughter and grandson. But the proximity to London meant that meetings with Wells were fewer because he greatly feared society's censure, should it become openly known that he kept a mistress and a love child. Rebecca wrote to Sylvia Lind in despair: 'I hate domesticity'.[13] She longed to go shopping and spend all her money on clothes from Bond Street. Tired of the deceit and her half-relationship, she longed above all for 'ROMANCE. Something with a white face and a slight natural wave in the dark hair and a large grey touring-car.'[14]

Rebecca was not alone in her suburban isolation; Anthony had a Scottish nurse, Miss Morrison, known affectionately as Nanky, and she employed two general servants. But to S.K. Ratcliffe, the American-based British journalist who was a friend of the Fairfield family, she wrote of her loneliness and Wells' growing detachment: 'Now I am hardly ever allowed to see the Great Man, and when I do it is usually in a public hall or on some similarly intimate occasion . . . I am in the most miserable state. Everything emotional that has kept me going through the worries and hardships of the last three or four years has suddenly failed me.'[15]

The mounting difficulties in Rebecca and the 'Great Man's' relationship were really only alleviated on their brief, infrequent trips to Monkey Island. This was a quiet and secluded spot on the Thames, beloved of Wells in his childhood, and would become the inspired setting of Rebecca's first published novel, *The Return of the Soldier*.

Anthony was the great pleasure of Rebecca's life. She devised games for him and humoured his childish delight by alternating Wagner's *Tristan and Isolde* with Harry Lauder's popular song 'I Love a Lassie'. Work, however, went slowly and as the months went on she lamented her difficulty in completing *The Return of the Soldier*.

But she had completed *Henry James*, and it was published in 1916. The biography caused Rebecca some notoriety among London literary society, which was shocked that such a young woman should criticize an acknowledged master. However, the book also had its admirers and Marie Belloc-Lowndes, a successful, and fashionable, thriller writer told her she thought it 'one of the best critical works in the language' and was touched when her compliment made Rebecca blush.[16]

Wells spent much of that year amidst the horror of the French and Italian fronts, taking notes for a proposed book. Rebecca's concerns were closer to home, and her situation seemed to be crystallizing her thoughts on the position of women. In an essay for the *New Republic*, she regretted her own concern over the ink stains on her dress which she saw as a by-product of her profession, and railed against women who seemed driven by the quest for elegance:

I have told how women infected with elegance hand down the bad tradition in our schools and teach girls to live not for life's sake but to be desired . . . To every woman who desires her sex to be more than a perishable article hawked to uneager buyers at a penny plain and two pence pretty, who would have her sex engage in humanity's conspiracy to thrust disorder on the dark, disordered universe, elegance is the enemy.[17]

On Wells' return, he rented rooms in Claverton Street, Pimlico so that he and Rebecca might meet in London. There they occasionally dined with Wells' friend, Arnold Bennett, whom Rebecca detested, finding him mannered and ponderous. Wells still visited Hatch End, as did both of Rebecca's sisters, Violet Hunt and the novelist G.B. Stern. Rebecca had met Peter, as G.B. Stern was known, through Violet Hunt, at a South Lodge tea party and the two had struck up a close friendship. Wells, typically, was less enamoured of Rebecca's new companions, and in particular, demanded that her housekeeper, Mrs Meikle, be dismissed. Caught between the demands of domesticity, the tyrannous Wells and the need to finish her novel, Rebecca agreed to move again. Wells took her to the Essex coast and drove her around but, in pain after an injury to her hand, Rebecca found herself uncharacteristically sentimental and with 'an indisposition to burst into loud tears'.[18]

Nevertheless, at the end of February 1917, Rebecca and Anthony moved to a small house in Leigh-on-Sea in Essex. Southcliffe towered above the Thames estuary with panoramic views and Rebecca immediately took to the house. Her dear friend, Peter Stern, whose husband, Geoffrey Holdsworth, was at the Front, came to stay and seemed to take over much of Mrs Meikle's role, leaving Rebecca free to resume her work. But, as the warmer weather approached, with its long beach walks on the shore of the Thames, so too did the bombing raids, which came ever closer to Rebecca's home. The air raids terrified Rebecca, which in turn irritated Wells. He preferred to 'alter and avoid disagreeable things' if possible, or if not 'to sit tight and jeer'. Once, Rebecca, panicking, had rushed out to the passage at the back of the house and spoken to all the neighbours who were similarly gathered there, seeking reassurance. When the raids persisted in the following nights, sleep-deprived, exhausted and scared, she cried out repeatedly. Wells detested this, seeing it as melodramatic weakness. He wrote to her afterwards: 'You go out to get the fullest impression of any old black thing. Every disagreeable impression is welcome to your mind, it grows there.'[19]

He went on to say that what was a 'love adventure' for him had been turned into an 'utterly disagreeable story' by her 'peculiar genius'. He was tired of what he regarded as her negativity, her pessimism, her need to see everything in the blackest light.

The raids continued until finally, one weekend in early October 1917, Southcliffe was narrowly missed by an aerial torpedo and the bay itself was bombed. Grabbing Anthony, Rebecca left the house, intending to go to Pimlico. Instead, Peter dragged them off to an old mill at West Wycombe. Later, Rebecca learned she had had a close escape; the pet cat at Southcliffe had been killed and Claverton Street had been bombed and flooded by a resulting burst water main.

Despite the attacks on Pimlico, this spate of bombings made Rebecca feel that London was safer than the coast and she decided to evacuate Anthony there, enrolling him in a Montessori Boarding School. Rebecca stayed close by for his first week at the school in case he found it difficult to settle in, but Anthony immediately took to his new surroundings and she delightedly wrote to Sylvia Lynd, 'Anthony has absolutely abandoned me. From his first loud, glad shriek – "There are little girlies here!" he has preferred his school to his home.'[20] Although later Anthony claimed that he hated being sent to boarding school at such an early age; he was only three.

With Anthony settled at the school on weekdays, Rebecca had a double reason to be in London and spent more and more time in the rooms Wells had rented at 51 Claverton Street. She was able to go to the theatre again and did so with various friends, including Ibsen's translator, William Archer. But post-birth insecurities and the instability of her relationship with Wells made her compare herself unfavourably with the women she saw there. She found herself longing for 'eyes like saucers' and a neck like 'any metaphor out of the Song of Solomon'.[21]

Just as Rebecca's life seemed more and more fractured, divided between London and Essex, evenings with Wells and weekends with Anthony, her sister Winnie was planning to settle down with a man called Norman Macleod. Perhaps a little envious of her sister's stable relationship, Rebecca merely noted the fact in letters to her friends, without elaboration or celebration.

Laid low with an eye infection, Rebecca once again retreated to Southcliffe, in autumn 1917, feeling ugly and miserable. She wrote to a new woman friend, Sally Melville, of another new acquaintance, Commander Kenworthy, who she described as having 'the bounce of the Old Testament God'. While professing a fascination with her 'wonderful mind', the commander had shown more than a little interest in Rebecca's body. She had rebuffed him but admitted that this might have had as much to do with his incredible ugliness as out of any regard for Wells.[22] Although Rebecca was enjoying increased freedom, Wells continued to grumble that, despite his love for her, he also loved 'being with my work with everything handy'. He continued, 'I *hate* being encumbered with a little boy and a nurse and being helpful, I hate waiting about.'[23]

Before 1917 was out, the bombing in London became so severe that Anthony's school was moved out to the countryside. He enjoyed the farm animals and the change of scenery but his relationships with other pupils were not good. This was largely a natural consequence of a dispute between his parents. Rebecca had never acknowledged Anthony, who was now three, as her son, either publically or to the child himself, and he was still calling her Auntie Panther. Wells was adamant that this was wrong and that Rebecca should explain the situation to nurses and servants and allow Anthony to call her mother. The problem with this suggestion was that Wells himself still refused to admit publicly that Anthony was his; Anthony was 'expressly forbidden to call him "*father, papa or daddy*"' and referred to him only as

Wellsie.[24] Diffident and reserved, isolated by the oddities of his domestic situation, Anthony grew apart from children his own age, eventually escaping in invented fantasies about an imagined, more-perfect family life.

New Year's Day of 1918 was not a good beginning to the year. Wells did not visit. Rebecca was desperately lonely and in a state of despair over her work's lack of progress. She marked the day in her diary simply 'Bored to Death'.[25]

However, Rebecca was not short of other admirers, though not all of them were welcome. A fellow Fabian suggested going 'to the theatre together and then sin!' Rebecca was shocked at his presumption, conceding that some men might feel they have that right; 'men with square jaws who eat chops for breakfast and shoot and ride' but that this suitor was 'a Fabian and a vege-tarian!' and not her type at all.[26]

Two years before, in 1916, Rebecca had begun work on a new novel, *The Judge*. Its heroine, Ellen, is reminiscent of Rebecca in her suffrage days but undergoes a drastic change after her marriage to Richard Yaverland, competing for her husband with his overprotective mother. The depiction of the resulting *ménage à trois* contains many allusions to Rebecca's own triangle with Jane and Wells. She had hit a block; and now she lamented to Sylvia Lynd that it lay on her mental chest 'like an under-cooked suet pudding'.[27]

While Rebecca struggled to finish the new novel, *The Return of the Soldier* was published in London during May 1918. Within a fortnight 1,600 copies had been sold and after a month it had gone into a second printing. It captured the mood and pain of the age with its depiction of a shell-shocked soldier whose con-sequent amnesia returns him to an earlier, happier, more innocent time. Chris, the soldier, after losing his memory, returns to an old love, Margaret, and in doing so disregards the controlling claus-trophobia of his relationship with his wife, Kitty. The novel was small and sparsely written with an unmistakeable elegance that led to admiring reviews.

She had some problems with the publisher, the Century

Company, however. 'Bertie', their agent, took a verbal agreement she had given him as a commitment to allow Century to publish her next two books as part of the contract for *Return of the Soldier*. The solicitor of the Author's Society came to her rescue and Rebecca wrote to Sylvia Lynd that she was relieved to be free from Bertie's vulgar comments and bosom-staring.

Following the release of the book she spent the weekend with Violet Hunt and Ford Madox Ford but the visit was not a success. Ford was gently unkind about the novel, comparing it unfavourably with his own work, and Hunt's normally odd behaviour seemed to be heading towards madness as she repeatedly, and deliberately, dropped her lace-trimmed knickers from Rebecca's balcony onto the flowering petunias below.

But shortly after, Rebecca met an old friend from ADA, Greta Mortimer, by chance when she took Anthony to see a pantomime, and the two women rekindled their fond friendship. Greta's boy, Basil, was of an age with Anthony, and, for once, Rebecca was the better off of the pair. Greta helped her out by watching Anthony and giving her a little more freedom; in return, Rebecca donated Anthony's old clothes and his pram to Basil.

In September 1918, Wells, Anthony and Rebecca took a rare, short holiday together, in Hunstanton, the place of Anthony's birth. Rebecca was not particularly thrilled by the choice of location, referring to it as deadly in a letter to Sally Melville, but she took comfort in Anthony's joy at being part of a family, even if only temporarily. While they stayed there, at the Sandringham Hotel, the Allies finally achieved victory; the Great War came to an end.

∾◦∾

With the end of the war, and the new solvency afforded by the success of *The Return of the Soldier*, Rebecca finally left Leigh-on-Sea in 1919, to return to London. She moved into a new apartment at 36 Queen's Gate Terrace in South Kensington. Anthony's musical games to Harry Lauder and Wagner had turned into signs of real ability and Rebecca wrote to Shaw, with whom she kept up a scattered correspondence, for advice on how best to develop this. He recommended that Rebecca do all she could to encourage any latent talent.

In the spring of 1920, Wells and Rebecca took a brief trip together, driving down to Cornwall so that Rebecca could stay with Peter and her husband, who had returned from the war but was still deeply shaken by his years at the Front. An accident during her stay when she fell down an uncovered well shaft resulted in a septic wound and a necessary convalescence at a nearby nursing home. Wells, characteristically, found lots of reasons not to visit his ailing lover, and instead arranged a trip to Czechoslovakia, where he was delighted to be hailed as a literary superstar. During September and October, he followed this with a trip to Russia. On this visit he met Lenin and revised his negative view, finding him more willing to think outside of established Marxist doctrine than he had anticipated.[28] But while he was critical of Marxist theory, Wells took a much more lenient view towards the revolution than Rebecca would later express. He described Lenin's regime as the only possible Russian government, even going as far as to defend the Red Terror, because it killed 'for a reason and to an end'.[29]

On his return he confessed to Rebecca that he had had an affair, with the twenty-seven-year-old secretary of Maxim Gorky, Moura von Benckendorff. Rebecca was distraught but managed to react to the news defiantly; if Wells could see other people then so could she.

In the autumn of that year, therefore, she happily accepted an offer from the celebrated novelist Compton Mackenzie, proposing that she accompany his wife Faith to their house on Capri. Anthony would be cared for by her sister Winnie and by his grandmother when he was not at school.

Mackenzie, known as Monty, had been on active service in the war and had met Rebecca at yet another of Violet Hunt's South Lodge parties. Because of Rebecca's illness and her continued anxiety about her relationship with Wells, work on her new novel, *The Judge*, had been going very slowly. Wells had told her that it was 'an addled egg' that Rebecca should give up sitting on.[30] Monty, who had agreed to look at the first half of the manuscript, disagreed. He thought the book excellent, and he hoped that Capri would give her the time and respite to finish it. Perhaps in part because of his respect and concern, and also because of Wells' lack of attention, Rebecca was attracted to Monty. Their relationship, however, remained nothing more than a flirtation on both sides and Monty did not accompany the women to Capri.

The evening before she left for Capri, Rebecca and Wells dined with Max Beaverbrook. He was a close friend of Sally Melville, and Rebecca had met him, albeit briefly – they had been introduced by Shaw – two years previously. He frequently gave intimate dinner parties at his compact Victorian house in Fulham which his wife Gladys rarely attended. Like Wells, Beaverbrook spent much time away from his wife. Gladys lived for the most part in their much bigger house in Surrey, with Beaverbrook visiting her there almost every weekend. He also shared with Wells a reputation as a womanizer. He was not a particularly handsome man, short and stocky with a large mouth that was frequently rather cruelly caricatured, but he was intelligent, witty and charming. After the dinner Rebecca wrote to Sally, saying how much she had enjoyed the evening: 'I found him one of the most fascinating talkers I've ever met, and full of real vitality – the geniusy kind that exists mystically apart from all physical conditions, just as it does in H.G.'[31]

Capri was lovely in October. Casa Solitaria was accessed by a rough path cut through the shadowy cliffs, which, when they first arrived, were streaked with hues of lilac and rose from the morning sun. And the villa was beautiful. In preparation for Rebecca's arrival, Faith had asked the housekeeper, Carolina, to hang the best apricot curtains and to fill the rooms with huge bunches of flowers. But Faith's poor health let her down and, by the time they arrived, the train journey from Naples had taken its toll; she was suffering from a high temperature and a throat infection. She took to her bed immediately after lunch and did not get up for two days, stirring only from time to time to eat some broth or to gargle peroxide. It seemed to have little effect on Rebecca, however, who set up a space on the table in the main room. There, in her own very characteristic writing position, kneeling on a chair, never sitting, she recommenced work on her novel, muttering over her papers as she worked, oblivious to anyone else who came through the room.

When Faith recovered they held seances in the evening, a popular pastime of the day, placing cards on which were written the letters of the alphabet in the shape of a circle on top of the grand piano, and asking the spirits for messages. Rebecca was interested in spiritualism and the occult and resolutely believed she had psychic ability of her own, inherited from her mother.

As Faith recovered, the two women visited the small expatri-ate community on the island and Rebecca wrote amusing letters to her mother about their eccentricities. She was relaxed and happy: 'We are being so wholly comfortable that I can't help feeling (the universe being what it is) that somebody must be being very uncomfortable somewhere to make up.'[32]

As it happened, by coincidence, someone was. Jane Wells was extremely ill, having undergone a hysterectomy, and this, coupled with Wells' unease at Rebecca's visit to Capri alone, heralded a flurry of letters from him. Her threats of taking a new lover had deeply affected him, and he wrote, with typical double standards, 'It is much bitterer and more humiliating for the male and I can't bear the thought of it. I love you and I want to keep you anyhow, but I know that in spite of myself I shan't be able to endure your unfaithfulness.'[33]

His complaints continued in other letters. He was 'unendura-bly lonely'. He was miserable and tired, with a terrible cold and an ailing Jane and no one who could understand him. With a typical mixture of arrogance and neediness he wrote that he could not go on being a slave to the world, and that religion offered no consolation because: 'God has no thighs and no life. When one calls to him in the silence of the night he doesn't turn over and say, "What is the trouble, dear?" I'm miserable and lonely and disgusted and flat.'[34]

He was worried that Rebecca would find someone else to replace him in her affections and, speculating on the following year, when he was due to join her in Italy, he worried that he would find her involved with a new and handsome man. Jane did not recover well from her surgery. Indeed her condition was so bad that even Rebecca put aside her animosity to write to Jane wishing her better health. Wells' health also took a turn for the worse, as his cold turned into pneumonia. An impending trip to America had to be cancelled and he now proposed leaving Jane, still very unwell, to set out, earlier than planned, for Rebecca and the Italian climate.

Rebecca enjoyed the early part of her visit, the meetings with the various eccentric expats scattered around the area. Particularly fun were the days and evenings spent with the celebrated opera singer Louise Edvina, who had a house nearby. The three women eventually made music together, Rebecca on the piano, enjoying Fauré and Du Parc in Edvina's beautifully restored villa. Faith and Rebecca were adopted by a half-Siamese tortoiseshell cat with a huge bushy tail, who followed them round the hillsides and was consequently not only fed but thoroughly spoiled.

However, their gentle enjoyment was short-lived. One evening, while Rebecca was reading Hudson's *Long Ago and Far Away* aloud to her, Faith suffered from violent internal bleeding. A doctor was immediately summoned.

From being a companion and friend, Rebecca found herself thrown into the role of nurse and carer. She wrote to Monty, entreating that he come out and see Faith, but she received no reply. As Faith's health deteriorated, Rebecca grew increasingly worried and went to Anacapri to get the opinion of a well-known Swedish doctor, Axel Munthe, who speedily diagnosed a condition related to menopause. Christmas and New Year celebrations came and went and, while Rebecca enjoyed them, Faith remained very ill, and was increasingly distant towards Rebecca. As the days passed, her hostility and the reason for it became too obvious to be ignored. Faith suspected that Rebecca had had an affair with Monty, and Rebecca, aggrieved, moved out of Casa Solitaria and up to Anacapri, where she confided in the very sympathetic Munthe.

Rebecca then moved to the Hotel Cappucini in Amalfi, where she concentrated on her writing, worrying about Anthony and his progress in reading and her mother's health. She also had to try to allay the latter's concerns over her precipitous departure from Casa Solitaria. The hotel was an ancient convent, set in a terraced garden of orange and lemon trees. It seemed a suitably romantic place for her reunion with Wells, but after his arrival, in late January, the mood soon soured. Wells suspected Rebecca of infidelity. As a result, he vacillated between solicitous kindness and behaving like a domineering tyrant.

After a fraught month they moved briefly to Florence, by way of Rome, before Wells left for London. In Florence Rebecca met Reggie Turner, the curator of the Palazzo Horne, and Norman Douglas, the celebrated author of *South Wind*. Reggie had been a close friend and champion of Oscar Wilde, even sending him an extravagant dressing case from Bond Street when he was released from prison. Wilde had loved the case, despite its complete impracticality. Norman Douglas, a notorious paedophile left impoverished after various legal cases arising from his predilection, was indebted to Rebecca because she had launched an appeal to help him financially. As a result of this, Somerset Maugham had offered to 'assume total responsibility', on condition of anonymity.[35]

Reggie and Norman introduced her to D.H. Lawrence, whose work she already admired. Lawrence had arrived just six hours earlier and was staying in a run-down hotel overlooking the Arno. His room was at the back of the building and was small and dimly lit, but in it Lawrence already sat steadily pounding away at a typewriter. He stopped writing when his small group of visitors arrived, but only so that he could read them the article he had been working on in the hours since he had arrived. Shocked by his emaciated appearance but entranced by his genius, Rebecca found 'his conversation perpetually made and unmade the world until late in the afternoon'.[36]

◦◦◦

She found Lawrence 'one of the most polite people I have ever met'.[37] He made friends with her, shyly, 'as a child might do', and the day after their first meeting they went walking in the countryside, past the Certosa. Rebecca was delighted to leave Florence; she always preferred Rome, describing herself as 'so enamoured of Rome' that she could not submit to the enchantment of Florence.[38] And, in the sunshine that followed the torrential rain of the day before, she observed Lawrence's interaction with the changing weather and scenery, his intensity as if he was 'speeding faster than spring can go from bud to bud'.[39] Their tentative friendship would last until Lawrence's final days, so that, just a few months before his death in 1930, he wrote to her: 'Tell me if ever I can do anything for you, in any way. I'm sadder and wiser and perhaps might.'[40]

But even this meeting did not change Rebecca's humour; Florence displeased her. In general she found the expatriates she met there were either 'very vulgar and fast, like the sort of people who go to Cannes' or 'lost in the past with houses like museums'.[41] Her mother's health had deteriorated; she was homesick and missing Anthony. Wells sent her long letters, reminiscing about their time together as perfect, seemingly forgetting the squabbles, and entreating her to come back to 'some more love'.[42] He wrote adulatory pages, filled with the depth of his affections and his need for her, declaring 'I'm not really happy except when you are about'.[43]

Wells' devotion continued after Rebecca's return to England and they spent the summer together with Anthony, during the school holidays, on the coast at Norfolk. It was the kind of family life that Rebecca longed for, the idyllic summer marred only by her mother's rapid deterioration, her illness now diagnosed as Grave's Disease. In August, Rebecca wrote to Wells from her mother's home in Chatham Close. Isabella had been in terrible pain all weekend but Lettie and Rebecca agreed that giving her morphine might hasten her death. Although weak, Isabella could not rest, distractedly climbing in and out of bed, unable to find any respite. Another doctor arrived and Lettie finally agreed to administer the morphine. It brought immediate relief, but as the sisters had feared, Isabella did not wake up from the sleep it induced. Rebecca was overwhelmed by the loss of a 'queer passionate genius', acknowledging that they had only quarrelled so intensely because they loved each other so much. She helped lay out the body and begged Wells to join them, telling him that Lettie had collapsed, both from grief and from the strain of continually nursing her mother in the weeks preceding her death. Grieving, Lettie turned to religion and, in the period following Isabella's death, converted to Roman Catholicism. Perhaps frustrated by her inability as a medic to alleviate their mother's suffering, or indeed to save her, she also began studying for the bar.

After the funeral, Rebecca went to Weybourne where Wells joined her. In spite of his differences with Isabella, he recognized that 'in a passionate quarrelsome way the two were extraordinarily attached to each other' and Rebecca needed support.[44] In September, she settled for a few weeks with Wells in Norfolk, where she met Charlie Chaplin for the first time. He charmed her and she wrote to Reggie Turner in Italy that she thought him 'a very serious little cockney' and a darling.[45] It was the beginning of a friendship, a friendship that would later develop into something more.

⁂

In her grief, Rebecca drew closer to Wells than she had been for some time. Wells spent companionable hours with Anthony, producing drawings of 'Auntie Panther', and Anthony and 'Wellsie' on their excursions together, as well as a cartoon strip depicting Anthony as a cowboy on horseback. Wells' trip to the United States had been rearranged for the autumn and he begged Rebecca to accompany him, but she refused. Instead they arranged a holiday in Spain together to take place early in the New Year. Wells' devoted letters to Rebecca from the States, declaring how much he loved her both intellectually and physically, belied the fact that he was having a relationship there, with the New York radical Margaret Sanger. Sanger was notable for her forthright advocacy of birth control but also for her interest in eugenics. Her contradictory views – that on the one hand women should have greater freedom and independence, while on the other that 'undesirable' or 'unstable' women should be sterilized to prevent them from conceiving at all – were a mirror for Wells' own rather conflicting views on the emancipation of women.

In early January 1922, Rebecca, still seemingly unaware of the affair, was missing Wells terribly. In her diary she wrote that she was thinking of him, her 'heart was lonely', until 'a kind letter' from him cheered her up.[46] Her pensive mood endured – she was 'longing for Jaguar', dreaming of him – until Friday the 13th, when he would be back from the States, and she could at last write that she was going to meet him and that they would travel together to Algeciras.

It was an ominous day to start a journey and proved to be so when a storm blew up just as the boat they were on sailed out of the Bay of Biscay. Wells was grumpy and seasick. By the time they arrived in Algeciras, he demanded a naval doctor, who prescribed an antiseptic gargle for his sore throat. Wells refused to accept that his illness was minor and demanded that Rebecca act as his nurse. His trip to America had been a success and pleased by this and, no doubt, by his romantic conquest, he treated Rebecca not merely as a nurse but as a servant. In a letter to her sister Lettie she complained that he ordered her around, expecting his every whim to be attended to. However, there were moments of respite and Rebecca's diary is punctuated, although less and less frequently, with the good days, when 'darling Jaguar' walked with her or was 'naughty'.[47] When they reached Granada, Rebecca had had enough of the tyranny and rebelled, accusing Wells of behaving more like a schoolmaster than a lover. But

Rebecca's letters and cards to Anthony, who was being looked after by Lettie, were full of funny descriptions of flamenco dancers; the tantrums and tears that made up most of the holiday were well hidden.

Throughout the spring and summer of 1922, Rebecca attempted to recreate idyllic past days, taking trips with Wells in the English countryside, but without much success. As the days lengthened she visited Porlock in Somerset, to stay with Peter Stern and her husband, Geoffrey Holdsworth. Wells arrived to take Rebecca away for a few days but, as usual, his resentment over the time she was spending with other people made their relationship tense and tiring. *The Judge*, which Rebecca had dedicated to her mother, was published during these difficult days, but what could have been a shared celebration became yet another source of acrimony between them. Wells disliked its rambling effusiveness. And he was not alone. In marked contrast to the precise, almost delicate structure of *The Return of the Soldier*, this new novel was a rambling, almost shambolic book, likened by Virginia Woolf to an 'over-stuffed sausage'.[48] Somerset Maugham was also critical of the book, and wrote to her from Thailand, warning her that her use of metaphor might destroy her reader's absorption in the plot and remind the reader that 'it is not life that he is living but a book that he is reading'. However, he also said that Rebecca's talent shone through, adding that he didn't think that 'there is anyone writing now who can hold a candle to you'.[49]

Chapter Six

DIFFERENT KINDS
OF DEPRESSION

Despite her growing recognition as a writer of note, Rebecca's personal situation in 1923 was bleak. She was single; she was a mother. Her lover was married and unfaithful to both her and his wife. In her younger years, she had written to her sisters with hopes of the 'boofs', their pet word for beautiful men, they might meet, but now the possibilities of her youth seemed to elude her and she longed for someone to change her life. The First World War had seen the loss of almost three-quarters of a million British men and, by the 1920s, the female population far outweighed the male. They were known as 'the surplus women' and according to the 1921 Census, there were 1.75 million of them.[1] Newspaper headlines abounded with the plight of the 'Two million who can never become wives'.[2]

Rebecca was one of many, born of a generation who assumed they would marry, but whose hopes had now been shattered. Friends who had married before the war were widowed, or if their husbands had survived they were now broken, reliving the horrors of the trenches. For Rebecca a part of Wells was better than nothing at all. In spite of their deteriorating relationship, and his increasingly bad behaviour, she did not end their almost ten-year affair.

Instead, she sought an escape from her emotional turmoil. She had recently taken up riding and very quickly became passionate about it, racing around the countryside. Her boldness and apparent lack of fear earned her respect from other riders and, despite her inexperience, she joined a local hunt.

The ultimate test of her unusual domestic arrangements came in early 1923, when they threatened to affect her professional life. She had planned to visit the United States but was deeply troubled when a prominent American socialite tried to have her banned from the country for her immorality. This sparked a new determination in Rebecca to resolve the awkwardness of her position and she issued Wells with an ultimatum: either he must divorce Jane and marry her, or they would permanently separate.

Wells indignantly dismissed her anxieties:

> It's your business, in my idea, to disregard these fool scandals and go to America and succeed, as you certainly will do if you go, in spite of them. It's not your business, it's not playing the game, to lacerate me about it. For ten years I've shaped my life mainly to repair the carelessness of one moment. It has been no good and I am tired of it.[3]

But Rebecca was adamant. Wells bombarded her with letters: perhaps she would not find that marriage brought all that she expected it to, perhaps if he improved her living conditions with a 'comfortable home in the country' and 'a little flat in London' then all might return to normal. Rebecca did not go as far as to make any public declaration of independence, but the distance between them was obvious to friends and troubled Wells, who found himself deeply jealous of this new Rebecca who was acting like a single woman in his company.

It was at this time that Rebecca renewed her acquaintance with Max Beaverbrook, who had so fascinated her before the Capri trip. This time the attraction was mutual; one night, Beaverbrook asked Rebecca if she would be his mistress.[4] Rebecca 'woke up entirely happy and only distressed by what I was to tell H.G., how I was to protect Max from H.G.'s vindictiveness'.[5] But then almost immediately she received a message saying that Max had been called overseas and would not be able to see her after all. Perplexed, Rebecca was forced to acknowledge that she was in fact in love with Beaverbrook. For the second time in her life, she was contemplating an impossible emotional situation. She would write later to her sister that 'I cannot help feeling there is evidence that I am hounded by a malevolent fate in the way that I have twice found people who could have satisfied me completely – one H.G. was [sic] possessed by a devil, and Max by one of another sort.'[6]

In typical fashion, Wells reacted to the unsettling state of affairs by striking up a relationship with yet another woman. But this time both he and Rebecca would pay the consequences. What started out as a casual sexual encounter ended as an almost fatal attraction, and a scandal worthy of the newspapers.

In the spring of 1923 a young Austrian widow 'with a face like the Mona Lisa' wrote to Wells requesting a meeting so she could avail him of the troubles in her country. He invited Hedwig Verena Gattenrigg to have tea with him and Jane at their flat in Whitehall. She took advantage of the meeting to urge him to allow her to translate one of his books into German and, having had no interest from a German publisher, Wells quickly agreed. Her next meeting was also in Whitehall, but away from the watchful eyes of Jane who had by then returned to Easton Glebe. According to Wells, any literary interests quickly turned to romantic ones and she declared a great passion for him. She sent him love letters confessing the extent of her infatuation and Wells slept with her on numerous occasions, even at one point spending a weekend with her.

On her return to Vienna, she found that far from their liaison being a casual thing on her part, she had been deeply affected. Refusing to accept that her departure was the end of the affair, she immediately returned to London to press upon the now reluctant Wells the possibilities of their future together. Disturbed by her insistence and the inconvenience of an overeager woman in whom he was no longer interested, Wells resolutely refused to see her. She settled in a boarding house off Euston

Square and, undaunted by his lack of continued interest, visited his flat unannounced and haunted the streets where he was likely to be. Wells instructed his staff not to admit her under any circumstances, avoided her when he could, and waited for the problem to disappear, preferring instead to endeavour to address the problem of his ever more difficult affair with Rebecca.

One evening, as he dressed for a scheduled dinner with Edwin Montagu, the former Secretary of State for India, he turned abruptly on hearing someone enter his study. Going through, he found Hedwig sitting on the rug by his hearth, with a raincoat wrapped around her. As he approached her, she flung it open to show herself naked bar her shoes and stockings and confronted the shocked Wells with the words, 'You must love me or I will kill myself. I have poison. I have a razor'.

Wells called for his maid to get the hall porter but while he did so Gattenrigg removed a razor from the coat and proceeded to slash her armpits and wrists. Wells managed to get the razor from her and rested her on a chair, while she bled profusely and repeatedly cried that she wanted to be allowed to die. Wells' very competent porter had meanwhile arrived with the police who carried her off to Charing Cross Hospital.

Later it transpired that Gattenrigg had visited Rebecca first. Wells had effected an introduction between the two women and she had arrived distraught at Rebecca's flat. Charitably, when asked about the incident by the *Westminster Gazette*, Rebecca defended her, saying: 'Mrs Gattenrigg however was not abusive and there was not a scene. She is a very intelligent woman, doing really beautiful work and I feel very sorry for her.'[7]

Wells told Rebecca that there had been nothing but a trivial, brief fling with a woman who was clearly unhinged; Rebecca believed him. He also assured her that it was Jane, and not he, who had called the police after finding Gattenrigg at the flat. Consequently, Rebecca stood by him, making a very public show of lunching with him at the Ivy and, the day after the scene, attending an opening night at the theatre. Only years later, after

Wells' death, would Rebecca learn the extent of his betrayal, the nature of his affair with Hedwig Verena Gattenrigg, and be hurt even then that she had been so deceived.

Gattenrigg seemed in time to recover from her melodramatic encounter and, at the end of July, wrote to Jane Wells begging for forgiveness, hoping that she could continue her translation work, and pleading: 'I am very, very sorry to have caused all this sordid mess – but I had come to a point where the wish to blot out my consciousness was overwhelming and made me disregard all possible consequences . . . I was ill and helpless.'[8]

For Rebecca, while she continued to display public loyalty to Wells, the incident had in some way resolved her dilemma about her feelings for Beaverbrook. If a romantic affair did develop in the way that she hoped, Wells was going to have to put up with it.

For the rest of the summer, Rebecca planned to concentrate on Anthony, moving with him and his governess to a house in Swanage, in the hope that the countryside would do him good. Anthony was now ten and proving to be a troubled child. Winnie's daughter, Alison, saw him as a menace and lived in fear of his bullying whenever Rebecca and her sister visited.[9] Anthony would later attribute this to his unconventional family and his illegitimacy. Rebecca hoped he might calm down away from the city. At the same time she was making plans for her American tour, where she would lecture on feminism and on the modern novel, and arranging to board Anthony at St Piran's preparatory school in Maidenhead. Wells' fits of moody jealousy persisted and Rebecca grew more and more irritated by his possessiveness. She wrote to friends complaining of 'his absolute dependence on her' and that he was 'tiresome and jealous and quarrelsome'.[10] She felt prohibited from seeing anyone else and longed to end the relationship. Attempts to do so, however, always seemed to fail. Wells would either write pleading letters or promise better provision for Anthony. At one point, he even offered to leave Anthony the same sum of money as he planned to leave his other sons. Rebecca wrote to Sally Melville:

I am as miserable as Hell. I have gone back to H.G. I am going down to the country with him this evening. What else can I do? He says that if I go back to him he will leave Anthony as much money as his other boys – that will mean about £20,000. I daren't gamble on making that myself because I feel dead beat and though I might marry I could never get any man to give Anthony £20,000.[11]

Rebecca added that Wells was even considering divorcing Jane but that she had vetoed the suggestion. It had come too late. The compromise, the constant unease of being in a relationship that she no longer wished to continue, was beginning to impinge on Rebecca's work. From Swanage she wrote to her sister Winnie, complaining of the way Wells jeered at her, seeming to resent any letters she received admiring her work. He refused to read or work around her, instead demanding constant attention. Exasperated, Rebecca longed impatiently to leave for America, to get relief from his 'constant disturbance of my work', to be away from his 'dreary whingeing egotism'.[12]

By the end of October 1923, Rebecca had finally had enough and she sailed for New York on the *Mauretania*. Just after her arrival she wrote delightedly to Winnie, sending her first impressions of the city. The view as they sailed into the harbour was 'gorgeous', buildings were 'incredibly strange erections of a Robot civilisation' and the skyscrapers rose gracefully above them, 'white and slim like lilies'.[13] She was immediately welcomed into American literary society with a tea in Somerset Maugham's apartment. Maugham had taken up temporary residence in New York while his play *The Camel's Back* was being produced. Through him, Rebecca met a theatrical manager who was keen to put on a dramatic version of *The Return of the Soldier*, but the woman explained that in spite of paying various playwrights $3,000, she had yet to receive a suitable script based on the book.

Rebecca was by turns enchanted by the architecture and the atmosphere of the city, and critical. She found the women far uglier than their European counterparts and very careless in their appearance. And this female apathy, she thought, matched the general lack of vitality in any of the men she met. She found them ponderous in speech and action and generally boring as a result. Rebecca's London literary agent, Andrew Dakers, was also in New York with his wife. He took the opportunity to arrange for Rebecca to meet his American business partner. When both his wife and partner had left, he also took the opportunity to declare his passionate love for Rebecca. In a letter to Winnie, she recounted how he had 'flung himself down on the sofa and buried his head in the cushions and made noises like a sick cow'.[14] A horrified Rebecca was forced to watch while Dakers 'writhed and panted and kept on kissing [her] hands'. Eventually she was able to escape only because a journalist arrived to conduct an interview with her. Rebecca then embarked on her strenuous lecture tour, finding that the effects of fatigue and travelling meant that the lectures did not always go as well as she had wished. In the hope of gleaning an idea of what older American audiences might expect and appreciate, Rebecca attended a lecture given by William Lyon Phelps. Phelps was the Lampson Professor of English at Yale and had instigated Yale's first course on the novel. However, rather than find anything to admire, Rebecca was shocked by his moralizing and his anti-Semitism. The night was further ruined by the arrival of Dakers, who had travelled from New York specifically to say goodbye to the object of his adoration. Exhausted and angry, Rebecca spent the evening with him, albeit in the company of others, too, listening to jazz and drinking several very unpleasant temperance drinks.

At Christmas, Rebecca returned to New York – not just to the city, but to Max Beaverbrook. He had charged his secretaries with finding her and, when they did, he turned up at the Ritz ready to resume their flirtation as if there had never been any interruption. To Rebecca, it really felt that the dark days of Wells were over, that this was the beginning of a serious relationship, and she confided in one of her new American friends, the novelist Fannie Hurst, that she felt she really had something to offer him. For Max, however, grief-stricken by the recent death of his great friend, former prime minister Bonar Law, it may have been a temporary madness.

The idyll was short-lived and, after just two weeks, Max announced his intention to return to London. Later she would realize that they were 'completely unsuited to be man and wife'.[15] But after his departure Rebecca, feeling abandoned, was distraught. She immediately fell ill with influenza which in turn gave way to bronchitis and colitis. Weak and tearful, she postponed the remainder of her lecture tour and stayed in New York to recuperate. Fannie Hurst became her mainstay throughout her convalescence and Rebecca confided in her about all that had happened, taking comfort in Hurst's opulent world. Her apartment was richly decorated with icons and tapestries, and despite prohibition, her home was always well stocked with alcohol for visitors. Rebecca's other new confidante was the writer and biographer Emanie Nahm Sachs. She had recently completed a novel entitled *Talk*, which on its release the following year would be both a commercial success and critically acclaimed, with the *New York Times* even drawing comparisons with F. Scott Fitzgerald. Emanie was married to Walter Sachs, whose family owned the banking firm Goldman Sachs. She was only a year younger than Rebecca and the two women became the closest of friends, and would remain so until Emanie's death in 1981. Indeed their friendship was so intense that, shortly after they met, Emanie told Rebecca she had fallen in love with her. In 1924 she wrote to her wondering if Rebecca's romantic adventures were perhaps a sign that she did not want a peaceful life, adding, 'if you are so fascinating when you are living through a tragedy, you must be dangerous indeed now that it is over'.[16]

∽∽

But cosy evenings in Hurst's apartment and intimate lunches with Emanie were counterbalanced by several less-successful New York encounters. Despite having broken with Wells, Rebecca was nevertheless still the subject of moralizing gossip about their liaison. At a society party, Ruth Hale, the wife of the writer Heywood Broum, humiliated Rebecca by addressing her before the assembled company:

> Rebecca West, we are all disappointed in you. You have put an end to a great illusion. We thought of you as an independent woman, but here you are, looking down in the mouth, because you relied on a man to give you all you wanted and now that you have to turn out and fend for yourself you are bellyaching about it. I believe Wells treated you too darn well, he gave you money, and jewels and everything you wanted and if you live with a man on those terms you must expect to get turned out when he gets tired of you.[17]

Other meetings were equally unsuccessful. Rebecca had met the Fitzgeralds and liked both Scott and Zelda. They reciprocated, holding what Zelda remembered as their biggest party of all in Rebecca's honour.[18] But there was a misunderstanding. Rebecca dressed and waited in her hotel room for Scott to collect her and take her to the party. When he did not arrive, she began ringing friends in a desperate but futile attempt to find out where she was supposed to be. Fitzgerald had either forgotten his promise or Rebecca had misunderstood. Across town, guests gathered at the party, but Rebecca never showed up. Fitzgerald made fun of her, mimicking her over dinner, and the New York literary scene was soon buzzing with gossip about the English writer's apparent rudeness.

Once she had fully recovered, Rebecca travelled to California to resume her tour. While she was there she took comfort over Max's rejection, in Charlie Chaplin's ardent pursuit of her. In Los Angeles, Chaplin tried to get her to sleep with him but she refused. But her rejection only seemed to encourage him. Finally, in order to escape his attentions, Rebecca travelled on to Santa Barbara without telling him. Chaplin frantically tried to track her down, but failed. Rebecca didn't discuss the events with anyone until three years later when she confided in Lettie. Chaplin later told her that he was terrified of being impotent and had wanted to have sex with Rebecca to prove that he was not.

Rebecca's time in America extended with the success of her lecture tour but her triumph was blighted by tales of Anthony's problems back in England. The headmaster of St Piran's reported early in 1924 that Anthony had cut up his sheets with a pair of scissors. Anthony later remembered that he was beginning to question the notion that Rebecca was his Aunty Panther and he struggled to understand the true nature of his familial relationships. He longed for Panther and wrote to Lettie that he was counting the days until her return.

Chapter Seven

ANTHONY'S AWAKENING

❧❧

In March 1924, five months after she'd set sail, Rebecca was still in America, and Anthony, increasingly confused and longing for his mother, wrote some 'pathetic letters' entreating her to come home.[1] She was reluctant, complaining to Lettie that his problems were 'terribly inconvenient' but conceding that if he really was as miserable as he said he was then she didn't have a choice. That said, though, she would finish her tour first, which meant remaining in the States until the beginning of May. She also had a new anonymous suitor and described him to Lettie as 'the sweetest, quietest creature in the world'. However, he was, she wrote, a 'very Jewy Jew', which she thought might stop Anthony getting into a good school.[2] The new boof also had a daughter by a previous marriage, and perhaps in acknowledgement of the difficulties she was having with Anthony, she worried too that she was 'no good with cubs'.[3]

Anthony's view of his childhood was that it was one of isolation and rejection. He recalled abject bewilderment and great loneliness. The way in which his classmates regarded his unconventional family situation only added to his misery. Bullied and tormented at school, he finally gave his mother an ultimatum, on her return from the States: he wanted to know just exactly what his domestic situation was. Reluctantly, Rebecca told him that she was his mother and Wells was his father, but she attached a condition to her imparting of this information that the little boy saw as terrible. He must never, ever share the secret with anyone until he was grown up, 'because the story was one that ordinary people wouldn't understand, and because it would get me, and her, and my father into terrible trouble if it were to get about'.[4]

Anthony took 'refuge from his mounting anxieties' by announcing that he was interested in becoming a Roman Catholic.[5] Rebecca had no objections and suggested he get in touch with Lettie to discuss it with her (Lettie had converted after Isabella's death and continued to practise). She did, however, quite rightly worry that Anthony's decision might 'raise an awful dust with H.G.'.[6]

Rebecca was forced to deal with the difficulties that had prompted her departure from the States in the first place. Anthony was unhappy and confused. The promise she had extracted from him, about keeping his true family situation secret, had proved impossible to keep. Anthony had instead invented ever more elaborate stories about his parentage and when he was caught out in the lies, became the brunt of even more bullying and scorn.

In her absence, Wells had started to show considerable interest in Anthony, albeit mainly in his letters, a situation that only changed when he learned of his son's growing interest in Roman Catholicism. Indeed, in a letter sent while Rebecca was in the middle of her tour, he had even vaguely threatened that he might adopt his son. He told her that he had informed his eldest son, Gip, about Anthony and said he would also tell Frank in due course.

A chance meeting in a West End theatre, soon after Rebecca's return, precipitated yet more declarations of love in the days that followed. Wells claimed their meeting had left him 'sick and sorrowful with love' and called her 'the woman of his life', saying he loved her very much.[7] These avowals continued throughout the early summer, culminating with a note sent at the end of June in which he described a 'day of longing for her' and his conviction that he would be her lover until the day of his death.[8]

But for Rebecca, a romantic drama of a different kind was unfolding. Max Beaverbrook had got back in touch for the first time since his precipitous departure from New York almost six months previously. Beaverbrook telephoned, asking to meet. They duly did, at his house in Fulham and, much to Rebecca's surprise, they were not joined by anyone else. After lunch they strolled round the garden, in pale sunshine, and to Rebecca's great distress, Max spoke lightly of their relationship as 'if it were a tremendous joke'.[9] It seemed, she confided to Fannie Hurst, as if he felt no physical attraction at all towards her. Max even implied he was drunk when they made love in London and was consequently embarrassed when she took it seriously. He had, he claimed, 'the greatest friendliness' for her. 'What about New York?' she wrote to Hurst, agonizing over why he had bothered to send secretaries to pursue her if he really had no interest in her at all.[10]

Later, rumours reached her that Max was in fact conducting a full-blown love affair with the actress Gwen Ffrangcon-Davies, currently enjoying a successful run as Juliet opposite John Giel-gud's Romeo. Rebecca was hurt by his dismissal, but she was most upset by his claim that he had only seduced her because he was drunk. He was 'vile', she felt she might die, and if it wasn't for Anthony, she wasn't sure she could go on.[11] Her reaction to his rejection drove her to acknowledge that Max was the first serious emotional attachment she'd had since H.G. Yet with that came the pain of the realization that, for Max, it may not even have been a relationship at all.

Rebecca might have moved on to another disastrous affair, but Wells still hadn't lost interest in her. He visited her fre-quently over the summer, irritating her by hanging around the house. But by August, Wells seemed at last to have accepted that the affair really was over, and sent Rebecca a very pointed letter: 'Cicely Fairfield is just a Fairfield and Rebecca is a wilful, impulsive bitch and Panther . . . Panther is my lost love and a black hole in my heart.'[12]

Rebecca's deteriorating love life was in contrast to her professional one and at this time a surprising alliance struck up. The anarchist Emma Goldman had arrived in London, and, on the recommendation of her niece, Stella Ballantyne, who had met Rebecca in New York, Goldman wrote to Rebecca for advice and support. Rebecca replied immediately that she would be 'so interested' to meet her, not only for Stella's sake, but for her own, and offered to help in any way she could.[13]

Emma Goldman was a Russian émigré who had lived in America for thirty years, until she was imprisoned both for her anarchist sympathies and because she openly advocated birth control for women. On her release in 1919 she was deported to Russia, full of hope that the new revolutionary regime would offer a natural home for her beliefs. But instead she 'Saw before me the Bolshevik State, formidable, crushing every construct-ive revolutionary effort, suppressing, debasing and disintegrating everything.'[14]

Disillusioned and now as vocal a critic of the communist regime as she had ever been of the capitalists, she sought refuge first in Berlin and France and then London, where she hoped to drum up support for her political cause. In late October 1924, Rebecca and Goldman spent the day together. They went to see an amateur drama play put on by a group of doctors and nurses in St Paul's Cathedral and thought it silly. After the performance they laughed about it together, while enjoying a long talk over tea. Rebecca then introduced Goldman to Lettie, who also offered to help her. Goldman was impressed by Lettie, thinking her obviously capable, but was bewildered by her Catholicism, which she found anachronistic. Rebecca, however, she thought the 'most interesting and vital person' she had met in London.[15]

Equally impressed with her new acquaintance, Rebecca immediately set out to launch Goldman in London by making a series of introductions for her, albeit with varying degrees of success. Shaw refused to meet her at all and the *Daily Herald* and the Labour Party hierarchy were openly rude. The *Daily Express* – a Beaverbrook newspaper – ran a story headlined with a reference to the 'Red Virgin'. Rebecca retaliated with a letter to

Max 'of such unparalleled venom' that he did not reply:[16] 'I know that your interest in politics is restricted to personal gossip, but you might try to understand and sympathise with people who are interested in deeper issues.'[17]

Goldman's anarchism had been born out of her dismay at the tyranny of Bolshevism; she found 'reality in Russia grotesque'.[18] For her, anarchism was 'the only philosophy of peace, the only theory of the social relationship that values human life above everything else.'[19] When the communists brutally crushed the anarchist-inspired Kronstadt rebellion in March 1921, her rejection was total. Max and others' dismissal of what Rebecca saw as a reasoned political position based on first-hand experience seemed ridiculous. Emma was 'Russian and speaks Russian as her native language'.[20] Rebecca wrote the foreword to Goldman's book My Disillusionment in Russia (1925), predicting that 'uncritical admiration' of Soviet Russia could destroy the Labour Party, stressing that it was important to be aware of how the regime denied expression of thought rather than to romanticize any of its ideals. She went on to justify her support further: 'Her anarchism predisposed her to admiration of the new Russia, only contact with and extremely unpleasing reality would have disenchanted her.'[21]

It was a position that put Rebecca at odds with the Labour Party she had championed at the end of the war and alienated many of her former political allies. When Labour had taken power in 1924, they attempted to build, and justify, a relationship with the Soviet Union. The Conservatives, riding on the back of popular anti-communism, exploited this position, and defeated the newly elected opposition after just nine months. Rebecca seemed to be agreeing with the Conservatives, but she justified her position, saying it was ridiculous to reject a correct belief just because you didn't like the politics of the people who shared it with you. Like Goldman, she hated communism, seeing post-Revolutionary Russia as an example of a state that 'has bled away its intellectual vitality by suppressing free expression of thought'.[22]

On 12 November 1924, Colonel Josiah Wedgwood, a Labour MP who was nevertheless a great supporter of Goldman's, hosted a dinner for her. It was organized by Rebecca, who gave a speech, as did Bertrand Russell, which guaranteed a huge turn-out. Wells did not attend but sent a very charming note, thus avoiding Rebecca's wrath. Even Max seemed to have relented after Rebecca's attack and published a glowing account in the *Express*. The evening was a great success despite the lively heckling from some of the attendees who were shocked and angered by Goldman's views on Russia.

Goldman wrote to Rebecca to thank her and to say that she had been overwhelmed by the 'strength and beauty' of her personality, how it shone in her speech, and that she had wanted to embrace her, but was afraid that the audience might misunder-stand.[23] Rebecca was equally taken with Goldman's strength, and wrote 'I do not know how one would set about destroying Emma, except by frequent charges of high explosive, carried on for a very long time.'[24]

And she wrote, too, to Wells, thanking him for his letter and agreeing that for her, too, 'free speech, liberty of discussion' were paramount and that there could be no real order in the world, and no true communism when people were being forced to follow Russian leaders 'at the point of a gun'. Goldman saw herself as a true revolutionary. For her, the problem was that the Bolsheviks weren't revolutionary at all; the ideals of the revolution had been lost to Leninism.[25]

Rebecca used her contacts to try to help Goldman set up a series of lectures, although she did warn her about the difficulties of making an income on the lecture circuit. She introduced her to Lady Rhondda, the editor of *Time and Tide*, which was widely read by educated women. Rebecca believed the judicious placing of articles in the magazine might help Goldman get an audience for her lectures. But she also tried to make Goldman feel that she had a friend in London, inviting her to dinner to meet Anthony, who Goldman thought seemed 'affectionate and un-spoiled'.[26]

John Gunther, an American journalist who had interviewed Rebecca for the *Chicago Daily News* during her American tour, was in London and had attended the Emma Goldman dinner to report on it for the *Chicago Evening News*. John was tall, blond and handsome; Rebecca later nicknamed him her 'Gothic angel'.[27] She sent him an amusing note shortly after the dinner which delighted him. John wrote to his girlfriend, Helen Hahn, back in Chicago, that Rebecca had asked why she had not heard from him since the dinner and worrying that he had 'so soon starved', and, if so, would he like her to despatch his bones somewhere.[28] She went on to offer herself as 'mother, grand-mother, aunt, sister, and all other discreet female relatives' during John's stay in London. Stunned and delighted, John telephoned her and they arranged that he would visit her in Queen's Gate Terrace the following Sunday, the last before Christmas.[29]

John was charmed by the elegance of Rebecca's top-floor flat and by the casual dinner she had prepared. She had forgotten the salt and asked John to carve for her, enchanting him still more – so much so that he offered to wash the dishes; she refused. Instead, they chatted for hours. Later in the evening a succession of guests dropped by, including Lettie. Afterwards, John wrote to his girlfriend telling her that Rebecca was both 'pretty as a picture' and a brilliant conversationalist, adding, perhaps to reassure her, that he was to become part of Rebecca's family.[30] Rebecca seemed to have enjoyed the evening as much as John, and invited him for Christmas. He was sad to have to refuse, but though he liked Rebecca, as with so many people, he was also a little afraid of her.

Early in the New Year, however, they met again when John, who was far from wealthy, splashed out to take Rebecca to dinner at the Ritz. They drank Chablis and ate sole in champagne-and-mushroom sauce and, more importantly perhaps, talked intimately for two and a half hours. Rebecca listened as John spoke about his ambitions, his work plans and his girlfriend. While his letters to Hahn hint at the developing intimacy between them, he also mentions Rebecca's age – 'she's just thirty-two, older than

I thought' – again trying to set her mind at rest about the nature of their relationship.

On the next evening out Rebecca took John to dinner at Claridges. He was due to leave in March and just before he did so, they spent a last mad day in Mayfair, acting like playful teenagers. They took lunch together, afterwards visiting all kinds of shops; they tried on extravagant hats and fell about laughing, John played with a huge elephant gun. They tumbled into perfumiers and dabbed each other with scent.

It was a day of more fun and laughter than either of them had known for a considerable time. At first they bought nothing, then at every corner flower seller they started to amass flowers. It was daffodil season and they stopped again and again to buy 'great glowing yellow flowers'.[31] They filled Rebecca's flat with them, before calming down sufficiently to talk 'seriously, very seriously, for an hour or more'.[32]

It was the beginning of a love affair that would outlast so many of Rebecca's other relationships. As late as 1961, John would write to Rebecca, 'My God, I have loved you for damn near 40 years'.[33]

That same spring, another enduring friendship was blossoming. Vyvyan Holland was a successful author and translator – and the son of Oscar Wilde. Widowed in 1918, he pursued a lively social life in the same circles as Rebecca. Now they began a flirtatious correspondence, which at times even hinted at a relationship, although there is nothing more to suggest that they ever became lovers. Nonetheless their friendship would flourish as long as they both lived. They were both competitive, albeit in a rather light-hearted fashion, with Rebecca asking Vyvyan if he had a secretary then answering her own question with an arch, 'No, I thought not'. They often had dinner together or went to the theatre; Rebecca even introduced him to John Gunther, and, assured that the meeting had been a success, the three of them went to see a West End play.

Rebecca was still in touch with her old friend from ADA, Greta Mortimer, and was deeply distressed when, after a visit to her London doctor, Greta arrived at her home feeling unwell. Rebecca urged her to spend the night and then sat up with her while she miscarried a three-month pregnancy.

But romantic liaisons and the social whirl were only a partial distraction from her continuing troubles with Anthony. His reports from St Piran's had improved but she dreaded having him home over the holidays, fearing a lack of adult companionship, and again expressed her concerns, writing to Lettie 'how dreadfully inconvenient that will be'.[34] She had no support from his father, who was still irritated by Anthony's interest in Roman Catholicism, blaming Lettie for it, and taking less and less of a role in his upbringing. He seemed to have come to the reasoning that if he couldn't live with Anthony then he couldn't be much good to him. Anthony later recalled that his father had reacted to his Catholicism by spending three successive visiting days presenting 'the rationalist case for treasuring intellectual freedom'.[35] Wells also made his feelings plain in a letter to Rebecca:

> I hate the Church of England about as much as I hate the Roman Catholic stunt . . . You've got him on your hands. I'm not very likely to see much of you from now on and I don't see how we can hope to cooperate in so subtle and complicated a matter as his upbringing. And what is the good of my writing letters to him? What is there to write about now? We've broken. Am I to tell him that? He's not going to see me again for years.[36]

However inconvenient the school holidays might be, Rebecca took Anthony – accompanied by a tutor because Rebecca had concerns over his progress at school – to the Riviera and wrote to Lettie that he was very happy and enjoying swimming. This was followed by a trip to Padstow in August.

But even a few summer weeks without adult company was irksome to Rebecca; as she had suspected, a holiday with a young boy was not conducive to adult socializing. She missed her friends and wrote to Vyvyan that she was 'pining for companionship'. She added that the house was too full for her to invite him and that he would have to choose between sleeping with her or with Anthony's tutor. The choice, she wrote, 'would inevitably be followed by ill-feeling in the evening by the one who was not chosen, and in the morning by the one who was'.[37]

At the end of the summer Anthony returned to school and Rebecca returned to London. Rebecca's social life continued at a frenetic pace, so much so that friends like Greta Mortimer worried that she was overdoing it.

In January 1926, she sailed for a six-week trip to New York. One of the main purposes of the journey was to try to finalize a deal for the dramatization of *The Return of the Solider*, but the negotiations were plagued with difficulties. Moreover, the weather was terrible and when John Gunther flew to New York to spend a weekend with her, he ended up in bed with bronchitis. Once it became apparent that the talks with producers had broken down, Rebecca sailed home on the *Olympic*, catching up en route with Somerset Maugham and his wife, Syrie.

While she was in New York, Lettie had written to her about Anthony and how unhappy he was that he saw so little of her. Back in England, Rebecca's worries about Anthony continued to grow. She attended a prize-giving at the school, which left her feeling uneasy. Moreover, Major Bryant, the headmaster, had taken to censoring the boys' outgoing letters, which Anthony had reported to Rebecca, who was left in a quandary – she was sympathetic, but she did not wish him to flout the school rules, by refusing to have his letters read. Once the holidays had begun and Rebecca had again taken Anthony to the Riviera, Lettie went to Maidenhead to see the headmaster and check on Anthony's progress. While there, she was shown a letter Rebecca had sent him in which she made some reference to Lettie's overbearing qualities.

The results were unsurprising. Lettie wrote to her sister to complain and Rebecca retaliated with a full-scale attack. She told Lettie that, because of their father's problems, she – as the eldest – had been given too much authority in the house when they were growing up. As a result Lettie had developed an authoritarian manner that had persisted in her adult life and her dealings with other people. Rebecca felt that her sister did not act like 'a woman moving among your equals' but rather like a bossy prefect.[38] Furthermore, she claimed that Anthony too had noticed and had mentioned during the holidays that his Aunty Lettie seemed to think she was better than them and behaved 'like a teacher' when she was with them.[39] She did soften her criticism somewhat by conceding that their mother had been too distracted by troubles to correct them when they were growing up. But she added that she was worried about Lettie's tendency to 'irritate people not by being exactly rude' but by being superior.[40] She conceded that Anthony was devoted to her but also insinuated that his enthusiasm for male company was perhaps due in part to Lettie's behaviour towards him.

Her deteriorating relationship with Lettie wasn't the only blight on Rebecca's holiday. At first the weather was awful, with interminable rain, until, at last, Rebecca could write to John Gunther that she was working while sitting on the beach in a swimsuit. John was in Genoa and while she waited for him to travel up to Antibes to join her, she wrote him a long and despondent letter. She felt she was on the edge of a breakdown because of all the stress with Lettie. Rebecca felt that Lettie disapproved of her, and lamented that 'she hasn't a thought about me that goes more than two centimetres below the surface which isn't dislike and shame'.[41] She confided that she thought Lettie was actually embarrassed by her and had wanted to stifle her since they were children.

After a romantic interlude with John, she returned home, resolved to make a decision about St Piran's. A newspaper article about the headmaster's arrest for drunk driving was the spur she needed. With Wells' agreement Anthony was enrolled at The Hall in Hampstead. Anthony later wondered how the headmaster's alcoholism, noticed by 'every boy at St Piran's' had been completely missed by both his parents.

The Hall was very different from St Piran's, with a more liberal environment. The headmaster, Gerald Wathen, had brought the school from modest beginnings to be the leading prep school in North London, and it had close links with Stowe, the public school Rebecca hoped Anthony would attend.

The contact with Wells over the matter was civilized and seemed to herald a dampening down of the overt hostility between them. Wells even wrote to Anthony telling him that he was proud to be his father, and the relationship between mother and son also improved now that Anthony was free from the bullying and the unhappiness of St Piran's.

Wells turned sixty in 1926, but his love life continued to be as complex as ever. The ever-acquiescent Jane remained the calming centre of his activities but, as his relationship with Rebecca had waned, he had moved on to other women. The socialist writer Odette Keun had largely taken Rebecca's place. Parts Dutch, Italian and Greek, she had been raised in Istanbul and married previously to a Georgian prince, a blend of exoticism and intelligence Wells found very attractive. Some years earlier he had written a favourable notice of one of her books, and indulged in a brief affair with her in Geneva when 'a dark slender young woman in a flimsy wrap and an aroma of jasmine . . . flung herself upon me with protests of adoration'.[42] They established a house near Grasse which gradually became Wells' winter home, until he bought a farmhouse south of Lou Bastidon and settled down to enjoy keeping a wife at Easton and a mistress in France. The new place was known as Lou Pidou, derived from 'Le Petit Dieu', which was Keun's very apt nickname for Wells.[43]

Rebecca, too, had a new lover.[44] Steven Martin was a banker she had known for three years. They had struck up a relationship on Rebecca's second New York trip of 1926, for which she had set out in the autumn, as soon as Anthony was settled at The Hall. Steve Martin was also a gambler, who veered between being a millionaire and having almost no money at all. Rebecca loved his Californian drawl but worried that her feelings might prove to be nothing more than infatuation.

Accordingly, she found this new adventure perplexing. It was not, she realized, the same kind of relationship she had enjoyed with Max. It was much less serious, and with that realization came an admission: she still had feelings for Max. She was pragmatic about Steve: 'I don't know if it will last, I don't want to marry him, but I definitely want to be with him for some time to come.'[45] There was also the question of her relationship with John Gunther. She now wrote to him, saying that she wanted to be honest about her new circumstances, adding reassuringly that it shouldn't necessarily affect 'the essentials of our relationship'.[46] In essence she wanted to continue to see John too, for him to be 'the nice sweet friend' he'd always been; after all, he 'really did fill my flat with yellow flowers'.[47] He seemed to accept the situation and they remained on excellent terms.

Steve, however, remained ignorant of her entanglement with John. Rebecca deliberately hid it from him, thinking that when he and John met, Steve might be predisposed to dislike him if he knew of their history.

The American trip was not an unqualified success. Various problems had prevented the dramatization of *The Return of the Soldier* from going ahead and the project was now abandoned. However, *Cosmopolitan* magazine approached her with a very lucrative offer. If she would agree to ghostwrite a four-part serial based on the memoirs of a First World War nurse, they would pay her $10,000. It would be called 'War Nurse: The True Story of a Woman who Lived, Loved and Suffered on the Western Front'.

She spent the Christmas holidays in London with Anthony but when he returned to school immediately sailed back to New York, and to Steven Martin. But Steve had been diagnosed with cancer. Rather than enjoying a lover's reunion, Rebecca found herself nursing him until his death in the spring, while writing reviews for the *New York Herald Tribune* and finishing 'War Nurse'. She wrote very little to her friends or family about her last days with Steve, but immediately following his death, she confided in John Gunther that she had suffered temporary deafness for almost a month as a result of the shock of the experience.

She left America shortly after Steve died and travelled to

Florence, where she underwent psychotherapy and continued work on a novel she had briefly begun some months before but had subsequently abandoned when faced with the combined workload of 'War Nurse' and reviewing for the *New York Herald Tribune*. The novel was called *Sunflower* and was a thinly disguised account of her affair with Max Beaverbrook. Sunflower is an actress who recognizes that her lover, Lord Essington (a character similar to Wells), is not able to give her the emotional commitment that she needs. Her new lover, Frances Pitt, seems to embody sensitivity and sexuality, in contrast to Essington's old-fashioned ideas and moodiness. In her notes, Rebecca scribbled that she hoped to develop one theme of the book to illustrate that 'Women have remained close to their primitive type because doing the same job – wifehood and motherhood. Men have departed from the primitive type because they are doing utterly different jobs.'[48]

Rebecca never completed *Sunflower* and wrote to G.B. Stern that she was sure it would never be published because it contained a much-too-recognizable portrait of a political figure. Thus Sunflower's sexual desire is never fulfilled in Rebecca's text, but is instead presented as an impossible fantasy: 'She wished that a magician would change her into a cat, so that she could come and live in this house without the question of love being raised; for of course nothing like that could ever happen, not the way they met.'[49]

Rebecca spent the summer in southern Europe with Anthony, staying in Italy then Cap Ferrat, which she dismissed as 'a kind of drearier Bournemouth', then finally Agay.[50] In Agay she found a delightful house called Fri Fri Palace, with lots of balconies and an avenue of palm trees leading up to it. Agay was in a then-unfashionable part of the Riviera and the house was well priced at £6 a week. It was also close to the beach, surrounded by pinewoods and hills. Rebecca's attic bedroom had two balconies and she spent much of her time there continuing to work on *Sunflower*. G.B. Stern came to visit to recover from her difficulties with her husband, who once again was suffering badly from shell shock. There, in a reverie of writing and swimming and sunshine, Rebecca entered a state 'more beautifully near pure living than anything I had known for years'.[51]

Before her return to England, Rebecca dallied in Paris, and had a brief affair with a dashing Romanian prince called Antoine Bibesco. Bibesco was married to Elizabeth Asquith, daughter of the Liberal leader, but was well known for his promiscuity. Rebecca thought him the 'most beautiful human being she had ever seen'.[52] The love affair was delightful but ended badly with a 'nightmare horror' of 'brutal repudiation'.[53] Rebecca felt Bibesco implied that she had forced him to have the affair; she went home to London and wept. A torrent of letters of apology followed, and while Rebecca largely ignored them, she came to regard their affair with amusement rather than sorrow, simply because she encountered so many other women over the years who had also shared his bed.

In the spring, Wells' wife, Jane, had been diagnosed with cancer. She was beyond help, but nonetheless underwent radiation therapy, which left her so debilitated that she had to use a wheelchair. Initially Wells was solicitous of Jane, but as weeks became months, he grew restless and made frequent trips to town, and eventually started going back to Lou Pidou to see Odette once or twice a month. When he was at Easton the house was often filled with visitors, in an almost party-like conviviality, something that was noted with displeasure by Arnold Bennett, who added 'H.G. likes a lot of people to distract him'.[54] But there were quiet times, too, and Wells recalled sitting with Jane in the summer sunshine, 'listening to Beethoven, Bach, Purcell and Mozart' and later watching the wood fire burning at dusk.[55] Frank Wells' wedding was scheduled for 7 October and in the days leading up to it Jane managed to order the wedding breakfast. But she did not live to see her younger son's wedding and on the eve of his nuptials, in the early evening, she fell asleep for the last time. The wedding was not cancelled but was rescheduled for early in the morning, to keep it as quiet as possible, with few mourners. Jane was cremated, as she had wished to be, at Golders Green Crematorium.

Wells wrote to Rebecca to inform her of Jane's death. She in turn confided in John Gunther, with a lack of compassion, about her own concerns, chiefly that Wells might, as a result, 'become tiresome in various ways'.[56] But rather than pursuing his former lover, Wells instead made provision for his son, contacting his solicitors, Messrs Gedge, Fisk and Gedge, to draw up a settlement for Anthony. Two trusts were set up for him for a total of £5,000; he would receive the interest from the first at eighteen, from the second at twenty and inherit the capital amount on his thirtieth birthday. There was no independent settlement for Rebecca. Angrily, she wrote to Wells: 'I hope you're giving me the life interest on this £5,000? It is going to be difficult if after A. comes of age I am dependent on him for the rent of the house. It's not a good or normal relationship.'[57]

Wells was adamant, replying that Rebecca might marry again (ignoring the fact that they had never been married) or 'bring off a big success'.[58] Odette Keun intervened and persuaded Wells to settle '£14,000 on Anthony'.[59] Despite the size of the new agreement, Rebecca's solicitor was far from happy, mainly because, if Anthony died, the money would revert to Gip and Frank, and not to Rebecca.

Before he returned to France and Odette, Wells asked Rebecca if she would help arrange a meeting between Gip and Anthony. Jane's death made the situation easier; he felt that the two young people had much in common and Gip himself had suggested that it might be good to get to know his half-brother. Rebecca agreed at once although the encounter had to be postponed because Anthony was ill at school with chickenpox. She visited him frequently and was very impressed by the beautiful drawings he had taken to making while convalescing, writing to Wells that she believed he was gifted.

Rebecca was also in the process of moving, to 80 Onslow Gardens in South Kensington. Standing on a wide corner with an open outlook, her new flat was on the first floor of a large house. It came with a large roof garden which she thought Anthony would love.

Eventually, it was arranged that Gip would take Anthony to the zoo. They got on famously. Spurred by this success, Wells invited Anthony to Easton Glebe for Christmas at the last minute, and Rebecca, cross at having her plans disrupted and warily jealous of Wells' new interest in his illegitimate son, wrote to protest. Early in the New Year, Wells wrote 'Evidently it is no longer possible for us to correspond.'[60] This particular argument proved to be short-lived but it did set the tone for 1928, which would be a year of continual battles between them. It seemed that Rebecca had been right to worry about what Jane's death might precipitate.

⌾

That spring, Rebecca had some positive news to report to Fannie Hurst. A book including a long essay on art and her *New York Herald Tribune* articles was to be published by Jonathan Cape. Putting the book together had meant leaving off the work she had begun over the summer on *Sunflower*, but she intended to return to it in due course. Anthony had settled well at The Hall and was soon to start at Stowe. Mother and son were enjoying spending time together at Onslow Gardens, and had acquired a Sealyham puppy. Relations with Wells had settled too and they now entered into a frank correspondence about how Anthony was to be known at the new school. Wells was at last prepared to acknowledge his son openly and Anthony would no longer have to hide, or invent, his family background.

A collection of Rebecca's criticism, *The Strange Necessity*, was published in May. Rebecca thought it the best thing she had ever done, but the reviewers were far from convinced. Arnold Bennett deplored her need 'to perform' in his piece for the *Evening Standard* and the *Bookman* critic said simply 'she writes very badly'.[61]

The month also brought serious concerns over Anthony's

health. He was very pale and coughing incessantly. Amid suspicions of TB, an X-ray and an appointment with a specialist
were arranged, and Rebecca made plans for a trip to a Swiss
sanatorium. She kept news of Anthony's decline restricted to a
very few close friends in the first instance, for fear it might
jeopardize his place at Stowe, if indeed he was well enough to go.

The specialist confirmed that Anthony was indeed suffering
from TB but did not recommend Switzerland, and instead suggested a sanatorium on the east coast, in Kelling, Norfolk. It was
run by a Dr Morris, who had gained an excellent reputation for
his success in treating the disease, particularly when the patients
were young. Rebecca wrote to Wells to warn him of the severity
of Anthony's predicament and he immediately replied, with great
warmth and sympathy: 'this misfortune of yours reopens all sorts
of shut-down tendernesses and I feel like your dear brother and
your best friend and your once (and not quite forgetting it) lover.
Count on me for any help you need. I'm still very hopeful about
the case, for what comes as suddenly may go as suddenly.'[62]

Accompanied by Gip, Wells immediately travelled to London
to visit his sick son. Anthony would later say that he was acutely
aware of his father's far more optimistic outlook on his future in
comparison with his mother's worries and fears. Wells reassured
Anthony that he would be well in no time, and seemed, to the
twelve-year-old boy, to offer a new possibility, one that had been
lost in his mother's sense of doom: that getting better lay within
his own power.

Rebecca was recovering from a bad bout of flu, struggling to
care for her son, making travel arrangements for visiting him in
Norfolk and trying to keep up with her work. She was, understandably, a little taken aback by Wells' joviality. Shortly after
his visit he wrote her a letter in which he dismissed her worries
a little offhandedly, and Rebecca replied angrily that the specialist had told her the most optimistic prognosis possible was to
prepare their son for life as an invalid.

Once Anthony was settled in the sanatorium, Rebecca began
to make the trip every two weeks to be with him, spending a few

days at a time in a nearby hotel. Throughout August, she commuted between the Station Hotel at Cromer and the flat in South Kensington. Wells visited only once, when Anthony had recovered sufficiently to be allowed to leave the sanatorium for outings. He took his son to the little resort of Wells-next-the Sea for the day. They walked along the salt marshes, had a casual lunch and Anthony photographed his father standing by the roadside, saying now he had 'a picture of Wells-next-the-sea at Wells-next-the-sea'.[63] This was the father of Anthony's dreams.

Very gradually, Anthony did recover and was able to start at Stowe the following year. But it was Rebecca who paid the bill of over £200 for Anthony's treatment. And his illness marked another stage in hostilities within the little family. Anthony in later years resented what he thought of as his mother's dramatization of events, while seeming to romanticize his father's role. For Rebecca it was a 'black experience'. Anthony, unable to see how his recovery could be anything but joyous, refused as an adult, to acknowledge the emotional, logistic and financial difficulties of having a son in a sanatorium, some way from home, with a potentially fatal illness, while struggling to pay for his care.[64]

The squabbling over Anthony was concurrent with a separate argument between Rebecca and Wells. Amongst its pieces of literary criticism, *The Strange Necessity* included an account of Wells' work and style. It was on the whole not a critical piece. Indeed it praised Wells as one of the 'Big Four', the four literary figures who were like 'visiting uncles': Wells, Shaw, Galsworthy and Bennett, with their 'loquacity and charm'.[65] She went on to say that she felt she was lucky to 'be young just as the most bubbling creative mind that the sun and moon have shone upon since Leonardo da Vinci was showing its form'.[66] However, she then poked fun at Wells' rather florid and melodramatic love scenes, the passages where his prose became 'like blancmange', by writing a parody of them.[67] She referred to *The Passionate Friends* as a 'large blond novelette with a heaving bosom', mentioning dismissively that 'all the uncles have written twaddle in their time'.[68] Wells retaliated in a letter. He resented the name 'Queenie' given to the heroine of Rebecca's parody, and didn't like Rebecca's remarks: 'And good critics, Pussy, when they want to show a novelist writes about mawkish love affairs, don't invent a silly name for a heroine and silly things she is supposed to say. They quote.'[69]

It was the first of a barrage of letters. In another he defended his female characters, saying that she hadn't quoted because she wouldn't find evidence to support her criticisms in his books. He also protested that she would turn people who hadn't actually read his books against him. In yet another letter he called her criticism 'slighting and slovenly', reiterating his own poor opinion of *The Judge* – 'a sham' – calling her 'ambitious and pretentious' and saying that she lacked humility. Rebecca told her sister Winnie that he was 'writing me an insulting letter by every post' and resigned herself to his behaviour, saying 'all men are mad'.[70]

The row with Wells was not the only issue raised by *The Strange Necessity*. Arnold Bennett reviewed it rather harshly in the *Evening Standard*, dismissing much of the content as 'silliness'. An *Evening Standard* reporter came to interview Rebecca about her reactions to the review before she had even read it. When the interview appeared in the paper, Rebecca found it to be 'a tissue of lies, simply beyond belief', which claimed she had insulted Bennett.[71] Rebecca now wrote to Winnie to reassure her, saying 'of course, I said *none* of these things'.[72] She appealed to the *Evening Standard* to write a retraction and when they did not, served them with a writ for libel. She then wrote to Arnold Bennett telling him that she had done so and reassuring him that she had not insulted him in the interview. She sought damages, but asked her lawyer to decide on the amount, and refused to allow the paper 'to waive their obligation to make a public statement in court'.[73] The *Evening Standard* was a Beaverbrook paper, so throughout the dispute she was in contact with Max again. So much so, in fact, that when the paper's solicitor sent her a draft of an official apology, claiming to have checked the wording with Max, Rebecca pointed out that this was highly unlikely as Max was in the West Indies.

Rebecca had come to the usual uneasy understanding with Lettie, and leaving Anthony with her, she made another trip to New York in the autumn to discuss 'War Nurse', which her *Cosmopolitan* editor, Ray Lang, wanted her to turn into a novel. She also continued reviewing for the *New York Herald Tribune*. Rebecca was still excited by New York, and loved the new architecture that was springing up, part of a citywide building expansion that, in just a few years, would include the Chrysler Building and the Rockefeller Centre, but she was shocked by the level of crime and gang warfare, and especially by her perception that the New Yorkers she met found it amusing. The 1920s also saw an explosion in the use of the motor car, thanks to both mass production and a reduction in price. The sheer number of automobiles shocked Rebecca and, in a letter to Lettie, she lamented the busy roads and the difficulty of crossing them. Her work fared well and a new editor at the *New York Herald Tribune* gave her an $800 contract for four reviews, as well as a 'pocket money job' for every week of her stay.[74] *War Nurse* was published as a book in 1930 but Rebecca did not put her name to it. Despite her unwillingness to acknowledge the work which she regarded as little more than a financial necessity, there are passages that reflect her own relationship difficulties with Wells. Corinne Andrews, the heroine, reflects that her lover 'respected nothing but his own desires and convenience ... But he had in him an enormous vitality; a spring of life within him, that was like salvation in a world which was being swamped with death.'[75]

The real nurse whose memoirs were the inspiration for *War Nurse* was from Chicago, and Rebecca planned to visit the city during her trip. She also hoped to learn more about bootlegging, which she described as 'beyond anything in history'. She was coming to the realization that, although she had briefly toyed with the idea of moving there, she could never settle in the

States because it was no place to bring up Anthony, 'even though his adult life may possibly lie there'.[76]

When she returned to London, while Anthony was preparing to start at Stowe in the New Year, Rebecca began work on what she intended to be a short story. She called it *Harriet Hume*, and kept working on it until it was a 'fantasy, not a novel' of 70,000 words, rather than the 5,000 she had intended.[77]

Harriet Hume was set in the period immediately after the First World War but an element of comic whimsy is added by the mannered style, which is more reminiscent of Wells and Bennett. There are four encounters between Harriet, with her stylized femininity and her belief that public events are important only as a backdrop to the immediate sensations of life, and Arthur Condorex, a politician who finds his own value solely from his position in relation to public events. Harriet can read Condorex's mind and sees how he is deceiving himself. In the final encounter they are spirits, in harmony. The two opposites who could not agree in life find peace with one another as ghosts. The careful, almost loving descriptions of London, where the book is set, are one of its most memorable features. They give some indication of Rebecca's great ability to evoke a place and time, a talent that would come to the fore just over a decade later, in what was arguably her greatest work, *Black Lamb and Grey Falcon*.

At Christmas, Wells again invited Anthony to Easton Glebe, but smarting at the short notice and their arguments throughout the year, Rebecca refused. She had made other arrangements. A friend had loaned her a lovely apartment in Paris and she was resolved to take Anthony with her. Wells was furious, and told her that her refusal was one of the most malicious things she had ever done and was, moreover, depriving Anthony of a good time with his half-brothers.

With Jane's death, Wells seemed to take a livelier interest not only in Anthony but in his illegitimate daughter by Amber Reeves, whom he now also introduced to his son. But, as

Anthony later recalled, the gulf of six years age-difference and a consequent lack of anything in common doomed the siblings' relationship from the start. Rebecca was growing increasingly uneasy about Wells' new and intrusive interest. In the earlier, more difficult years she had had to fend for Anthony alone, but now that he was 'no trouble and a very desirable object' Wells wanted to step in and take over.[78]

She consulted the lawyers who had represented her and won her earlier suit against the *Evening Standard*. In January 1929 Theobald Matthew, of Messrs Charles Russell Solicitors, instituted proceedings so Rebecca could legally adopt her own son. This legal option existed in order that an adoption certificate could replace a birth certificate that stated that a child was illegitimate. But the point, for Rebecca, was undoubtedly not only to spare Anthony and herself the shame and discrimination that resulted from the circumstances of his birth, but also that she, as the boy's mother, would be named as sole parent and guardian of her adopted son. She discussed it with Anthony, who agreed to the proceedings; Rebecca paid a fee of £60 and then answered a series of questions about her undertaking as guardian. Wells, however, was incandescent and employed Gedge, Fisk and Gedge to oppose the proceedings. He maintained that Rebecca was motivated by jealousy of his literary career and by a desire to hurt him.

He started writing to Rebecca to question Anthony's apparent lack of academic success at his new school, a rather inappropriate gesture, given that Anthony had just missed several months of schooling because of his illness. He even threatened to stop paying school fees and go to the headmaster, Dr Roxburgh, to discuss the matter. By the time the case came to court in June the relationship had reached an all-time low. At the hearing, Wells' solicitors told the court that Rebecca was 'living a frivolous life among a circle of idle second-rate friends' and suggested that their client was distressed to see his son surrounded by 'all these seedy people'.[79] In the end the adoption was granted but with conditions; Rebecca was compelled to consult with

Wells about Anthony's education, allow him to spend time in the holidays with his father, and, most worryingly for Rebecca, designate Wells as his guardian should she die. Wells settled £8,000, a portion of the originally agreed sum, on Anthony when he was twenty-one, but in a revocable trust so the various conditions relating to access had to be met.

By the end of June the process was complete. Wells made the most of his 'victory' and asked that the boy spend three weeks in September with him at Easton Glebe, a time during which Rebecca had already arranged a stay on the Riviera. As soon as Rebecca had left England for Agay, Wells headed to Stowe for the very first time. Anthony's first report had indicated a weakness in Mathematics and Latin and stipulated extra tuition over the break. His father now told Dr Roxburgh that Rebecca refused to let Anthony have a tutor in the holidays and that he was consequently insisting on three weeks at Easton Glebe with a tutor that Stowe would send. Anthony was at first overjoyed at the idea of spending three weeks with his adored, and usually absent, father. However, Wells let it slip that the weeks Anthony was to spend at Easton he himself would in fact be motoring in Switzerland and Italy with Odette. Anthony would therefore be alone in the house with Gip's wife, Marjorie, and a strange tutor. Rebecca, unhappy at this thought, insisted that the tutor join them in France presumably so that Anthony could get to know his tutor.

In July, just seven days before Anthony was due to join her from school, she wrote to him from France, urging him to write and tell his father that he wanted to spend September with her so that he could enjoy the swimming, and, if need be, he would go to Wells at either Easter or Christmas.

Wells insisted that after July Anthony should come to stay at Easton, but agreed that he would return to England when Anthony and his tutor did, thus circumventing Rebecca's arguments that Anthony would be alone in the house. There were problems with arrangements for the tutor, however, and it wasn't until later in the holidays that he was free to join Rebecca and

Anthony in France. The holiday month was a great success. Rebecca's friend Pamela Frankau, just twenty-one, went for 'wonderful swims' with him. Rebecca too enjoyed swimming and joked in a letter to Lettie that they were turning into 'quite a marine family'.[80] Anthony later recalled that summer of 'beautiful bodies of young women baking in the sun' and wrote of how he fell in love with the beautiful, almost childlike, Pamela.[81] They shared confidences and spoke for hours and continued to be friends long after the holiday, when she visited him at Stowe and took him for long lunches in Thame.

In the second week of September, Anthony travelled back to Easton, leaving Rebecca in Agay. It was not an easy arrangement. Rebecca sought assurance from Wells that he was indeed returning to England and details of an exact date, so he might travel with Anthony, at least from Paris to London. But he was maddeningly vague and Rebecca suspected that he didn't want to meet up with Anthony while he was still with Odette. Prior to sending him off she wrote a list for Wells of the practical things that would need attending to before Anthony's return to school. A visit to the doctor to check on his health, and to the dentist, and she suggested a trip to buy any new school clothes that Anthony needed and to arrange to have the appropriate tags sewn onto them (which she then conveniently enclosed). Wells was furious at being asked to do these tasks, which he seemed to regard as more suited to Rebecca, and immediately sent a letter telling Rebecca to return from her holiday to do them. He very soon after retracted it in a telegram, though – presumably, Rebecca thought, under advice from his family or his lawyer. As well as worrying about what might happen if she died, Rebecca was also concerned about the kind of life Wells led at Easton Glebe, which she thought permitted him all the enjoyment of a country gentleman but none of the responsibility of a landowner, an example she was afraid Anthony might try to emulate. She thought Wells was obsessed with material things and might nurture a taste for extravagance in Anthony, one that she could not meet, and that belonged to a world – that of Easton – in which she did not feel welcome.

~∞~

That same month, *Harriet Hume* was published by Hutchinson and Rebecca dedicated it to her friend, the writer Sylvia Lynd, and Sylvia's husband Robert, the editor of the *Daily News and Leader*. Although Virginia Woolf was less than appreciative, calling it 'tight and affected',[82] the *Morning Post* and *Sunday Times* reviewed it favourably and Rebecca was delighted to receive a royalties cheque for £224. Nonetheless she wrote to A.D. Peters, her literary agent who had replaced the amorous Dakers, saying she was annoyed by a letter from Wells wondering how she had been capable of writing it, given her 'sloth and bad habits'.[83] In fact, Wells had also praised the book enthusiastically, adding that he was pleased to be able to do so unreservedly, proclaiming that with this 'charming' book she had finally found her own voice.

Distressed and indignant at Wells' remark about her supposed indolence, especially since he was now ensconced at Easton Glebe with Anthony, Rebecca wrote to Bertrand Russell. The letter gave an account of recent events and what Rebecca saw as the increasingly unbalanced nature of Wells' dealings with her. It ended with a request for Russell to act as a second named guardian in her will. 'I do not feel the smallest confidence in leaving H.G. as a guardian of my only child. I think that if I died he would get bored with the boy, and would get his fun by frustrating him at any crisis.'[84]

She continued that she thought Russell the 'best person in the world' for the task and offered to add a codicil to her will to the effect that so long as Russell was acting as Anthony's guardian, money would be paid into the experimental school he had set up with his wife, Beacon Hill. She added in a postscript that another deciding factor was that Wells was afraid of him and wouldn't oppose him in any outlandish way.

However, Russell rejected her request and in later years she regretted asking him, saying that she had thought Russell was 'an angelic being' as well as a good friend.[85] Instead her solicitor, Theobald Matthew, was appointed as an additional guardian in the event of her death.

In the summer of 1929, Rebecca had made her usual trip to the Riviera and there she had met up with Vera Brittain. They knew each other well through their work at *Time and Tide* magazine; they were both on the board. Vera was very taken with Anthony and wrote to her dear friend Winifred Holtby of his 'charming composed and mature manners, and very dark hair'.[86]

In the autumn she invited Rebecca to dinner at her home in Chelsea. Vera's husband, the political philosopher George Catlin, also invited his Oxford friend Henry Maxwell Andrews. Henry spent most of the night talking to Rebecca about the places they had travelled to, their likes and dislikes. The only real point of disagreement seemed to be their feelings about Oxford, which Henry loved with a passion and about which Rebecca felt much more ambivalent. Henry was tall and distinguished and impeccably dressed. She described him as 'rather like a dull giraffe, sweet, kind and loving'.[87]

The next day, Henry sent Rebecca a beautiful bouquet of red-and-gold flowers and asked her to dine with him. She immediately wrote back, addressing him as Mr Andrews and saying that she would be delighted. Afterwards, he was obviously concerned that he had spent too long with her, but she reassured him, saying 'it was a great pleasure to meet someone who felt about life' as she did.[88] They began a relationship, slowly at first, attending other dinners at the Catlins' home and writing one another frequent notes.

Henry was a very different personality from Wells. He was the head of a department in Schroders, the merchant bank. Years later, Rebecca seemed almost embarrassed by the fact that he had worked in a bank, and would immediately answer any questions about his profession by saying what he would have done, had he had the chance – academia and the art world being just some of the careers he'd had in mind. Rebecca thought that he was 'a delightfully funny man' who was 'scholarly' and 'very generous and very kind'.[89] But her friends were less taken with him. Vera Brittain wrote in her diary that the writer Phyllis Bentley had remarked that 'Henry's conversation with Rebecca, her and myself was just like one bad player in an otherwise good tennis four.'[90]

Vera also noted that she could understand Rebecca's attraction to Wells with his 'young and very vital' manner and 'his eyes vividly blue' but she was surprised that she could settle with Henry afterwards. Perhaps Wells had been exhausting, like 'living in a perpetual hurricane', she speculated.[91] The idea that Rebecca saw Henry as a safe haven was undoubtedly true and a few months after they met she wrote to him, 'I can't tell you how safe and comforting the thought of you is'.[92] On the surface, Henry did seem a strange match. He was regarded as a charming if somewhat dull man and was nicknamed 'the Elk' by Rebecca, while his mother became known as 'the Elk's Dam'. Letters from Rebecca to Winnie calling him her Elk were all destroyed when they were eventually married.[93]

However, there were similarities in their backgrounds. Henry was not as English as he seemed. He was born two years after Rebecca, in 1894, in Rangoon, Burma. His father's family were part-Scottish, part-Danish. His mother, Mary, was half-British, half-Lithuanian, but had been brought up in Hamburg where her Lithuanian father was responsible for building the tramway system. One brother worked in Germany but Henry's father and Uncle Ernest worked in the export/import business in Burma, where Henry was subsequently brought up and learned to speak fluent Burmese. A change in fortunes, which Rebecca herself said she never really understood, meant that the wealth which all three brothers shared was lost. Only Uncle Ernest remained a very rich man. When Henry's father died, Ernest invited his widow and her two sons into his home. Despite the invitation, he did not welcome them warmly, and the boys were sent not to a London school but to a school in the Midlands where they were regarded as 'rich German Jews of no importance'.[94] The boys were happy enough at school but Henry's mother struggled against the restrictions of her new life. They were placed in a house in an area where she knew no one, but she assured the boys that Ernest was sacrificing a great deal for them and that they should try to please him, a request that seemed to haunt Henry until his uncle's death.

Both boys went on to Oxford, although Henry's elder brother, also Ernest, was subsequently expelled for cheating in an exam. In 1914, Mary was forced to go to Hamburg to sort out the sale of a house she and her husband had lived in shortly before his death. She took Henry, her youngest but most reliable son, with her. Henry was oblivious to the talk of impending war between Britain and Germany, largely because his Uncle Ernest dismissed the possibility as highly unlikely because 'peace was essential to the well-being of each', a belief that continued to bewilder Rebecca throughout her later life.[95] Once in Germany, however, the reality and likelihood of war was obvious. The owner of the hotel where they stayed warned Henry kindly that perhaps he should go home given that he was of military age. But Henry stayed; his mother needed him to support her until the sale was agreed.

Henry was a British subject, like his mother, but with the sudden declaration of war, they found that Britain would not recognize their status because they had been domiciled in Germany when war broke out. They had purchasers for the house but the sale had not been completed. They were effectively trapped in Germany. Eventually, friends arranged for Mary to travel to Amsterdam, which she did, but Henry was to be interned for the duration of the war. Originally, because of his Burmese birth, and despite the fact he was six feet tall with blue eyes and pale skin, he was held in a camp for natives of British colonies. The guards tried hard to persuade the inmates to transfer their loyalties to Germany. At first Henry adapted. He spoke Burmese and convinced his captors it was his only language. But when he was eventually asked if he would fight for Germany, he refused, and said simply that he would rather die than betray his country. Just before Christmas 1914, Henry was put on a train to Spandau, on the outskirts of Berlin, and taken to a camp close to the point where two rivers met. It was called Ruhleben, which means Peaceful Living, and it was where he would spend the war, an experience that would indelibly mark his personality.

Henry later published a chronicle of those years under the pseudonym Richard Roe. *In Ruhleben* is a collection of the letters he wrote to his mother while he was interned. Deprived of a university education, Henry and his fellow internees established a university at the camp, offering lectures and classes in a variety of subjects. Henry lectured in English Literature and History and also taught French and Latin. As a result he was both popular and greatly respected, so much so that when friends of his mother procured him an order of release, he refused to take advantage of it. Rebecca suspected he had homosexual relationships in the camp and some of his letters to Mary do indeed hint at this: 'At times some men seem more beautiful than you could imagine anyone being. It is at such moments that we feel the love that tried to hide itself, the tenderness that came unsought.'[96]

Although he felt his role there was important and that he helped many of his fellow prisoners, the years in the camp were, for Henry, ultimately lost years. When at last the war was over and he was released, he was a quieter, more withdrawn man, and confided in Rebecca that he lived in 'a state of hating the world that had gone on while their lives had been smashed'.[97]

Against his uncle's advice, but buoyed by his role at the camp's university and convinced that he was destined for an academic career, Henry returned to Oxford. However, he was unable to cope with the stress and strains of examinations and could live up neither to his own expectations nor to those of the people closest to him. He failed his exams. It was the great disappointment of his life and, while he pursued his career in banking through friends he had made at New College, he longed to be a real part of the university there. Rebecca wrote in her memoirs that 'He ached for its privileges; sometimes I suspected that much of his eccentricity was assumed, that he fabricated in a continuing dream that he was the Warden of New College or All Souls and famed as an Oxford character.'[98]

Henry's great similarity with Rebecca, and their strongest affinity, was that they both struggled to find a place in the society they lived in. Rebecca was painfully aware of her background, spending much of her time in later years trying to trace grand antecedents, and dismissing the fact that she had never been to university. Henry was a reluctant banker, a graduate of a mock university in a prison camp, with only a pass degree from Oxford awarded to those coming back from the war.

When they first got together, Henry was a wealthy man in his own right, but his money had been made by gambling on stock in Schroders. After the markets crashed, he was left in debt, with only his salary to live on. He was still living with his uncle, in Cavendish Square, and though he had every expectation that he would in time be his heir, he still believed that he might at any moment be 'precipitated into friendlessness and destitution'.[99] The touching nature of their relationship in its early days is apparent in the frequent letters between them, filled with endearments and gentle insecurities. Henry's work at Schroders caused him to travel frequently and Rebecca listened to the wind while he sailed overseas and hoped that his crossing was safe. She wrote to him after one such trip, 'I hadn't betrayed that I was worried before you left, and was so glad that you exist.'[100]

The arguments with Wells continued, but now she was able to tell Henry that 'it's certainly true that you and your sympathy has [*sic*] made the difference between heaven and hell!'[101] They called one another 'Ric' and 'Rac', nicknames taken from a French cartoon about two dogs.[102] More tellingly, Henry also called Rebecca the name by which only her family had ever really known her: Cicely.

Henry was indeed a sanctuary for Rebecca. The year after

they met saw her troubles with Wells and Anthony continue, and she was forced to resign her position at the *American Bookman*; she had been writing a literary column for them since late 1929, which had made up a sizeable portion of her income. She wrote to her sister Winnie that they had 'gone humanist', which she described as a 'foul American form of Catholicism' that induced its adherents to write attacks on modern writers.[103] Meanwhile Anthony's devotion to Catholicism had been replaced by a complete rejection of the Church. When he went to the headmaster at Stowe asking to be allowed leave from chapel on the grounds of an objection to Christianity, in particular the Church's attitude to birth control, Rebecca began to worry that he was 'ineducable'.

The death of D H Lawrence in March affected Rebecca deeply and led to another quarrel with Wells when he seemed to make a joke about it. One of her last pieces for the *Bookman* was dedicated to his memory. It was subsequently published in the collection *Ending In Earnest*, along with rewritten versions of her other *Bookman* pieces. In it, Rebecca recalled their meeting in Italy, and the tragedy of his loss. His work had attempted to take 'sex and those base words for it' and 'hold them up before the consciousness of the world' but his spirituality was at odds with the contemporary focus on naturalism: 'Even so did those of us who heard of Lawrence's death feel that from the spectacle of the universe, by the incredible stupidity of a destroying angel, the best thing had gone.'[104]

Rebecca's usual summer Riviera trip was punctuated by letters to Henry telling him how much she missed him, and a nasty bout of bronchitis which laid her up, prompting an offer from him to travel down from London to France to visit her for the day. She wrote delightedly in reply that he really shouldn't trouble, 'What a journey to think of!', and confessed 'I am feeling so fond of you I can't bear to be away any longer'.[105] Henry in turn confessed the reality of his precarious financial situation and she wrote back at once telling him that together they could manage. Henry 'was filled with gratitude for your gracious reply'.[106] He spoke to his uncle about the relationship and Uncle Ernest wrote a slightly formal but very welcoming letter to Rebecca saying that he would rejoice if the bond between them made for 'much happiness and contentment for you both'.[107]

Finally, in August, she wrote to her American literary agent, George Bye, that she was about to be 'led to the altar', calling Henry simply 'the nicest man I ever met'. She explained that while they had intended to wait until the following spring to marry, Henry's long working hours meant that dashing between his home and hers was far too much and they had thus brought everything forward. She was looking for a house for them to share, but this did not prove easy and it was decided that initially at least Henry should move in with her at Onslow Gardens.

The idea of Henry as a refuge from the troubles of the past year was borne out when Rebecca confided in her journalist friend, S.K. Radcliffe, that Henry had done so much to build her up after the terrible events of the past two years that she would marry him as a sign of gratitude, even if for nothing else.

∽≫

On 1 November 1930 Rebecca and Henry were married in an Anglican ceremony before only a very few guests at Newland's Corner, Abinger in Surrey. Anthony remained at school. She dressed simply in a beige velvet dress, carrying a sheaf of lilies and red flowers reminiscent of those Henry had sent her after their first meeting. Rebecca looked radiant; Henry seemed the perfect backdrop for her stage. The wedding was reported on by the newspapers, which seemed to concentrate on the changes the couple had made to the traditional wedding vows; Rebecca had chosen to omit the word 'obey' from the vows and Henry promised to 'share' his worldly goods with her, rather than to endow them upon her. Rebecca wrote the following day to her sister Lettie, who had given her away, that she was 'full of gratitude' and that 'no two people ever enjoyed a wedding so much'.[108] Towards the end of her life, Rebecca recalled: 'My marriage was certainly the most important thing in my life though I never understood why it had that primacy.'[109]

They honeymooned blissfully in Genoa, although Rebecca did send a letter home to Lettie complaining about how the newspapers had reported the wedding, exclaiming it to be ridiculous that they had made so much of her refusal to 'obey' Henry.

Chapter Eight

HARK THE HERALD ANGELS SING, MRS SIMPSON'S STOLE OUR KING

❧

The newly wedded couple returned to London and moved into Rebecca's flat together, but it was immediately apparent that it was too small and so they decided instead to live temporarily with Henry's mother, Mary. She lived at 94 Queens Gate, an elegant terraced town house, round the corner from Rebecca's old place in Queen's Gate Terrace. Mary's home faced a church, St Augustine's, which may have been in part the inspiration for Rebecca's next book, a biography of the saint. Rebecca, not surprisingly, did not enjoy sharing a house with her mother-in-law, and told Winnie that there 'was growing hysterical horror at living in this horrible flat'.[1] So she was much relieved when they eventually found a flat that seemed perfect, both for them and for Anthony when he was on holiday from school. Near Portman Square, 15 Orchard Court was a magnificent, modern place, which, by sharing the cost of £400 a year, a bargain due to a low housing market, they could afford.[2] Rebecca told Winnie that it would take six weeks to have it decorated and that until then they didn't want anyone to send them furniture. She despaired that nothing from Onslow Gardens, not even the beautifully made curtains, would fit the new flat. Only the prospect of escaping from Mary's home quelled 'her horror at the expense'.[3]

When Henry travelled to Basle for work, Rebecca spent most of her time at the flat. Eventually, she announced proudly that it was 'beginning to look as if some day they might live in it'.[4] Rebecca took time from the chaos of setting up home to honour Arnold Bennett, despite the difficulties of their relationship. He died in March 1931 and Rebecca wrote a pamphlet for the John Day Company entitled *Arnold Bennett Himself*. Rebecca paid homage to his talent, the way that Bennett 'painted life in brilliant, savage strokes'.[5] For Rebecca, his commercialism raised the question as to whether art 'can be based on pure sensationalism' and rendered his position as an artist uncertain. But he had 'the first necessity for a novelist in his insatiable appetite for life'.[6] Above all Rebecca lauded his personality. Bennett was 'the perfect Londoner', and, as a man, 'he was great, he was grand: he was Coquelin's Cyrano De Bergerac, but tenderer, more lovable'.[7]

Once the flat was completed, Rebecca and Henry planned a summer holiday together in Switzerland and, before they left, Henry wrote a letter for Rebecca to be opened by her in the event of his death. He had made a will in her favour and continued:

> All the best that life gave me until I met you, all generous thoughts and efforts, seemed to find their true value in whatever ability they gave me to understand you and to love you. If ever you should feel lonely and disheartened I hope you will recall how when I was lonely your work recalled me to the ideals and enthusiasms of my youth and gave me strength not to compromise.[8]

As head of the European division of Schroders, part of Henry's job involved reorganizing the German economy. His work frequently took him to Germany and Rebecca sometimes accompanied him but, as she reported to Winnie, she 'never loathed any place so much as Berlin'.[9] She despaired of the fact that Germany had got itself into so much financial difficulty. Part of

Henry's work was to try to come up with some solutions for this, but the German leadership seemed intent on getting the funds from other nations to help them out. With a great deal of prescience, she worried over the way they seemed to look forward to a 'Hitlerite government': a government that would surely 'shoot all the Jews' and bring no relief to the crisis at all.[10]

The one shadow over these early married days was the tension between Henry and Anthony, and, of course, Wells. Anthony was jealous of Henry's demands on his mother's time, and later Rebecca suspected that her son had actually exacerbated the situation by lying to Wells about Henry and Henry's wishes for his future. Henry had none of Wells' charisma. In fact Anthony thought that Henry had a 'Midas touch of boredom', that he 'bored for England'.[11] Rebecca described Anthony as acting like 'a raging fiend and hysteric'.[12]

When Anthony was sent down from Stowe for failing Latin, any hopes that he might go to Oxford were dashed. Rebecca believed that Anthony had assuaged Wells' disappointment by telling him that Henry had been pushing him to study Classics; as he had no interest in doing so, he had made no effort to succeed. Given Wells' disapproval of the study of classical languages, this was a winning tactic.

Wells invited Anthony to join him and Odette at Lou Pidou. Anthony enthusiastically agreed. He later wrote that he had merely exchanged the tension in one house for that of another. Rebecca resented the visit, which had led to an uneasy atmosphere in London during the days before his departure. Anthony had not reckoned on a similar situation when he arrived in France. The relationship between Wells and Odette was going through a volatile phase and Wells, never good at suffering in silence, was suffering from haemorrhoids, which made him even more ill-tempered than usual. Anthony confessed to his father that he was unhappy at school and that he wanted to be a painter. He even asked for advice about a love affair. Odette, sensing all the usual adolescent conflict in the boy, got straight to the point, suggesting that the problem was probably more to do with a desire for sex than anything more complicated. Being English, she reasoned, would make it culturally difficult for him to separate the longing for sex from love, and a quick sexual relationship would sort it all out. Wells found this notion deeply upsetting and flew into a temper. Anthony, lying awake in his bedroom upstairs, was forced to listen to them shouting at one another. Nor was it the end of the matter; comments about his innocence were to plague him for the rest of his stay. A few days later they all had lunch with a former mistress of Wells', Elizabeth Russell, and the Aga Khan. Odette steered the conversation to the breeding of livestock, much to Anthony's embarrassment. When Odette noticed, she pointed at him, teasing 'Anthony is blushing. He is really blushing!' before adding that it surely meant he was a virgin. Wells told her off, but she simply turned to the Aga Khan, asking him to back up her opinion that the English were prudish in public but 'lubricious in private'.[13]

Anthony was also worried about his financial position and when he wrote to Wells about how difficult he had found his time in France he also sought assurance as to what arrangements had been made for him. At first, Wells was unsympathetic but he later reassured his son that there were three trusts in existence, all in his favour, as well as various 'holdings of securities' which he claimed were for Anthony.

Yet Anthony's general anxiety did not seem to lessen and an increasingly worried Rebecca referred him to the psychiatrist Hanns Sachs. Sachs' first diagnosis was that the whole issue of education was such a traumatic one for Anthony that he should not take any more exams for at least the first six or seven months of his therapy. When Sachs left for the States he recommended that Anthony follow him to continue his treatment, and Rebecca reluctantly agreed, seeking advice from American friends on how he might best continue with some schooling while he was there. But Anthony was not Rebecca's only problem. Perhaps the strain of their domestic difficulties, or perhaps Henry's propensity to flirt with other women, meant that the couple's sex life, which had at first been so fulfilling, was already almost non-existent.

Rebecca later recalled one of the last times they ever made love, in early 1931; they had been married only a few months. Rebecca fell pregnant but an ectopic pregnancy necessitated an abortion. Henry's lack of interest in her haunted Rebecca throughout their long marriage and even during her fondest recollections she lamented that he had utterly failed her sexually.[14]

❧

What was meant to be a relaxing visit to Switzerland with a concerned Henry left her exhausted and suffering from digestive problems, as well as a propensity to faint. She booked in for a cure at Dr Lahmann's Sanatorium in Bad Weisser Hirsch. Once there she settled in, taking long walks to Dresden along the bank of the Elbe, admiring the 'baroque towers and spires' as they were lit by sunset hues and declaring it 'more park than city'. The tension that had existed between Henry's mother and Rebecca had dissipated, now that they no longer lived in the same house, and Mary wrote kindly letters, and also sent a 'very strange' underskirt of black artificial silk and coffee-coloured lace.[15]

However, Rebecca worried about Anthony, who had written her a letter hinting darkly at taking his own life and saying goodbye to her. She confided in Dr Lahmann. His jocular advice that it wouldn't be healthy if an eighteen year old wasn't 'thinking of suiciding himself' allayed her concerns just a little and she reasoned that perhaps the only thing to do was go on calmly, hoping that the worst of the moods and despair would pass after adolescence.[16] However, Pamela Frankau, with whom Anthony was a little in love, had received a similar letter and immediately taken it to Henry in London to see what should be done.

Henry rushed into action, eventually finding that his stepson was at a Thanksgiving party in New York, at the house of Emanie Sachs, Rebecca's novelist friend, where he was a guest. After speaking to Anthony on the telephone, Henry quickly sent a telegram to Rebecca to reassure her. Overwhelmed by his kindness, she thanked him for the 'sweetness and thoughtfulness' of the gesture.[17] Despite her protestations that Anthony's angst was a natural part of adolescence, she had actually been tormented by worries for his safety. By being aware of her fears, Henry was showing an understanding 'close to genius'.[18] But the drama was not completely over. Anthony wrote again to Pamela, this time claiming to have attempted suicide by throwing himself in the Charles River. According to his account of events, a passing policeman had rescued him and then, in an act of pity, let him go. Anthony's therapist, Hanns Sachs, assured Rebecca that the story was a complete fabrication and that it had been designed specifically to hurt Rebecca, in retaliation for a financial squabble. Rebecca was annoyed at Anthony's extravagance in spending £28 on a model train and had written to him, berating him for being a spendthrift.

Stressed, and preoccupied with her anxiety about her son, Rebecca responded slowly to her treatment, continuing to faint even while she was a patient at the hospital. But Lehmann assured her that the main cause of her ailments was extreme tiredness, and recommended that she rest even more. While pointedly acknowledging that Henry seemed to be having quite a busy social life without her in London, she conceded that this was the right place for her. There was a week of injections when her period prevented her taking the full cure, then a rigorous regime of exercise in the sunny but bitterly cold weather. She missed her husband on the long forest walks, lamenting that such ambles should never be 'a solitary vice'. At night she collapsed, exhausted, in bed, with a copy of *Time and Tide* or the *West End Review*, filled with gratitude to Henry because she could finally rest without fretting about where Anthony was staying or if he might be in danger.

In time, she found sufficient energy to continue work on her book on St Augustine, writing to Henry that her subject's life was 'so African – so Islamic' that he could be called the non-Semitic 'precursor of Mohammed'.[19] In Rebecca's biography, Augustine is described as one of the greatest of all writers, obsessed by sex, dominated by his mother, but unsurpassed by later novelists. His influence permeates literature, from Shakespeare – 'the Augustinian content to Shakespeare alone is impressive' – to Joyce, Proust and Lawrence.[20] Augustine had propounded 'The idea that matter, especially matter related to sex, is evil; that man has acquired guilt through his enmeshment in matter; that he must atone for this guilt to an angry God; and that this atonement must take the form of suffering, and the renunciation of easy pleasure.'[21]

And in doing so, he had created a prison for the modern mind.

One interesting point she makes about St Augustine's *Confessions*, especially in light of the way Rebecca often reported her own life to others, is that it was 'too subjectively true to be objectively true'.[22] She elaborated that some things were just too painful to think about without some degree of falsification.

Rebecca finished her cure to more good news. Whether as a result of the psychoanalysis or the change of scene, Anthony returned from the States with a new focus in his life. He had always enjoyed painting more than the academic disciplines so beloved of his father, and enrolled as a student at the Slade. Anthony later recalled of his father, 'I don't think he liked me very much because I was so like Rebecca and because I was arty.'[23] Rebecca was impressed by his work and always insisted that painting was Anthony's true, natural talent. Her delight at his new direction was short-lived. In less than two terms, Anthony dropped out of art school. He refused to answer Rebecca and Henry's concerned questions as to what the problem might be, or even so much as comment. Instead, he retreated further from them and took up the lease of a small house called Quarry Farm, just outside Salisbury. Again, Rebecca and Henry proffered help and advice, offering the services of the family solicitor, but Anthony, wilfully independent, refused and stormed out of their house every time such suggestions were made.

But it was not so much his independence that troubled Rebecca as the sheer irresponsibility of Anthony's way of life. On his eighteenth birthday Anthony began to receive an income from one of the trusts set up by his father. As a birthday gift, Rebecca gave him the interest on some of the savings she had put aside for him, so that he might enjoy some little indulgences without dipping into his allowance. It amounted to some £300, which he immediately spent on more model trains from Bassett-Lowke in Holborn, which was renowned for the exquisite precision of its models. Rebecca was shocked, thinking at first, when the receipt arrived from the shop, that there had been some error. Then finding that the cupboard in his bedroom at her house was filled with boxes from the store, she confronted Anthony. She warned him that he needed to show more prudence, that this kind of extravagance would infuriate Wells and thus endanger any further settlement coming to him.

Once he settled into his cottage, his relationship with Rebecca and Henry was amicable enough, but they continued to fret that he was making no attempt at all to establish a career. They warned him that the income from his allowance was barely enough for him to live on as a bachelor and would be woefully inadequate if he decided to marry. Anthony paid no heed, buying what Rebecca admitted was very beautiful furniture for his new home, and allowing her, for once, to join in. She filled in 'the obvious gaps' in his domestic arrangements with bedlinen and very pretty and brightly coloured, but flimsy, Indian rugs.[24]

Beyond her troubles with her son, Rebecca's social and professional life blossomed with her marriage and, just as her review of Wells' book had led to their momentous meeting, so, in 1932, another review led to a new friendship. Rebecca wrote a review of several books for the *Daily Telegraph*. Almost in passing she praised a new book about D.H. Lawrence by a 'lady with the fascinating name of Anaïs Nin'. According to Rebecca, Nin's book, *D.H. Lawrence: An Unprofessional Study*, discussed Lawrence 'more brilliantly and profoundly than ever before'.[25]

Their first meeting got off to a shaky start. Almost a year after the review had appeared, Anaïs Nin arrived at Rebecca's apartment, hoping to use the encounter to promote Henry Miller's work. While she admired the beautiful decoration and the view from the wide windows, she found it cold and too majestic with a '*grand monde*' atmosphere. Lunch was formal. When Rebecca spoke, Nin thought that she did so far less well than she wrote and that she was a mixture of insecurity and uneasiness. But then, she wrote in her journal, there was more, when she was quiet she glowed; she was the 'fox and mother with earthy hands'.[26]

Rebecca was rather more positive about the encounter and immediately invited Nin to return for dinner. This time, Rebecca struck Nin as 'sumptuous'. She had changed out of a green dress and looked magnificent in black velvet, with silver necklaces draped over her full breasts visible at the dress's square low neck. But although she was generous with offers of help and contacts to further Henry Miller's work, she still seemed uneasy. Then, on Nin's last night in London, the two women at last opened up to each other. They found that, with their difficult relationships with their fathers and their lack of conventional education, they had much in common. Over dinner at the Ivy, Rebecca seemed to lose her inhibitions and Nin noted that 'in one instant we stood where it takes others years to stand'.[27] When Rebecca expressed surprise that Nin had brought two manuscripts written by Henry Miller with her, saying that she found Nin to be the better writer because she was 'so much more mature', their friendship was cemented. It was breathless and sensual and Rebecca exclaimed that she felt as if she was having another love affair.[28]

Old friendships blossomed in this period too. Ever grateful for their first introduction, Rebecca and Henry often visited Vera Brittain and her husband. Marriage was agreeing with Rebecca and Vera often commented how well she looked. In return, Rebecca wished only success for *Testament of Youth*, which she admired tremendously, and worried that her friend looked tired with the strain of bringing up her children and working at the same time. The relentless social engagements that preoccupied Rebecca at this time were noted by Virginia Woolf, someone she had known since 1928 and who was yet another of her circle at this time. Woolf shared Nin's initial impression of Orchard Court and found something a little empty in the formality and lack of intimacy that characterized dinner with the Andrewses. There was 'nothing said of any naturalness or spontaneity'.[29] It was a sentiment Woolf had expressed before, referring to the 'fish blooded' Andrews, but she had other reservations about Rebecca, too, thinking her 'a hardened old reprobate'.[30] Rebecca was similarly unconvinced by what she saw as Woolf's pretentiousness.

Class undoubtedly played a big part in their mutual distrust. Woolf seemed to sneer at Rebecca's attempts, now she was married, to aim at middle-class respectability, something that had so eluded Rebecca both while she was growing up and as a young woman entangled with Wells, but which Henry offered. When they first met, Woolf wrote to her sister Vanessa Bell that Rebecca was 'a cross between a charwoman and a gypsy', who looked shabby and had dirty nails.[31] Now Virginia criticized what she saw as a facade, 'the social strata they live on – appearances'.[32]

Above all Rebecca hated the fact that the Bloomsbury set condescended to her. Even in indomitable and rather revered old age, she never condescended to anyone, not even to the least celebrated of her employees. Although what she said about them in private was a completely different matter.[33]

She admired Woolf as a writer, but later recalled that she'd never found anyone in the group entertaining because their experience of life was so limited.

Rebecca's social status might have been a subject of mockery for Virginia Woolf but it was a source of some pride for her. She wrote to Henry while he was on one of his business trips that the Prince of Wales had been at the same party as her. Not only that, but the prince was accompanied by his 'new artificial Rac'.[34] Ric and Rac were not only Rebecca and Henry's nicknames for one another, but they were also used as shorthand for male and female, man and woman, in their letters. Mrs Simpson, Rebecca told her husband, was clever but also 'very common and trivial'.

Rebecca thought her a social climber who had mercilessly aimed to seduce the prince. It was a popular view at the time, but one that Rebecca would soon drastically revise when she got to know more of Wallis Simpson and her circle.

Despite the apparent success of the spa cure, Rebecca's health was still troublesome. Finding what she thought was a lump in her breast, she at first suspected the worst, confiding in Anaïs Nin that she thought she might die. It turned out to be mastitis and an operation was scheduled with a plastic surgeon, Thomas Pomfret Kilner. Pomfret Kilner, whom Rebecca called 'Tommy', was just two years older than her and a senior surgeon at St Thomas's Hospital. Physically he was very similar to Wells with his small stature, twinkling eyes and boundless energy. Like Wells, he too had a wife, but Rebecca fell in love with him. They slept together shortly after meeting. They were lovers for only one night, but Rebecca was left feeling blissfully happy. Tommy did not seem to share her pleasure in what had occurred between them and immediately broke off the relationship, leaving her hurt and miserable and 'mad with loneliness'.[35]

Disappointed, Rebecca accepted a commission to write a series of articles for the *New York Times* and in March 1935 sailed for New York on the RMS *Olympic*. From the ship she wrote to Henry. The letter was initially apologetic, ostensibly over a bottle of wine she was meant to buy for a friend of his: 'I shouldn't have failed you. Do, please, please forgive me. I won't do these things when I come back.'[36]

But as the letter continues, it hints at her indiscretion and pleads 'forgive me if I have failed you in any other way as well as the wine'. She goes on to say that she hated leaving England with the feeling that she had let him down, adding 'I do love you so but the world's just too much for me just now'.[37] She promised to 'tidy everything up' when she got back and to be a 'perfect Rac', saying how she appreciated how he had been in the past few months.[38] Once Rebecca was settled in New York, she began work on a new novel, *The Thinking Reed*, a comic portrayal of the French Côte D'Azur, an echo of Maugham's famous remark that it was a 'sunny place for shady people'. But beyond its funny portraits of expatriates, there was also the story of a marriage, of an incompatible couple who somehow got on. When the book was finally published, in 1936, it was tellingly dedicated to Henry. The trip was also an opportunity for Rebecca to catch up with friends, including Anaïs Nin, who was staying nearby and to whom she lamented over the shallowness she thought was starting to characterize American society, where 'everything that's deep is lacking'.[39]

She returned to London by way of France, met up with Henry, and together with him, saw Nin, this time in Paris with Henry Miller and her husband, Hugo Guiler. They spent a light-hearted time, shopping for lipstick and bath salts, painting each other's eyes. She wore Nin's nail polish and a little white hat identical to hers. Nin loved Rebecca's 'earthy, fulsome' body, her tanned skin and soft breasts, and noticed that in spite of her humour and glitter, her eyes were filled with melancholy. At night the women left the men and huddled in Rebecca's room, sharing confidences, marvelling at the similarities in their lives, their loves. Rebecca spoke openly about her failed love affair with Tommy and admired Nin's ability to grab hold of life.[40]

The two women were once again entranced by the 'vigour and warmth' between them. Nin loved Rebecca's ardour, her humour and irony, and Rebecca felt giddy on Nin's beauty and charming accent. They sat up late at night and Nin listened as Rebecca spoke endlessly about Tommy. They walked around Rouen, losing themselves in their conversations about shared experiences, Rebecca mercilessly describing mutual acquaintances and making Nin laugh at her sharpness. Then later, lying in Rebecca's room, Nin found herself tempted to make love to her as she rested on the couch opposite her, 'untidy and slack, with her very strong legs and accentuated curves'. The rhythm of life with Henry was broken and Rebecca felt her imagination stretched. Despite the fact she was ten years younger, Nin felt protective, that she might influence Rebecca 'towards freedom'.[41]

But while Rebecca dallied with Nin, Henry's professional

situation deteriorated. He had appointed a local man, a Jew, to look over the Berlin operation. But with the Nazis' seizure of power, Henry's appointee vanished. Schroders continued their relationship with the new ruling party; Henry, however, refused to associate with them and was consequently fired. The columns hinting at the dangers of Nazism which Rebecca wrote for the *New York American* between 1931 and 1933 had been prophetic, but she had not imagined that developments would impact on her own financial security. Her monetary worries were reflected in those of the characters of her latest book, *The Harsh Voice*, a collection of Rebecca's longer short fiction.

Towards the end of the year, Anthony surprised Henry and Rebecca by announcing that he was going to be married. His bride was Katharine Church, an artist who, at twenty-six, was five years older than Anthony. He had only met her a few weeks before, at a Christmas party, but had known immediately that he wanted to spend his life with her. The wedding took place in February. Shortly afterwards, Rebecca wrote to her American friend Doris Stevens that Anthony had 'up and married a pretty blonde after my own heart'. She was a 'fine painter' and 'very funny' and Rebecca was just hoping against hope that it would all work out well.[42] Kitty, as she was known, had studied at art school and was one of a group of avant-garde artists that included Julian Trevelyan. Both Henry and Rebecca admired her 'physical grace and loveliness' as well as her paintings and were gladdened by her very obvious affection for Anthony despite his moodiness.[43] Later, when the marriage was over, Rebecca thought she had missed one of the great similarities between them. Kitty, like Rebecca at the same age, was fatally drawn to men who were difficult; Kitty loved Anthony because he treated her badly, not in spite of it.

On 20 January 1936, George V died and Rebecca's acquaintance, the erstwhile Prince of Wales, succeeded as Edward VIII. Rebecca saw Wallis Simpson socially from time to time through their mutual friends Katherine and Herman Rogers whom Wallis had stayed with in Peking in the twenties and continued to visit in Cannes. Rebecca now found Wallis very charming, 'smooth and passive and yielding, a sort of gentle massage'.[44]

Then, in the spring of 1936, Rebecca received an invitation from the British Council to make a lecture tour of Yugoslavia. It was intended as a short and interesting trip but developed into a project that would consume the next five years of Rebecca's working life. The first days of the trip went well, with Rebecca writing to Henry about her travelling companion, a 'most extra-ordinary' person, Stanislav Vinaver. He was half-Jewish, half-Serbian and at forty-five just two years older than Rebecca. Vinaver was short and fat with black curly hair; she later described him as a 'Jewish Mr Pickwick'.[45] The chief of the Yugoslavian Press Bureau, he was a successful poet and had been travelling Europe independently for some years. His wife was German and they had two children. The tone of her second letter to Henry was markedly different. She was delighted by Skopje, now the capital of Macedonia, but at that time part of Yugoslavia, and had loved the medieval feel of the Easter ceremony with its candles and processions which were so redolent of St Augustine. With Vinaver she visited the mosques, monasteries and local festivals, and enjoyed his brilliant conversation, although wondered if his garrulousness bordered on abnormality. By the time they had moved on to Ochrid, and a lakeside hotel, she was reconsidering her earlier enthusiasm; Vinaver was behaving strangely. When they returned from dinner, Vinaver apparently made pressing advances to her. When she resisted, he persisted until she found herself hammering him with her fists to try to get him away from her. When she finally got him out of her bedroom, she took stock of her rather dire situation. No one in the hotel had come to help her or even shown any concern at the obvious row from her room. Vinaver was an important government official; her passport was with the owner of the hotel; she had very little cash. Her first impulse, to leave the hotel and try to walk the huge distance back to Skopje, gave way to the realization that she would never be able to get past any of the military checkpoints. She remained in her room until morning to find an apologetic and subdued Vinaver at breakfast. At night his attentions began again, but thankfully he was forced to desist when they went to stay at a monastery.

All of these events Rebecca recounted to Henry in a letter, but surprisingly, given the drama of the events, she reconciled herself to Vinaver. She thought he had become rather fond of her and in any case was always 'delightful' during the daytime. She also justified his behaviour by saying that the French women journalists he had accompanied previously had all slept with him so it was perhaps unsurprising that he expected her to do so. There is one other factor rendering her subsequent reconciliation and friendship with Vinaver less puzzling; Rebecca was conscious of her age, unsure of her sexual attractiveness and worried about her husband's attentions elsewhere. She may have been trying to show Henry that she too was desirable, especially when she added in the letter, 'after all there can't be many Rics who have to worry about the dogstealers when their Racs are forty-three years old'.[46]

In Belgrade she was introduced to Vinaver's wife and agreed to have lunch. She found her 'dotty', a German woman who was so distraught at the fact that her husband was half-Jewish that previously she had put her head in a gas oven and threatened to kill her children.

It was at this time that another calamity was to befall Rebecca. She came down with a heavy cold and then with something far more serious. Realizing she needed medical attention, she called the British embassy, and the chargé d'affaires, John Balfour, arranged for a doctor to visit her. He diagnosed bronchitis and, most worryingly, erysipelas. This latter was an infection characterized by high temperatures, shaking, vomiting and a painful red swelling which, in Rebecca's case, covered her face. Rebecca panicked: not only was she disfigured but she knew erysipelas could be fatal. She asked Balfour to help her be admitted to a clinic, but the condition was so infectious that none would take her. Vinaver visited constantly, his ardour undimmed; Rebecca lay in bed and groaned. The only food she was able to keep down was yoghurt. Finally, after a few days, it was deemed safe to admit her to hospital, although the rash on her face was as bad as ever. Thinking that this would prevent Vinaver's unwelcome fussing, Rebecca was at first relieved but soon disappointed to find that even there he continued to press his suit. In despair she begged Balfour to help her and, with enormous kindness, he invited her into his home. There, at last, she felt she was able to start recovering, even though she looked 'as if a hyena had clawed half my face'.[47]

The illness had deeply affected her. She felt she had aged, that the lines on her face were more ingrained, and that her hair had turned much greyer. When she had recovered a little she went to the spa at Kurhaus Semmering in Austria to recuperate sufficiently to be able to make the journey back to England. She was diagnosed with anaemia and undernourishment. Rebecca longed to go home but felt both too exhausted and too worried about Henry's reaction to her appearance. The worst of the rash had healed but the right side of her face was still unsightly.

Yet, in spite of it all, Rebecca had fallen in love with Yugoslavia. She found its dramatic history captivating. She worried only that the place was 'lousy with Italian propagandists' and that the Italian threat was preventing any possibility of internal peace in the country.[48] She agonized too over what she had seen in Europe, the way Germany was 'rearming and planning for conquest'.[49] A Viennese manufacturer she met at Kurhaus Semmering told her that he was producing pumps so that Germany might empty numerous reservoirs of water and use them to store gas bombs in preparation for an attack.

Henry came to Austria to collect Rebecca, the idea being that they might spend a few days together before he accompanied her on the journey home. But the trip was cut short by a telephone call from England; they had to return at once. Uncle Ernest was dying. Henry visited his uncle's bedside several times a day; Rebecca developed what she called 'a lighthouse keeper's wife character' and heated soup on the stove at home ready for his return.[50] Ernest's death was slow. Rebecca wrote to Winnie that she felt as if they were in Purgatory, as he eventually slipped into unconsciousness but still did not die. They grappled with his estate which they expected would be worth 'very little money'.[51] There was a house in Crawley which Rebecca hated and which, although it had cost £4,000, was now valued at around £1,000. Henry's speculations since leaving Schroders had not gone well; an investment in a Turkish mine had failed and money was an issue; they were largely subsisting on Rebecca's income alone.

When Uncle Ernest eventually died, in May 1936, Rebecca and Henry were astonished to learn that the estate that they had expected to be worth a pittance was an inheritance of £170,000. They were rich. They could, if they wished, sustain their current way of life without working at all.

But Henry was worn out from caring for Uncle Ernest, traumatized by watching a protracted and painful death. Worried by the seizures and the mental confusion that had tormented his uncle, he made a confession to Rebecca: his father had committed suicide and another uncle had been placed in an insane asylum.[52]

Rebecca was stunned and when Tommy suddenly wrote asking to see her, she immediately agreed. But six weeks passed before Tommy wrote again to make arrangements. When at last they did meet, Tommy confessed his dilemma: he loved her but was terrified of the consequences, the danger of being caught in an illicit affair. He begged her to write again but when she duly did, once again the letter went unanswered. Rebecca was frustrated, as well as angry at the waves of vacillation that seemed to characterize their relationship. Perhaps unsurprisingly, given the events of the previous months, Henry was still not making love to Rebecca, and she wrote to Emanie that she was puzzled by his lack of desire when he so obviously had 'great devotion' for her.[53] She was further hurt by the fact that Henry seemed to be taking an ever-increasing interest in a Finnish opera singer. She had noted Henry's interest in young women before, but she worried that his latest infatuation seemed intent on making disparaging comments about her being old and unattractive. Most ominously of all, Rebecca wrote to Emanie, Henry seemed to almost derive a kind of 'vicious teasing pleasure' from the way the opera singer put her down.[54]

Her difficulties with Tommy continued and took a bizarre turn when the two of them sat down with H.G. to discuss the situation. Rebecca was forced to acknowledge that Tommy really wouldn't be her lover again, he was too afraid, and confessed to Emanie that she was sad because she 'adored his little podgy person as I've never adored anyone else'.[55]

Rebecca sought solace in writing and travelling. Despite growing international anxiety over the political situation in Yugoslavia, Rebecca planned another trip to the Balkans with Henry to coincide with Easter the following year.

Henry continued to do what he could for friends and relatives in Germany but became increasingly exhausted as the situation in Europe escalated. Hitler had introduced compulsory military service in Germany thus revoking the Treaty of Versailles. Rebecca arranged to take Henry to Austria to recuperate from his fatigue, lamenting the fact that she felt sure Mussolini was about to capitulate in Italy, thus enabling the Germans to move into Austria. 'If only we had put man, woman and child of that abominable nation to the sword in 1919,' she wrote to Winnie of Germany.[56]

⚮

On 25 October 1938, Rebecca's prophecy came to pass. Mussolini's new foreign minister brokered an agreement between Germany and Italy creating what Mussolini referred to as 'the axis of the new Europe'.[57] The Balkans were now surrounded on all sides, by the Germans and the Italians and, to the east, by Russia.

Rebecca spoke out against the British government's decision not to allow the Spanish republic to buy weapons to protect itself from Franco's forces and described herself as 'passionately anti-Franco'.[58] She wrote a statement on her position for *Authors Take Sides on the Spanish War*, a pamphlet of 126 views. Rebecca's statement was unequivocal: 'I am for the legal government of Republican Spain against Franco, since Spain herself, at a properly conducted election, chose that Government and rejected the party which now supports Franco.'[59] Other contributors, among them Ezra Pound and T.S. Eliot, remained neutral.[60] The end of the year was marked by an incident which Rebecca described as bringing her 'the deepest pain': the king abdicated in order to marry Wallis Simpson. Rebecca felt betrayed, and surprised herself by realizing 'how much I am a part of my country'.[61] The match itself was of interest to her and she wrote gossipy but astute letters about it.[62] Rebecca noted that most of the friends she shared with Wallis had noticed that she seemed far fonder of her husband than she was of the King. She had revised her earlier opinion that Wallis was a social climber, and described what she called the King's 'imbecility' both in his passion for Wallis and in the way he naively believed there was any chance of his union with her being popular. She thought that the abdication was the work of the prime minister, Stanley Baldwin, who was determined to get rid of the King at any cost. Rebecca felt that the King's suggestions of a morganatic marriage was far preferable. She lamented his going to Austria and, again with foresight, was convinced that it was only a matter of time before the Nazis would use him to their advantage.

Despite the escalating tensions between Yugoslavia's ethnic and political factions, coupled with the geographic vulnerability of the region, the majesty of the mosques and the blueness of the River Ochrid had left their mark on Rebecca. As she later wrote: 'I am never sure of the reality of what I see, if I have seen it only once; I know that until it has firmly established its objective existence by impressing my senses and my memory, I am capable of conscripting it into the service of a private dream.'[63]

❧

And so, once again, she set off on a journey to Yugoslavia. She took Henry, and this time she was working on a book about her experiences. 'I resolved to put on paper what a typical Englishwoman felt and thought in the late 1930s when, already convinced of the inevitability of the second Anglo-German war, she had been able to follow the dark waters of that event back to its source.'[64]

Black Lamb and Grey Falcon is a masterful albeit somewhat rambling book. Defying genre, it is part-history, part-travelogue, and importantly, a deeply intimate picture of a marriage. Many of the characters she met during her first trip, and again on her return, were renamed and recast as caricatures of themselves, subtly changed to carry the plot or make a political point. Vinaver became Constantine, his German wife became Gerda, and Henry – a gentle, questioning version of Henry – accompanied her through the pages. The great strength of *Black Lamb and Grey Falcon* is the way that its text became the thread that bound together West's public and personal worlds, her political judgements and her private tenderness.

It is astonishingly predictive, presenting a country of disparate, quarrelsome peoples on the brink of dissolution. Even today, Rebecca's stated intention 'to show the past in relation to the present it begot' still stands up, but from a twenty-first-century perspective it is perhaps harder for the reader to make such a clear distinction between the wronged and the wrongdoer or to escape from what West called 'our modern disposition to pretend that public actions must be inspired by simple and superficial motives'.[65]

For West, however, some beliefs were genuinely intolerable and would eschew our modern tendency towards extreme tolerance or political correctness. In *Black Lamb and Grey Falcon*, written before the outbreak of the Second World War, she warned against false and uneasy acceptance of ideas that were, quite simply, unacceptable.

> The past had bade us overlook racial and national differences because they had then no significance to compare with that which must follow from the clash between one man's good faith and another's roguery; for all Europeans

were agreed in their ideal of a moral society. Since then the world had altered. Now different races and nationalities cherish different ideals of society that stink in each other's nostrils with offensiveness beyond the power of any but the most monstrous private deed.[66]

It is a sentiment reiterated, in 1987, by the novelist Hilary Mantel, in an article about her experience of living in Saudi Arabia:

When you come across an alien culture you must not automatically respect it. You must sometimes pay it the compliment of hating it.[67]

Perhaps most significantly of all, from a contemporary viewpoint, West offers a clear insight into current conflicts between Christian and Islamic traditions in Europe today. She questioned not only the possibility, but the wisdom, of integrating non-Christian Eastern European countries into the community of Western European nations, a situation that was almost perfectly mirrored in the fragmented and bitter religious conflict in the Balkans in the 1930s.

Yet *Black Lamb and Grey Falcon* was more than a commentary on the political situation in Yugoslavia, more than a historical travelogue. The characters she wrote about, and the depiction of her marriage, afforded Rebecca the opportunity to make shrewd observations about the male and female psyche. Women were, taking the definition from the Greek root of the word, 'idiots', private citizens concerned with small, personal matters. It was all very well discussing the defences of the country, but when there were several thousand people living without bathrooms, surely domestic issues ought to be dealt with first. Men, however, were 'lunatics' looking at a moonlit world, seeing the shape of everything but none of the details that made up the very nature of each individual thing.

Rebecca's second trip was markedly different from the first, not least because of the uneasy relationship between Vinaver and

Henry. Surprisingly, Vinaver did not seem to rein in his attentions, despite Henry's presence. Indeed, Rebecca seemed to enjoy
Vinaver's admiration rather more now that she was safely chap-
eroned by her husband. Henry was less enthusiastic and on the
long train journey to Split, she had to ask him to behave more
politely to Vinaver. Rebecca kept a notebook of her experiences
and impressions.[68] Tommy, referred to in the book as 'K' for
Kilner, was still much in her thoughts, and while she was grateful
for the little kindnesses Henry continued to show to her, she
continued to fret over her thwarted love affair.

However, both Henry and Rebecca were unhappy when
Vinaver's wife, Elsa, joined them for part of the trip. Her support
for the Nazis and the way she constantly contradicted her
husband made the journey tiresome and eventually, their tolerance exhausted, they insisted she travel on alone, by bus, because
the car was too small for four passengers and a driver.

By the end of the trip the tensions had exacerbated them.
Vinaver became unpleasant, bordering on rude, and Rebecca
excused his behaviour to Henry, saying that he must be ill. They
returned home at the end of May 1937. In December, after seven
months of writing intensively, Rebecca knew the book was going
to be hugely long, despite the fact that her advance from
Macmillan was only £200. It would also be late. She was due to
deliver the manuscript in June 1938, an impossible task for a
book that now extended to two volumes.

Not only that, but Rebecca realized she could not finish the
book without revisiting some of the terrain she had discovered
on her second visit. Henry, who was preoccupied with his own
work, could not accompany her, so Rebecca set off alone for
Yugoslavia. The world was changing rapidly around her and she
confided in Emanie: 'There's a turning away from life that first
turned men away from love, and is now turning them away from
all forms of civilization, and all the content, not of civilization
alone but of life itself.'[69]

If Rebecca thought travelling by herself would leave her more
time to write she was mistaken. Staying with friends in Skopje

she found that the conversations lasted throughout the day and ended at local cafes in the small hours of the morning, with glasses of wine and plates piled high with sausages. She left for Ochrid by way of a ten-hour trip on a crowded bus; the Bishop had invited her to stay at a monastery by Lake Ochrid. The monastery was also an asylum for the mentally ill, so invalids roamed the corridors and were prayed for at the services. There, she began to write again and found it heaven except for the fact that there was only cold water to wash in, hot water being regarded as a 'gateway to sin'.[70]

It was on this third trip that Rebecca saw the spectacle that would give her the title for the book. Early one morning, she and a friend came upon a pagan fertility rite. A huge stone shining with red blood stood in a valley. Since twilight the previous night, black lambs had been sacrificed on it. Ten thousand peasants, Rebecca claimed, came to perform the slaughter that they believed might bring them a child or better crops. Finding it idiotic, even barbaric, she felt as if she had reached the very base of human nature: 'On the sheep's field I had seen sacrifice in its filth and falsehood, and in its astonishing power over the imagination.'[71]

Yet, for all of that, she acknowledged that the primitive feelings it aroused were also part of her own nature. Here, at last, she found a little of the insight she had been seeking. The black lambs were a metaphor for Serbia's greatest loss, that of Kosovo. There, the defeat of the Slavs by the Turks over six hundred years ago was seen as a sacrifice. In Rebecca's account, although the Slavs believed they had right on their side because Christianity 'denounced the primary human fault, cruelty', they would never prevail because the noble ideal of sacrifice robbed them of the will to win. She felt, too, that in Western Europe, in the months before the outbreak of war, liberals were acting like lambs instead of like priests, passively holy, but forgetting to protect 'the works of love'.[72]

The grey falcon of her title is taken from a Serbian epic poem about Prince Lazar, who died at the Battle of Kosovo and was subsequently canonized. According to the poem Lazar was visited the night before the battle by an angel in the form of a grey falcon. The angel presented him with a choice: victory in battle or entry to the kingdom of heaven. Lazar sent his forces into battle to almost certain defeat, and thus, the poem claims, sacrificed not only his own life but also died with the blood of his people on his hands. This holy gesture has been venerated ever since and Lazar is still an iconic figure for the Serbs who, to this day, believe that the remains of his 600-year-old body possess great spiritual power. At a monastery on Fruška Gora, Rebecca held Lazar's blackened mummified hand and was moved by the fact that he was 'one of that company loving honour and freedom and harmony'.[73] He had gone to war to fight for something so worthwhile that losing was secondary to the glory of being prepared to defend it. Such conviction, for Rebecca, was part of the heroism of Yugoslavia. But she also saw its limitations: glory could never come from a failure to win freedom. Ultimately she rejected the idea that spiritual redemption was the greater end. For her the loss of Kosovo to the Turks was equivalent to the loss of Europe to the Nazis. She believed that there were 'certain ultimate human rights that must have precedence over all others', and that no one could find salvation by condemning millions to slavery. [74]

In Belgrade, she met up with Antoine Bibesco, her erstwhile lover. They spoke on the phone, teasing each other; he joked about Rebecca's greying hair, she riposted about the whiteness of his. They became lovers again, just for a week, and Rebecca joked to Emanie, years later, that she was testing to see if she was sexually satisfying to him or not, after the way he had treated her in Paris.[75]

Rebecca told Henry that she had met Bibesco, saying that he had been 'very severe' about her marriage and wondered if running away to Romania with him would make Henry divorce her. Pleased that she was still commanding such attentions, now that her fiftieth birthday seemed all too close, she nevertheless assured Henry that 'She prefers her Ric. Tho it's nice to have people showing an interest in the old premises'.[76]

Chapter Nine

WEST'S WARS

Today you can still see the traces of Rebecca's Yugoslavia, despite the ravages of its more recent conflict. Kalemegdan Park in Belgrade stretches out from the edge of the city, and the fort, where Rebecca walked on a sunny afternoon, is as majestic as it ever was. The frescoes too, in the sixteen monasteries perched on the mountain of Fruška Gora, show their medieval battles, saints and royalty in colours only slightly faded by time. Lazar's remains have been returned there, to the monastery of Vrdnik Ravanika where Rebecca saw them. And even now, if you are lucky, in the countryside of Macedonia or Montenegro, you can still catch a glimpse of old men and women wearing beautiful traditional costumes of the type that Rebecca brought back home with her.

When Rebecca returned to England early in 1939, she was more enamoured of Yugoslavia than ever. But war now seemed both inevitable and necessary. She opposed the Peace Pledge Union and in an article for *Nash's* magazine asked 'Do you believe you are going to abolish cancer if you get 100,000 people to sign a pledge that they do not intend to have cancer?'[1] In March, Hitler dismembered Czechoslovakia. While Britain and France did nothing, Rebecca worried that the Allies were also refusing to listen to repeated pleas from Yugoslavia and other central European countries. The Balkans became Hitler's bread basket as, caught in the middle of the fighting, they resigned themselves to his demands, remaining resolutely at peace, at least on paper. As a result the British considered Prince Paul, the regent of Yugoslavia, to be pro-German.

Rebecca and Henry now spent considerable time trying to get German Jews out of Europe and over to America. Even before Britain entered the war, Rebecca had been helping Dr Walter Landau, a specialist in the treatment of tuberculosis, and a Jew. Landau was the brother-in-law of Nazi journalist Raul Silex, who was in turn connected by marriage to Stanislaus Vinaver. In the first instance Rebecca offered to help Landau as a favour to her friend Vinaver. She later revised this, saying he was a delightful man, and she would have happily helped him for his own sake. She sent substantial amounts of cash, offering up to £500, to Ben Haubsch, her American editor at Viking, to help Landau establish himself in the US, and even offered to pay a yearly sum of $1,000 to an institution so they could employ him.[2] Their endeavours were wholly successful, although Landau found work of his own accord, and took up a position at a sanatorium in Baltimore. Once he was settled there, Rebecca sent more money and used her contacts to get passage for his wife and son.

With the advent of war, Rebecca spent more time with her family, taking Winnie's daughter, Alison, to the opera at Glyndebourne, which had opened two years earlier. The conductor and producer were both émigrés who had found themselves unable and unwilling to work in Nazi Germany. Rebecca thought Glyndebourne 'one of the best ideas human beings have had for a long time' and marvelled over the fact that its owner, John Christie, had amassed much of his fortune from the sale of cinema organs.[3]

Her relationship with her niece was troubled, however. It had never been good. When Winnie had looked after Anthony during Rebecca's frequent trips abroad, he had terrorized Alison. Rebecca always defended her son, and her difficult relationship with Alison continued into her niece's adulthood, aggravated, for Rebecca, by Alison's fascination with the Communist Party. To her despair, it seemed that Alison was not interested in the facts and was happy simply to follow authority.[4] Their relationship continued to deteriorate even with the signing, a month later, of the Molotov–Ribbentrop pact, the treaty of non-aggression between Germany and the Soviet Union.

When Britain declared war in September 1939, Henry got a job working for the Ministry of Economic Warfare. They spent the autumn at a rented manor house in Sussex and while Rebecca returned there every evening even after work necessitated time in London, Henry often stayed over in the London flat. He hated the blackout, as did Lettie, who was continuing to work in London, but Rebecca considered the atmosphere of the city surprisingly calm and thought the popular expression 'the Great Bore War' very apt.

Henry and Rebecca resolved to buy a house in the country, where they would spend at least part of the time, and where, Rebecca thought, they might support their extended family, living off the land as best they could during the crisis. Anthony explained that he had failed the army medical exam because of an irregular heartbeat and lung damage caused by his TB. To avoid the humiliation of being registered as unfit, he volunteered to join a group of 'promising artists, writers, actors, musicians' known as the Entertainment National Service Association.⁵ Their duty would be to provide entertainment to the troops, but despite the presence of many famous stars within its ranks, ENSA also included a number of amateur performers and the acronym was popularly known to stand for 'Every Night Something Awful'. While Anthony waited to see if his application was successful, Kitty and he were asked to billet a group of evacuees from London in their home near Salisbury – seven little Irish Catholic children. They found the children's parents rough and dirty and despaired that no sooner had they got the children clean and calm than the parents descended for a visit and made them filthy again. Anthony joked that he would speak to the Pope directly about it after the war was over. His failure to join the armed forces did not go unnoticed, though, and he, with several of his neighbours, was denounced as a Fifth Columnist.

His house was searched by the police and he was held for questioning, but eventually released, to a very relieved Kitty.[6]

Just before Christmas, Henry and Rebecca found exactly the kind of home that they had longed for. Ibstone Manor is set amidst rolling countryside, on the Buckinghamshire side of the Chiltern Hills. Rebecca wrote to her friend and erstwhile editor at the *New York Herald Tribune*, Irita Van Doren, that they had bought a 'derelict farm and put it on its legs'.[7] The house itself was late eighteenth century and was the fourth and sole remaining wing of a much larger house. The previous owner had fallen into financial difficulties, pulling down the other three wings one by one as his situation worsened. It suffered from rising damp as well as a roof that was in need of repair, but it was habitable and Rebecca described it as 'the sort of house you can imagine Alice in Wonderland living in'.[8] The house came with seventy acres of farmland, a small herd of cattle and some pigs which the couple decided to keep on. It cost just £6,000 and was bought directly from the bank that had repossessed it.[9] Ibstone was just forty-five miles from London; by car, the journey took less than an hour. But Rebecca never learned to drive, and they kept on the flat at Orchard Court. Buses to the nearest train station were infrequent and unreliable, the train tortuously slow. One of Ibstone's greatest benefits was its distance from the bombs and destruction of the city, but later, after they gave up the flat, the house's isolation left Rebecca feeling depressed and lonely. Yet its beautiful setting amidst the quiet countryside also gave her great joy, unsurpassed by anywhere else she had lived. Indeed, the house would haunt her until the end of her life, a metaphor for so many other unfinished projects and dreams unfulfilled. In an article for the *New Yorker*, a year after they'd bought Ibstone Manor, she confessed how deeply attached she felt to it. There was an air of dilapidation, of ruin, when they first took possession of it but she felt she 'was reviving something that was very precious and had been destroyed'.[10]

Ibstone is built on a ledge running along a hill, with wide

lawns leading down to a walled garden. The garden was a wilderness when they took the house but Rebecca always wanted to return it to the showpiece it had been in the previous century when William Robinson, the renowned author of *The English Flower Garden*, had laid it out.[11]

The winter they bought the manor was severe, with heavy snow and bitter cold. Before they had even completed the purchase, the snow entered through the damaged roof, ruining the wallpaper in the upper floors and flooding the kitchen.[12] Margaret Hodges, who had worked with Henry in the City in the 1930s, was employed as a secretary for Rebecca, and began the monumental task of typing up *Black Lamb and Grey Falcon*. When her husband was called up she moved into Ibstone and became a close friend of the couple, as well as their employee.

From Ibstone, Rebecca wrote articles for the *New Yorker* about living in Britain during the Blitz. This was not history, she wrote, as Gibbon liked to record it, but a history of the endless troubles of everyday living. In a letter to Henry's mother, she explained that one of her *New Yorker* stories was based on her own experience of the difficulty of finding good servants in wartime. In it a very beautiful Irish cook almost poisons an entire household by making a stew with laurel leaves, before becoming delusional and barring the bedroom door because she thought that the house was populated at night-time by naked, eight-foot-tall figures.[13] Rebecca's situation was in many respects as surreal as her story. Trying to buy cheap curtain material for their new home, she found that fancy brocades and heavy silks were being sold at the same price commanded by cheap simple fabric. In those first months, Ibstone might only have had an electric stove that worked somewhat erratically and a few kitchen chairs, but it also had yellow silk taffeta curtains trimmed with bottle-green ruching and amber-coloured slipper-satin, all bound with amber-and-orange silk cords. The incongruously lavish furnishings contrasted too with the dreary wartime reality of nightly air raids and constant scrabbling for food.

While the house still languished in a state of shabby gentility,

Lettie came to stay, having suffered what seems to have been a heart attack. Rebecca despaired of her sister's critical remarks occasioned by the disarray. As ever, Lettie's superiority and caustic comments were reminiscent of painful episodes in Rebecca's youth and she was relieved when her sister finally returned to London and her work. Yet, in part, Rebecca attributed Lettie's attitude to her fear of the war, which Rebecca described as being 'like an exhalation', so that you found it 'in your own nostrils'.[14]

In her articles about wartime life, Rebecca omitted any mention of what was, for her, the first real tragedy. Britain had only been at war a few months when Basil, the son of Greta Mortimer, her ADA friend who had helped her out so much at the end of the last war, was killed. Rebecca had looked on Basil, with his 'golden hair and twinkling blue grey eyes',[15] as almost a younger brother to Anthony. He had been in the RAF. Bored with being grounded because of bad weather and suffering from the after-effects of flu, he took his plane up as soon as conditions allowed, despite his poor health, and crashed. The men of Greta's family withdrew into their grief, so that it was left to Greta and Rebecca to go and identify the dead boy's body. The media was still referring to this early period of the conflict as a 'phoney war'. Rebecca now rejected such notions, saying resolutely, 'if anybody says this is a phoney war hit them from me please'.[16] In years to come, Rebecca would remark to her secretary that war was 'ten minutes of terror to fifty minutes of boredom. It's people being killed.'[17]

The war was affecting Henry, too. His health was suffering from a combination of bad weather, a draughty house and long hours at work. A bad bout of flu gave way to stomach pains which turned out to be a duodenal ulcer. Rebecca made him milk puddings and worried that he was putting on weight. However, he recovered well enough to take a position on the committee established to draw up the post-war recovery plan for Yugoslavia and to work as a fire-watcher one night a week.

In response to Rebecca's news of wartime deprivation and

danger, Emanie, newly divorced, had been trying to enable not just Rebecca and Henry but also Anthony and Kitty to come to the States. She now had sufficient funds in the bank to act as personal guarantor for Henry and Rebecca, but, embarrassingly, not enough to guarantee all four of them, and she was frantically looking for willing sponsors. Rebecca cabled to say they would remain in England, but Emanie insisted on completing the procedure as a safeguard, so that the possibility of escape always existed for them. Emanie was persistent and persuasive; Rebecca and Henry could have a lovely study bedroom with its own bathroom; she would be delighted to have their daily presence. If funding could be found, Kitty and Anthony would live in her Colorado house.

Rebecca's former lover and dear friend John Gunther immediately stepped in with an offer of financial support. Rebecca's feelings of genuine patriotism brooked any possibility of leaving her country while it was under threat from enemy bombs, but she did suggest America to Kitty, thinking she might consider it since she and Anthony were planning to have a family. Kitty reacted badly, however; her father had been killed in the First World War, and she was determined to stay through this one. Emanie reluctantly accepted the family's decision, but stressed again that all the necessary paperwork was with the American Consul in London, if Rebecca ever changed her mind.

Anthony had not succeeded in being added to the ENSA list and was now running a dairy farm that he had bought with some of the money from Wells' trust fund. He told Rebecca that he had at last found something he loved doing more than anything else and she was pleased and surprised at the way he rose every morning at 4.30 to start milking. Even more unexpected was the way that Kitty too seemed taken with farming life.[18] Rebecca, who was turning Ibstone into a very productive estate, understood that the war made concentrated artistic work almost impossible, so practical occupations like farming were perfect for keeping one occupied, as well as being useful. The house was busy, too, with two evacuees, three maids, Margaret Hodges and various other visitors. The evacuees were an old lady of eighty-one and her daughter who was sixty. Their personalities were in complete contrast and Rebecca railed against what she saw as the old lady's mean nature and constant criticizing, while admiring the younger woman's delightful manners and dedication to hard work.

Early in 1941, Rebecca needed treatment for a fibroid which was growing alarmingly quickly. She was sent to a nursing home in Reading where she underwent a hysterectomy to remove 'the fibroids, my uterus, my cervix and my appendix'.[19] Despite the fact that she was almost fifty, Rebecca mourned that she would never be able to give Henry the family he longed for. It was a nightmarish experience but one which Rebecca skilfully turned into a tale of great hilarity in a letter to Emanie. She lied to Henry about the precise time of the operation to stop him worrying too much, then was told off by the matron for doing so. She was shocked to discover that her nurses were not trained to deal with surgical patients; in fact her night nurse was a midwife. Rebecca lamented that her doctor seemed to have 'given way to some odd fantasy and treated me when I was about to abandon my uterus as if I were going to produce young'.[20] Just a week after the operation, Rebecca had more bad news. During the operation, the surgeon had noticed that a stone in her gall bladder, of which she was already aware, would need to be removed within the year. Still recovering from the pain and debilitating effects of the hysterectomy, she dreaded the prospect of another invasive procedure which the male doctor, showing a certain lack of empathy, advised her would be 'much more painful' than what she'd just been through.[21]

Anthony and Kitty visited her during her convalescence and delighted her with news that Kitty was expecting a baby in September. Wells even showed concern, expressing sympathy at Rebecca's slow recovery, while Rebecca found that, being largely confined to her bed, or later to her flat, made her reflect a lot on her past, and her disastrous relationships with Wells, Beaverbrook and Tommy. They were so different from 'sweet Henry' and, in their unwillingness to settle down and enjoy more conventional lives, reminded her of the continuation of a 'dreary' war, brought about by a desire, all too common in men, to turn living into something 'injurious and painful'.[22]

Greta Mortimer came to Ibstone to work for Rebecca, but in a delayed reaction to the death of her son, she suffered a complete breakdown. She lost Rebecca's tax papers, confused messages and sent out bills with unsigned cheques, until Rebecca sent her to the local doctor who advised a holiday which Rebecca then arranged.

Then, in March 1941, Yugoslavia erupted in an act of such drama and heroism that it exceeded even Rebecca's expectations. Prince Paul's government had granted some concessions to Hitler by entering into the Tripartite Pact, which allowed the Germans to transport war materials, but not troops, across the country. Appalled, the head of the Yugoslav Air Force, General Dusan Simovic, planned and executed a coup, supported by the British. Prince Paul, whose sympathies had long been viewed with suspicion, was deposed, his nephew, Crown Prince Peter, just nineteen, was put on the throne and a pro-Allied government was established. The BBC reported the uprising as 'one of the most magnificent gestures of this age'.[23]

It was a glorious but very short-lived victory. After only ten days the Germans invaded and assaulted Belgrade, razing much of the city to the ground and leaving 17,000 people dead in their wake. The Yugoslav army was destroyed and the country was occupied. For Rebecca the drama of the rising, the news of which 'travelled like sunshine over the countries which he [Hitler] had humiliated' was a return to glory.[24] The Yugoslavs were the last 'legatees of the Byzantine Empire in its law and magnificence'.[25] They had chosen defiance rather than see their country be destroyed entirely by a 'state based on hatred'. And though in the streets of Belgrade and throughout the country they repeated the poem about Lazar and the grey falcon, Rebecca rejected any parallel with the Battle of Kosovo. In this battle no one had risked their personal salvation by subjugating their people and there was 'no one who would not have preferred to be victorious over the Nazis if that was possible'.[26] They should celebrate their resistance, and lament their defeat.

The story of the coup formed the epilogue to Black Lamb and Grey Falcon, and it was the part of the book of which Rebecca was most proud.[27] The book came out in the autumn of 1941 and was enthusiastically received. In spite of paper rationing, Macmillan published it in its full and glorious entirety, some half a million words. Lovat Dickson, her editor, wrote: 'Who would not be [compelled] by a book which demonstrated by its argument that the East End of London would not then be lying in ruins if the Balkan Christian powers had not been defeated by the Turks in 1389?'[28]

The book – and its author – were feted. Rebecca told Henry's mother, who had moved to Australia, that it was a 'wild success' and that she had gone to Cambridge to lecture at a Yugoslav exhibition at which Queen Marie, the exiled mother of King Peter II, the last king of Yugoslavia, had personally thanked her for writing it. On 25 October, the New Yorker was lavish in its praise. The book's brilliance was astonishing; it showed the 'mind of a rich, various and fallible being revealed in a prose of fascinating complexity and beauty'. It was not just Rebecca's magnum opus but 'one of the great books of our time'.[29]

Black Lamb was also popular for a different reason. It offered a portrait of a continent, only temporarily lost in the war. In a letter to his wife, David Hopkinson, a serving soldier, said that the book gave him a sense that Europe, and its culture, was waiting to be discovered again, after having seemed in recent years no more than a torture chamber and a graveyard for Jews.[30] Rebecca had rescued the very idea of a free Europe.

Henry continued to help people escape from Germany when he could and refugees stayed in the London flat and at Ibstone when necessary. One pre-war colleague, the Jewish manager of the Berlin Light and Power Company, was settled by him in London with enough money to re-qualify as a Chartered Accountant, although he was knocked down and killed by a

London bus just after his final exam. Rebecca helped with the war effort, too, taking Red Cross classes and also carrying out other more confidential war work that she hinted at mysteriously in letters to friends.

Buoyed up by the reception of *Black Lamb*, Rebecca began work on a new book. It was to be her 'Russian novel'. She hoped it would 'equate sexual and political life' and show that 'if you go in for unhappiness in sex you'll go in for it in your national life'.[31]

In her usual fashion, she began by immersing herself in all things Russian; she rejoiced in the work of the nineteenth-century writer Sergey Aksakov, especially his greatest novel, *A Family Chronicle*. Tolstoy's writings, by comparison, were nothing more than pale imitations of this superb, psychologically acute account of family life.[32]

Her small domestic trials continued but they also provided some amusement against the dark streets and the constant threat of bombs. A discharged cowman had reported them to the local food office for butter churning. In a letter to Emanie, Rebecca described him as 'typically male', convinced that he knew a lot about cows, so much so 'that if the cows didn't know it was because they didn't know as much as he did. And if they up and died of what he did to them, that showed the extent of their ignorance!'[33] Henry and Rebecca had brought their cat from London, a large ginger tom called Pounce. Before they moved to Ibstone, Rebecca had cared for Anthony's cat, feeding it cold grouse in a saucer on the piano, much to her visitors' amusement. But when Anthony reclaimed him, Rebecca felt the loss keenly. However, the cat had fathered a litter and Anthony offered Rebecca one of the kittens. She was delighted. Pounce's presence reassured Rebecca, especially when she was alone at Ibstone, writing. Whenever her concentration slipped, fearful of bombs, or the consequences of losing the war, she would look across and see him curled up, asleep in an armchair. He gave her the assurance that everything would be alright in the end. When the writer Paul Gallico visited Ibstone as an occasional guest, he was also obviously in thrall to Pounce, and addressed his thank-you letters to him.

Henry's involvement with the committee for post-war Yugoslavia was voluntary, and he had no paid work. Rebecca found it difficult having him around Ibstone all the time, finding him fussy and impractical. For her part, Rebecca was proud of her new-learned skills; she could milk a cow and tended a vast vegetable garden which greatly improved the quality of their food.[34] Henry's lack of any income also meant that the flat at Orchard Court had become an extravagance rather than a necessity and with a great deal of sorrow, Rebecca gave it up. The air-raids had made her aware of how much she loved London, and she felt almost guilty at not being there when the city was under attack.

On 7 October 1941, Kitty gave birth to a little girl they named Caroline. Anthony's farm was close to Newbury in Berkshire. His arable figures for the year were excellent, while he estimated that his 'Panther herd' of pedigree Guernsey cattle would be a better long-term prospect. He had borrowed money from Barclays bank to buy a further eighty-nine acres but asked if this loan could be transferred to Rebecca's trust with any profit going to Caro, as Caroline was quickly nicknamed, on her twenty-first birthday, and she agreed. Less than two years later, Kitty had another baby, Edmund, and Rebecca wrote to congratulate her, expressing her admiration for how well she was coping. Anthony may not have been in the forces, but he was a busy farmer and was also now a sergeant in the Home Guard. But Kitty took it all in her stride. Writing to Mary Andrews in Australia, Rebecca told her that the house was 'a picture' and the children were always 'beautifully looked after'.[35] Rebecca's only regret was that she saw her son and his family all too rarely. If Anthony had to take a calf to Newbury market he could collect her from the station, but otherwise the farm was impossible for her to reach.

Henry's work on the reconstruction of the Balkans was going well, and Rebecca proudly boasted that he had managed to get the Poles, Czechs, Greeks and Yugoslavians into some kind of agreement. Henry's 'large calm' made him ideally suited to this kind of work. However, he was proving far less adept at the business of farming. On one occasion, they had a crop of onions that they wanted to take to Jacksons of Piccadilly for bottling. Rebecca pointed out that they were packing them on the wrong day, four days before the carrier was due to arrive. Henry replied that he intended to put them into two suitcases and take them to London himself. One of the suitcases was a very expensive present that Rebecca had given him the Christmas before and she was rather loath to have it smelling of onions for years to come. She joked to Mary that if Henry subsequently took the case on a weekend break, his 'fellow guests would be able to say "Ah here comes Henry Andrews" from quite a distance!'[36]

One of the other members of Henry's committee was Milan Gavrilovic, a member of the Royal Yugoslav Government in exile, based in London. Gavrilovic had been a leader of the Serbian Peasant Party and was also a representative of the Serbian Orthodox Church. In 1942, he wrote to Rebecca to express his own and his peoples' everlasting gratitude for her book.[37] Rebecca replied, arranging to meet him in London the following month. He and his wife, Lela, and in time their children, would become very dear friends of both Rebecca and Henry. Her friendship with Milan drew her even further into Yugoslavian politics, and into the divisions that existed between the exiled Yugoslavs – divisions that were as marked as they had been in the country itself when she had visited it.

With the devastation of the Balkans came another catastrophe. The route to the Aegean, carved out by the Germans and Italians, divided the single country of Yugoslavia into nine units.[38] The Ustase, the Croatian fascists, seized power in the newly formed Independent State of Croatia, which also included Slavonia and Bosnia and Herzegovina. Serbia fell under direct German military rule and resistance groups immediately rose up in an attempt to overthrow the invaders. The defeat of the Yugoslav army saw many of their number hide in the hills and forests, grouping together to form the Chetnik resistance. Led by Colonel Dragoljub Mihailovic, the Chetniks supported the exiled government. In Belgrade, another powerful resistance group formed behind a man with a markedly different ideology, Josip Broz Tito. The Communist Party's Partisans, led by Tito, set up their own concentrated programme of activities to fight the Germans. A tense truce existed between the two groups and, for a time at least, they conducted their operations in close proximity, under the uneasy slogan 'One Country, Two Masters'.[39]

However, the Partisans had a dual agenda: to defeat the Nazis, but also to implement a communist regime. Mihailovic, on the other hand, wanted the 'biological survival' of the Serbian race.[40] In late 1941, the British government recognized Mihailovic as the only legitimate resistance leader in the country. Mihailovic was lauded as a saviour of the Balkans, and the truce that had existed between the Partisans and the Chetniks was destroyed. The ideological differences between the royalist Serbian Chetniks and the pan-Yugoslavian Partisans meant they were as interested in defeating each other as they were in fighting Nazis.

Once Italy capitulated, Yugoslavia became the sole route by which the Nazis could get supplies to Greece and from there to the Middle East. Destroying the route would effectively mean liberating Greece, and as the Allies turned their sights firmly on the Balkans, British support for the Chetniks began to waver. It was suggested that the Partisans' resistance to the Nazis was more successful and Mihailovic's loyalties were called into question.* The Chetniks were also restricted by their ethnicity and were only really free to operate in the Serb areas of Montenegro, Bosnia and, of course, the whole of Serbia itself. The Partisans,

---

* It is a popular pro-Chetnik view that these reports may in part have been encouraged, even fabricated, by communist spies working in the British government, but the overwhelming advantages (mentioned above) offered by supporting the Partisans seem a far more pragmatic reason for Britain to have changed allegiance.

meanwhile, drew their numbers from all of the Yugoslav republics, and could travel freely to win sympathy and support from
local people in every region.

Over the course of two years, public opinion and British
government support had reversed entirely. Churchill supported
Tito; the Soviet Union was an ally. Mihailovic was at first
disregarded, then openly condemned as a traitor. Guy Burgess,
the former journalist now working for MI5 and later unmasked
as a Soviet agent, had approached Rebecca when she was having
lunch in the Ivy, asking if she had heard the latest news, that
Mihailovic was collaborating with the Germans.[41] In later years,
she frequently returned in her writings to Burgess' own betrayals.

For Rebecca, the British volte-face was a betrayal of the
country she loved. The war, when it ended, would leave Yugoslavia, or what remained of it, brutally oppressed and dominated
by the communists. The threat of one dictatorship had simply
been replaced by that of another. Both she and Henry held fast
in their politic allegiance to the royalist government, Rebecca
staunchly praising Mihailovic's anti-fascist heroism before the
war. But the couple's position drastically changed the way they
were received. Henry's committee was disbanded and Rebecca
felt personally threatened by undercover communists, a suspicion
that would remain with her for decades to come. After the war,
Rebecca began to vote Labour. While she believed Churchill had
won the war and accepted that she probably owed him her safety,
she told Emanie that there was no one to whom she would 'less
willingly owe her life'.[42] She thought him a vulgar bully who had
ruined British foreign policy.

≈∞≈

After the war, Rebecca was in no doubt that her stance was
vindicated. Stalin and Churchill had ostensibly divided Yugoslavia between them but, despite the Allied support he had
received, Tito refused to allow either the Russians or the British
into the country. In fact, he told Stalin that if the Red Army
tried to cross the border they would be attacked by the Partisans.

In the decades that followed, Tito brought unity to a country badly fractured by the war. Propaganda urged Serbs, Croats and Muslims to live side by side, and intermarriage and movement between the republics were encouraged, all in an attempt to create a single national identity. Free health care and education, new roads and electricity for rural areas, meant that Tito's rule is still remembered with nostalgia. The regime was ultimately unsustainable, but the communists' total rejection of Chetnik ideology was fundamental to its existence, and to the notion of a unified Yugoslavia. When, in the early 1990s, Serbia's Slobodan Milošević and Croatia's Franjo Tudjam reignited the old enmity between Chetnik and Ustase, the Croatian revolutionary party, the country was once more plunged into war.

Free health care and good roads made no impression on Rebecca, however. She refused to acknowledge any of the benefits provided by a government she would regard as ideologically unsound for as long as she lived. The Slavic 'inat' she had so admired, their almost stubborn belief in a higher aim, was part of her too.

The last years of the war brought other problems for Rebecca, ones which were much closer to home. At the beginning of 1944 she learned from an announcement on the wireless that Tommy, her former lover, had been given a chair in plastic surgery at Oxford, endowed by Lord Nuffield, who had also funded the creation of a dedicated new unit at the John Radcliffe Hospital. Oxford was barely twenty miles from Ibstone. It was the job Tommy had always wanted and Rebecca was thrilled for him, immediately sending him a telegram of congratulations. His reply was woefully inadequate, ending, 'I send you thanks and all my good wishes'.[43] Bruised, Rebecca felt that her passion for him had been ridiculous.

Anthony had taken a part-time job at the BBC and divided his time between there and the farm. The relationship between him and his mother was the best it had ever been. Relieved that the difficulties of Anthony's teenage years were well and truly over, Rebecca greatly enjoyed visiting her son and his family and loved seeing her grandchildren. But in late March, Anthony telephoned with bad news. Wells, now seventy-nine, had cancer; he was dying. He had been told by his son Gip, and had taken the terminal diagnosis well. Rebecca confided to her diary the confusion she had felt on hearing the terrible news. She acknowledged the pain that Wells had cost her, remembering bitterly how she had felt humiliated by Jane, and recalled the way Wells had isolated her from her friends and kept her short of money and thus dependent on him. Yet it was almost as if their troubled past was a story she had learned from a book. And what remained was a deep affection.

Rebecca visited him at his house overlooking Regent's Park. He was being cared for by his son Gip, Gip's wife and two excellent nurses. When at last Rebecca was alone with Wells, she was shocked by his appearance, and then, when he cried and admitted that he was terrified of dying, she was deeply moved. He was distressed that his doctors would not tell him when he would die and troubled further by a quarrel with a very old friend, Thomas Horder, who had once been his pupil, and was now one of his doctors. Rebecca knew Horder and resolved to try to effect a reconciliation, believing that he had 'the power to hold people's hands when they are afraid of the dark'.[44] She was furious that Gip had told his father that he was dying and wrote to Anthony expressing both her anger with Gip and her intention to intervene in Wells' disagreement with Horder. The moment he received her leter, Anthony left a message with Rebecca's secretary, Margaret Hodges, threatening never to see his mother again if she interfered in any way.

Mother and son met at the Lansdowne club a few days later. Rebecca was struck by Anthony's changed manner; he seemed silly and theatrical. He warned her against contacting Horder, saying that the quarrel was of a medical nature, but then became very emotional. He told her that if any decisions were to be made they were up to Gip, as head of the family, and himself. He claimed that he had been involved in making the decision to tell Wells about his diagnosis and that he and Gip were justified in

making it because of their father's love of the truth.[45] Rebecca
bit her tongue, although she later wrote that her immediate
response had been 'that my longstanding affection did not prevent me from seeing that H.G. was probably the greatest liar that
ever lived'.[46]

Anthony went on to insult her, calling her 'worthless and
repellent and frightful'[47] before pointedly adding, 'Long ago, you
may have been the centre of H.G.'s life, but that is all over.'[48]

Rebecca told herself that his behaviour, although alarmingly
reminiscent of his previous breakdown, was no doubt due to
grief at his father's illness and overwork from having both the
BBC job and the farm to run. Neither was she deterred from
seeing Wells. She visited him every week, taking him milk from
the farm, and began to think that he seemed better than the
prognosis suggested; she hoped that perhaps the doctors were
wrong.

Less than a month later, however, in the middle of May,
Rebecca received a letter from Kitty. Anthony had arrived home
from work at the BBC one evening and announced that he
wanted a divorce so he could marry a twenty-four-year-old
woman called Audrey Jones, who also worked at the BBC. In a
conversation with Henry, Kitty elucidated the odd events leading
up to this announcement. Anthony had previously told Kitty
that he had met a woman at a party and he wished to marry
her. Kitty had retorted jokingly that as he was already married
that might be rather difficult. He then met Audrey Jones at two
further parties before having a meeting alone with her. They
were not having an affair, yet after fewer than half a dozen
meetings he had asked Kitty for a divorce. Kitty was stunned.
She had had no inkling of any trouble in their marriage and
thought their eight and a half years together had been harmonious and happy. Worse still, Anthony not only wanted a divorce,
but he demanded that Kitty and his two children leave the
farmhouse so that his new love could move in. When Rebecca
heard that he thought Jones was just like he had been when he
was eighteen, she retorted that he had been nearly mad, so it

wasn't exactly a recommendation. Three other letters from Kitty followed, in which she stressed that she would not give in to Anthony's demand for a divorce. Rebecca replied sympathetic-ally, but heard nothing at all from her son.

She did however hear from Wells. On one of her visits he told her, with great distress, that Anthony had told him he was tired of Kitty and wanted to marry someone else. He reassured Rebecca that he had done everything he could to dissuade him, but without success. Anthony had explained that his new love was 'mixed up in a group of superior minds who despised the war and ignored it so far as possible'.[49] Wells went so far as to suggest that Anthony's manner and speech suggested a kind of madness, echoing Rebecca's impression that Anthony seemed ill.

Rebecca then confronted Anthony about the sudden turn of events, and was astonished by his apparently calm and matter of fact response, as if this was 'an ordinary, everyday action, like moving into a new house'.[50] Kitty wrote heartbreaking letters to Rebecca, pouring out her terrible sadness and confusion, at pains to say how passionately and deeply she still loved her husband. Rebecca tried to persuade Anthony to allow her to visit him, but he refused, saying that the atmosphere at the farm was awful because of all the bad feeling and tension between him and Kitty.

Eventually, worn down by Anthony's constant entreaties, Kitty acquiesced and agreed to give him a divorce. She immedi-ately wrote to Rebecca to tell her, adding that if she persisted in her refusal, Anthony might grow to hate her. She also feared he would in any case walk out on her as soon as the war was over and set up home with Jones, leaving her and the children in a financially precarious position.

Rebecca was appalled. She called him up to urge him at least not to send his children and Kitty to London where the bombing was now terrible. Anthony's response horrified her: he didn't care what happened to Kitty so long as he could have his divorce. Rebecca surprised herself by the extent of her own emotional involvement. She realized that her happiness was in fact dependent on that of Anthony and her grandchildren.[51] It was a revelation that would haunt her for the rest of her life.

In a last appeal, Rebecca wrote to Anthony, telling him he was making a terrible mistake and would bitterly regret losing his daughter. Caro, Rebecca thought, was the 'most exquisite creature ever', with that 'streak of genius' that ran through her family.[52] Anthony reacted with 'black fury' and he called her up, shouting insults down the phone at her before refusing to speak or write to her for several months.* By July, Kitty reported that Anthony had started seeing a psychoanalyst again, and was having relations with Jones, but was otherwise behaving very normally towards her. Rebecca remarked wryly in a letter to Marjorie Wells that perhaps Miss Jones should be put in bottles since her revivifying powers were so great.

However, this was not the sum total of the difficulties between Rebecca and her son. Word reached Rebecca that rather than having failed his army medical, Anthony was in fact a conscientious objector. This was confirmed by Kitty, who pointed out that his work on the farm had meant that Anthony never had to declare himself as such because agricultural workers were in any case exempt from conscription. Rebecca remembered the anti-war group that Wells had spoken of in connection with Audrey Jones and Anthony, and feared that Tito sympathizers in the government, who had long wished to punish her for her outspoken support of Mihailovic, might well use her son to get at her. She worried, too, that Jones might be in some way connected to a plot to damage her reputation and career that she feared was being hatched by the pro-Titoists. Anthony's questioning by the police in 1940 further concerned her, so she wrote to Marjorie Wells, Gip's wife, that she was worried that if he became involved with an anti-war group, Anthony might even end up in prison

She also wrote to Anthony himself, urging him to exercise

---

* In a letter to Alison Macleod, dated 22 September 1944 (Beinecke), Rebecca says she has not heard a word from Anthony since that conversation.

caution. Henry was away on family business and did not see the letter but knew that she was writing it. When Henry returned, he received a phone call from Anthony, inviting him to have lunch with Kitty at the Carlton Grill. Kitty would be in London meeting a solicitor about the divorce. The Germans had recently begun their V1 bombing campaign and London was increasingly dangerous. The 'doodlebugs' terrified Rebecca as the Blitz never had. Their awful droning that increased as they approached, coupled with the sudden silence just before they fell, made Rebecca feel it was far easier to know how close they were, and therefore how close one was to either being blown up or merely 'being a pin cushion for bits of broken glass'.[53] The idea of Kitty facing the very real possibility of being killed or mutilated just so Anthony could get a divorce seemed to Rebecca the worst injustice of all.

Rebecca decided to brave London with Henry so that they could speak to Kitty together. They hadn't booked a table at the Carlton, assuming the doodlebugs would keep people indoors, but Londoners were stalwartly going about their lives, so the restaurant was, in fact, full. They moved to the Ritz and, over lunch, Rebecca mentioned that she was concerned about Anthony's mental health. Kitty replied that this was a strange remark because it exactly mirrored what Anthony had said about Rebecca. Kitty was far from friendly towards her mother-in-law. She told Rebecca that she resented her interference, and most especially she hated the way she had used Caro to try to make Anthony stay with her. Rebecca, overwrought and in pain from a minor leg injury she'd suffered the day before, lost her temper, crying, 'Anthony is wicked, he is poison, the only good news of Anthony I could hear is his death'.[54] As she said it, Rebecca said she felt an almost physical pain as if her heart was breaking. Kitty collapsed onto Henry's shoulder. The rest of the exchange was difficult but restrained. When they returned home, Rebecca felt further aggrieved because Henry, while comforting her, seemed to be taking Kitty's side. He acted as if she had been horrible to a 'sweet little thing' but didn't seem to have heard any of the conversation from her side – although she did, in part, attribute this to his poor hearing.

Later Henry met Kitty alone, and she produced the letter that Rebecca had sent to Anthony with regard to the possible dangers of the pacifist group he had been consorting with. She said that Anthony had wanted him to see it, that it was obviously a lie, that she found the suggestion a ridiculous fiction, 'too like a detective novel'.[55] Anthony felt that Rebecca had made the whole thing up as yet another ploy to separate him from Jones, and that perhaps she was mad. For Rebecca, the fact that all of this had been done behind her back was the worst aspect of everything that had passed. It was, she believed, as if Anthony and Kitty were deliberately trying to cause trouble between her and Henry. Kitty had flattered Henry, making sure that he understood that their problem was with Rebecca, and not him, and that they still wished him to be a grandfather to the children. Henry again seemed almost to take their side, saying to Rebecca, 'My dear, I am afraid you have made a gulf between you and the young people.'[56]

Rebecca was hurt but she was also incandescent with rage; the blatant attempt to cause friction between her and Henry was unforgivable. Kitty responded to Rebecca's anger by emulating her husband; she ceased to have anything to do with Rebecca for a time, setting herself and Caro and Edmund up in a house in Eccleston Square with a friend who also had two children.

Rebecca still hoped that the divorce might not go ahead. Reports of Audrey Jones were not wholly favourable; perhaps Anthony would tire of her. Lettie tried to support Rebecca as best she could, but only ended up by fuelling her temper when she remarked that she thought the break-up was inevitable as the couple had been married in a registry office and not a church[57]

Rebecca appealed to Wells, too, asking that, if he had intended leaving any money to Anthony, he leave it instead to their grandchildren. Gip seemed to take Anthony's side, and attacked her for the way that Anthony had been brought up. Rebecca recoiled, seeing in him so many similarities to Jane, who was just as hateful to her dead as she had been when she was living.

By the end of the year, Anthony apparently came to his senses. He was diagnosed as suffering from a heart complaint and jaundice, one symptom of which was unpredictable behaviour and mood swings. Audrey Jones, it seemed, was living with another gentleman on the three days of the week she was in Manchester with her war work.[58] Anthony begged Kitty for a reconciliation but, perhaps understandably, she refused. Rebecca now vented her fury on Kitty. She could see no reason why Anthony should not be forgiven and reunited with his family. If Kitty really loved him surely she would be happy at this turn of events. But on reflection, Kitty decided, just as Anthony had previously, that the relationship had not been all that good for some time. Moreover, it had prevented her achieving success with her painting. Kitty refused to let Anthony see the children, and much to Rebecca's fury, also refused to give her an exact address where Christmas presents might be sent.[59] Kitty's withdrawal was short-lived; within a few months she was beginning to relent and reconsidering whether or not she might in fact allow Anthony to live with her and the children.

Through it all, Rebecca continued to work hard on her 'Russian novel', worrying that it might end up rivalling *Black Lamb* in length. She told Emanie that it might be like *War and Peace*, a comparison she did not welcome at all because she thought it a terrible novel, populated by young women who were 'characterless bundles of giggles'.[60]

The end of the war brought great celebrations at Ibstone. The lack of transport meant that Ibstone and the surrounding villages, a small community of 250 people, were effectively cut off from the wider world. Henry hauled logs with the village men, built a huge bonfire, and somehow managed to find two barrels of beer. Everyone crowded into the village church, before heading off to the local school to listen to the King's radio broadcast together.

As the villagers sang and danced around the bonfire, Rebecca was overwhelmed by the beauty of the lit-up hawthorn trees and a huge beech tree silhouetted by the fire. The next morning there was a communal meal and another dance, until everyone was exhausted.

Peace brought huge practical change for Rebecca, too. For ten years, Margaret Hodges had been her secretary. But now, with the demobilization of her husband, and in her mid thirties, Margaret wanted to set up home with him and start a family. Rebecca was torn between anxiety that she should leave and have her family before she became too old, and worry over how she herself would manage without her. Margaret had come to be much more than Rebecca's secretary, and Rebecca wrote to her friends on more than one occasion about what a good cook she was, how careful she was with delicate clothes, and how capable at dealing with the farm paperwork.

In her journalism Rebecca continued to rail against continued British support for Tito. Just as Britain had taken too long to stand up to the Nazis, it was now falling all over Soviet Russia: 'The Right generally and the Left Wing journalists . . . would lie down in the gutter if Stalin said he'd like it.'[61]

Anthony's illness meant he could no longer run his farm and he went to work full-time for the BBC as an editor in the radio news service. By the late summer of 1945, he had settled again with Kitty and their children. They bought a little house on the Finchley Road side of Maida Vale, and the grandchildren's visits to Rebecca and Henry at last resumed. While confessing to Henry's mother that their falling-out had scarred her relationship with Kitty, Rebecca happily admitted to once again admiring how well she looked after Anthony and the children and how she always seemed so cheerful, even in the midst of domestic upheaval.

Post-war politics depressed Rebecca, and she failed to find anything redeeming in any of the parties contesting the 1945 election. She believed the Labour Party was divided between

Stalinists and leaders who were terrified of an alliance between the Conservatives and the Soviets. The choice seemed to be between a party divided against itself, or a party in thrall to the communists.

1. R's father

2. R's mother

3. Father's drawing of R as sleeping toddler

4. R & sisters

5. Father's drawing of R & dog

6. Tish on the beach

7. R & friends

8. Wells in 1911

9. R in 1912

10. R with GB Stern and Wells

11. R with Anthony as a toddler

12. A with dog

13. R portrait in checked dress

14. At desk writing

15. Beaverbrook

16. Henry as POW

17. H & R wedding

18. Anthony at Ibstone

19. Emanie

20. Wells and R leaving Pen

21. Wells old

22. With Ingrid Bergman

23. Francis Biddle

25. Ibstone

26. H & R at Ibstone

27. R at Chatterley trial full page

28. Henry & Rebecca

29. Gerd Larsen

30. H & R at airport, 1965

31. At horseshoe desk

32. Lionhead chair

33. Turban and glasses

Chapter Ten

TREASON AND TREACHERY

෧ඟ৽

Not long after the end of the war, the *New Yorker* contacted Rebecca to ask her for more articles and it was agreed that she should cover the trial of William Joyce, better known as Lord Haw-Haw. Joyce's deep, reverberating tones had made his voice one of the best-known in Britain during the war. His broadcasts from Hamburg, spreading Nazi propaganda and disinformation about the war, had been compulsive listening since 1939. Lord Haw-Haw's 'Germany calling! Germany calling!' initially amused British listeners, but had increasingly threatened British wartime morale. In May 1945, Joyce was arrested by British troops on the Danish border and brought to London to be tried for treason. The crux of his defence rested on the fact that he was not British by birth but rather American and therefore owed no allegiance to the Crown.

Finding somewhere to stay during the trial proved almost impossible; now that the bombing had stopped, people were rushing back to London. To add to the difficulty, the restaurants around the law courts had very little food. Day in, day out, Rebecca sat on one of the tombs in St Sepulchre, thankful that it was one of the few churches that had not been destroyed by the Blitz, eating her hard-boiled eggs and chocolate biscuits.

Rebecca approached Marjorie and Gip to see if she might stay with them at Wells' house, which would also enable her to visit him easily. She had been unable to get to London for some months and was shocked when she saw him, as his health had deteriorated considerably. Rebecca was further distressed to learn from one of the nurses that he had been calling for her, but that no one had got in touch with her to tell her. Marjorie agreed that Rebecca might stay there and Wells responded by insisting that Rebecca share breakfast and tea with him every day. Wells also wanted her to care for him, asking the nurses that they allow her to put on his spectacles or fold his newspapers. Rebecca puzzled over Wells' regard for her now, in contrast to how he had been in the past, and also wondered at her own emotion: 'Why am I delighted, when I am dead tired and want nothing more than rest, that he should take pleasure in what I do for him and feel it the lifting of a load from my mind that he is dying without suffering?'[1]

She noticed that on the mantelpiece by his bed there was an engraving of a quotation from a seventeenth-century bishop. It read 'Teach me to live that I may dread the grave as little as my bed'. Rebecca wryly thought that while Wells did indeed seem now to dread the grave as little as his bed, his far from devout life was probably not what the bishop had in mind for getting to that state.[2]

The trial brought unexpected revelations. One of the most surprising was that Joyce's appearance was completely at odds with the voice that had boomed out from the radio throughout the war. He was not a 'big flashy fellow' but 'a little whippy, jig-dancing' man who was 'full of fight'.[3] And his face was badly deformed by a wide scar that ran across his right cheek from his lip to his ear. Nor did Rebecca expect to be so affected by the proceedings. Because of her father's Anglo-Irishness, she hated the 'Irish-Irish' with a hatred similar in intensity to the way that Southerners in the United States regarded Negroes. She believed implicitly that they could only be redeemed by turning themselves into 'faithful servants' of Britain.[4]

Joyce had grown up in Galway and both he and his father were Unionists, loyal to the Crown; so much so that they moved to England during the Irish War for Independence. Rebecca believed Joyce turned to Fascism as a way of 'reviving old

England'.[5] She admired his bravery and his composure but was convinced that he was guilty, albeit on only one of the three counts of treason with which he was charged. The first was that he had breached his allegiance as a British subject by broadcasting enemy propaganda. But in the course of the trial it emerged that Joyce was not in fact a British subject; he had been born in America, in Brooklyn. The second was that he had breached his allegiance by becoming a naturalized German in 1940. This did not stand up either. A British court had no jurisdiction over an American who wished to become a German citizen. But the third charge, and the one that condemned him, was that when he left England for Germany Joyce was carrying a British passport. He had travelled under the protection of the Crown, and owed it his allegiance.

Rebecca found the trial – and Joyce – fascinating, a subject that merited a deeper analysis than would be possible in the article she had been asked to write, and she resolved to write a book about him. The ignorance and behaviour of the American correspondents irritated her; they seemed ignorant of Irish history and unable to follow the legal argument, and one journalist got so drunk at lunch that she spent the afternoon expecting him to vomit on her shoes. She felt unequivocally that Joyce deserved the death penalty and noticed that the audience in the public gallery shared her conviction. Nevertheless the words with which the judge passed sentence were as 'awful as they will always be'.[6]

Rebecca's reporting of the Joyce trial was such a resounding success that she was asked to cover the trial of the British fascist John Amery, two months later. Other treason cases followed, all of which Rebecca gathered together in her book, The Meaning of Treason. For Rebecca, treason represented 'an attempt to live without love of country, which humanity can't do – anymore than love of family'.[7]

Her time with Wells continued to be fraught. He was continually cold, so his room had to be kept shut up, with windows closed and a fire blazing; Rebecca sat and sweated, feeling that she was in a 'hell of desolation'.[8] But compensation came from her relationship with Anthony and Kitty, which was blossoming. She went to an exhibition of Kitty's and admired her paintings, defending her against critics who 'just jumped on her body' and looked down on her because she was a woman painter.[9] Her grandchildren, too, delighted her by how well they were turning out. Rebecca's relationship with her sisters was less happy however. Since the war she had found Lettie even more difficult and critical, and while she continued to love Winnie, she was increasingly troubled by the behaviour of Winnie's daughter Alison.

Alison was still a communist, reporting regularly for the *Daily Worker*, and writing a novel. Rebecca admired neither her political persuasion nor her prose, dismissing her attempts at fiction cruelly, saying they would 'never interest a publisher'.[10] Recently Alison's behaviour had shocked her still further. Alison had been seeing a West Indian soldier in the Canadian army, Jim Hackshaw, the nephew of a friend of Lettie's, and during the Joyce trial Winnie had confided in Rebecca that Alison was now pregnant by him. Rebecca approved of Jim's family; his uncle was a distinguished lawyer who made immediate friends with Henry. However, he wholly blamed Alison for the unfortunate turn of events. Rebecca reported to Emanie that Alison was ugly and 'oafish' and in no way attractive. The young man was kind and good and had only had sex with Alison because she had persuaded him that abstinence might be bad for his health.[11]

Jim was adamant that he did not want to live with Alison, indeed could not support a wife or a family, but would agree to marry her to protect the child from the stigma of being fatherless. Henry and Rebecca wrote to him immediately, offering financial support, but Jim refused to accept it. Winnie's view of the story was very different. She felt that her daughter had been seduced, and believed a version of the story that gave Jim far less credit. Rebecca immediately worried that Jim might hear Winnie's view and refuse to marry Alison. Winnie avoided all contact with Rebecca as a result of the dispute, while Rebecca, failing to see how offensive her interference and condemnation was, ranted to her friends. Most tellingly of all, she confessed to Emanie that Alison, more than anything else, reminded her of herself. She thought Alison ugly and clumsy, but that Alison looked just as she herself had. She saw her niece's attempts to hold on to the father of her child as being reminiscent of her own attempts to keep hold of Wells; she saw too that Alison's long, sprawling novels were in some way reminiscent of her own. The thought of Alison, she told Emanie, filled her with self-hatred.[12]

In the dawn of the cold war, Rebecca's fear of Russian nuclear plots bordered on paranoia, so much so that in March 1946, she sent the first half of her 'Russian novel' to Emanie, with instructions not to read it, but to keep it safe for posterity in case she was killed by a Russian atomic bomb. She wrote a preface to Elma Dangerfield's book *Beyond the Urals*, which was an account of the deportation of over a million Poles from eastern Poland by the Soviets during their first occupation from 1939 to 1941. It was, as Rebecca pointed out, an 'unfashionable' topic for a book. Too many people believed that Russia had come to represent an attempt 'at the abolition of poverty and inequality' and that this in itself made them innocent of any past or present crimes. The hearts of the British people were 'full of love for Russia' and had thus given the Russians 'as secure a nook as remains in our troubled world', despite the danger that they represented. The position of Russia could serve as an example of the problems of imperialism: 'When a nation passes its own boundaries and invades the territory of another, it is inevitable that it will treat the invaded less kindly than it would treat its compatriots and that the standard of human relations will be degraded from the level at which it stood before the invasion. This is the whole case against imperialism.'[13]

Britain was in danger of forgetting its own past misdeeds if it failed to acknowledge what had happened and what was happening in Russia. And, if Britain did so, it would never 'rectify the errors our past has imposed on us in our empire'.

At Easter, Ibstone was filled with guests. Kitty arrived with the grandchildren, Lettie was staying because she was recovering from an operation on her leg, and Margaret Hodges had returned, albeit temporarily. She was now heavily pregnant and she and her husband had nowhere else to live while waiting for her husband's position at a new school to be confirmed. Rebecca generously offered to take them in. But as hospitable as she seemed on the surface, Rebecca worried that working would be impossible with so many people in the house and that her food reserves were being stretched to the limit.

On Good Friday Alison gave birth to a little girl, Cathy. Rebecca hoped that she would send the child to live with her father's family in the West Indies, fearing that the combination of her mixed race and her mother's communism might make any kind of satisfactory upbringing almost impossible. Alison, in turn, blamed Rebecca for interfering, and was determined to follow Jim out to Canada to win him back.

∽◦ℰ◦∾

In the late summer of 1946, Rebecca met an old acquaintance to whom she had been introduced by Doris Stevens some twenty years earlier. Francis Biddle, at fifty years old, was three years younger than Rebecca. He was a prominent American lawyer and the primary American judge at the Nuremberg trials. The *Daily Telegraph* had commissioned Rebecca to write three articles about the trials and when she met up with Biddle, whom she had seen from time to time in the past twenty years, he was rather shocked by her appearance, remarking, 'Why have you let yourself go? You could be as wonderful as ever?'[14] He did however compliment her on *The Meaning of Treason*, which he said both he and his wife, the poet Katherine Garrison Chapin, had enjoyed reading. Biddle seemed to understand that Rebecca's marriage was sexless, and she responded to his advances. She thought she'd 'put the shutters up' but he made her take them down again.[15]

Rebecca found the city of Nuremberg to be 'terrifically post-apocalyptic'. She walked through 'acre after acre of ruined Nuremberg' only to stumble upon 'a vast head of God, lying on the pavement'.[16] And she felt 'gloriously happy'; she was Biddle's 'dragonfly', so wonderful she had made him catch his breath. Biddle told her he'd known for years that they could have been happy together. However it was also clear that he adored his wife, speaking of her often. His wife, in Rebecca's eyes, soon began to seem like another Jane. And when Biddle told her that she had refused to sleep with him for eighteen months after the birth of their second child, Rebecca wondered what chance women like her had against 'alligators like these'.[17] Rebecca returned to London to file her articles, planning to visit Wells and show him the photographs of Nuremberg and of the trial that she had brought back with her.

During the spring and summer of that year, Wells was deteriorating rapidly.[18] Anthony visited him often, sitting for hours by his bedside, waiting for periods of lucidity, worrying that Wells seemed fixated on the idea that Anthony was involved with some anti-war, pro-Nazi group. Anthony was absolutely convinced that the idea had been planted in his father's mind by his mother, a conviction that was, for him, borne out by the letter that Kitty had presented to Henry. Anthony tried to broach the subject but Wells' consciousness was so intermittent as to make it impossible. When the weather grew milder, Wells spent his days in the sun lounge, still seeking warmth, in a house that both Anthony and Rebecca described as coldly elegant. He would doze in the weak sunshine, covered by a light rug, sitting in a large and very battered armchair, surrounded by pot plants. Anthony continued to visit, until one day, despairing at his inability to speak to his father, to reassure him, he hid his head in his hands in sorrow. He looked up to find his father's still piercingly blue eyes staring at him. Wells continued to look at him before muttering, in a weak voice, 'I just don't understand you'.

The morning of 13 August did not seem to herald any great deterioration in Wells' condition. In fact, he was alert and communicative. He sorted through his correspondence with his daughter-in-law, and even attempted *The Times* crossword. The exertions made him tired and just after 4 p.m. he asked his nurse to help him to take off his bed jacket so that he could have a nap. He dismissed her, after changing his mind about the jacket, and climbed into bed. Ten minutes later, she found him dead. Anthony had not seen him since he had uttered those last, disappointed words and he was bitterly angry and upset. The appointment that Rebecca had made for Friday so that she might share her photographs with him was three days too late. He had hurt her and ruined her, but he had been 'an unexhaustable source of love and friendship' for thirty-four years and she could not even think of going anywhere near Regent's Park without a 'black cloud' of sorrow hanging over her.[19][20]

⌒⟨◯⟩⌒

Biddle wrote several letters to Rebecca after Wells' death, filled with concern, hoping that his presence in her life might help to alleviate the pain of bereavement. In late August, Rebecca, still reeling from her loss, arranged to meet Biddle again, in Paris. They visited the Palais Royal and Rebecca basked in his company and how enchanting he was to her. Together they went to the novelist Colette's apartment to meet her, but Rebecca was insecure afterwards, fearing that she had talked too much and taking comfort only in the fact that Colette too seemed to be very taken with Biddle.[21]

From Paris they returned to Nuremberg together for the sentencing, after which Biddle was hoping for a 'last lovely fling'.[22] He flew Rebecca to Prague and they spent two days together exploring the city. It was unashamedly romantic. Rebecca was stunned by the city's beauty, by 'the clean farmlands that dropped in terraces to the heart of the capital'.[23] She thought it the loveliest city she had ever visited, with its magical towers and spires and 'gorgeous' bridge.[24] In the evening the couple watched *Brief Encounter* together. They returned to Nuremberg only for a final dinner and a last overnight stay before flying back to London together. But on the plane home Biddle's attitude changed completely. He became distant, 'atrociously cold'. Rebecca attributed his change in mood to the fact that she had been talking to a young, good-looking man on the plane and that he was jealous.[25]

Biddle drove Rebecca to Ibstone and left her there after just one drink, although she later comforted herself with the fact that Biddle had immediately noticed Henry's growing eccentricities, in particular his absent-mindedness. A few hours later he left her a phone message saying that he never wanted to see her again. But after just two days of silence he turned up at Ibstone and was once again 'heavenly' and 'devoted'.[26]

The state of Ibstone on her return quickly shocked Rebecca out of her post-affair happiness. Henry's hopelessness at practical things had meant that a new secretary had taken complete control of the estate, even going so far as to gossip to the servants about exactly what she thought Rebecca was doing in Paris and Nuremberg. Rebecca sacked the secretary, but then had to deal with an aggrieved Henry. She was beginning to feel that his incompetence tied her to the farm, which was increasingly becoming a prison. She was still fond of him and didn't want to leave him, and there was so much money tied up in the farm that, in any case, it would have been practically impossible. She struggled to write up an account of the trial and her trip for the *New Yorker*, certain that anything she wrote would give her away. Her affair had shown her what she was missing: 'I want to write nothing. I want to live and I have left it too long.'[27]

Wells might have hurt her but it paled beside what Henry – for all his unfailing and doubtless profound love – had 'done against her'. Her sexless marriage, and Henry's enthusiastic interest in younger women, had made her feel old before her time.

In the autumn Biddle's letters tailed off and Rebecca mourned the fact that his wife seemed to have his full attentions again. She continued to write and cable him, however, mostly about a position at UNESCO that he was interested in and about which she had some background information. She signed one cable 'R' and was shocked when Biddle wrote angrily telling her that this was unfair to Katherine and hinted at some intimacy between them, whereas the signature 'Mrs Andrews', or even 'Rebecca', would have been far more appropriate. He also added that he loved Katherine and wanted to do everything he could to protect her from what had happened between them. Particularly galling for Rebecca were his instructions that she should 'wait in the sidelines' and that he would 'attend to her when he had time'.[28] For Rebecca, it was far too reminiscent of her experience with Jane and Wells. She wanted to see him and be rude to him, but instead made do with putting his next letter in the coke furnace.

Rebecca's article on the Nuremberg trials was published in 1949, and six years later would feature in her collection of essays A Train of Powder, under the title 'Greenhouse With Cyclamens – 1'. The most striking feature of her account was her character sketches of the defendants. Hess had 'the classless air characteristic of asylum inmates'; Baldur von Schirach, the head of the Hitler Youth, was like 'a neat and mousy governess'; Goering recalled 'the madam of a brothel'.[29] She ended the piece with an account of the executions. Past research had shown that death by hanging was the quickest, most effective way, but that was not what she saw at Nuremberg. The eleven men slowly 'choked to death', one of them, Ribbentrop, taking twenty minutes to die. Yet, despite the horror of their deaths, Rebecca affirmed that justice had been done. Later she claimed that she had been troubled by the 'moral basis' of the trial, especially the irony of the Russians reading out a denunciation of the German importations for forced labour.[30]

Towards the end of the year, Henry received bad news; his mother, Mary, was dying. He flew immediately to Australia, leaving Rebecca to take care of the farm. But by the time he arrived, Mary had passed away. The doctor reassured Henry that his mother had taken comfort in the fact that he was on his way. He wrote to Rebecca that he would have the ashes sent back to England after the cremation because Mary had been in exile in Melbourne and would have wanted her remains to be laid with those of her brother.

Rebecca found a new secretary in Anne Charles, a woman who very quickly proved to be more like Margaret Hodges than Margaret's disastrous successor. She passed December quietly, going to see David Lean's *Great Expectations* with her new employee, proclaiming it to be the best British film she'd ever seen, and writing supportively to Henry. He was unable to return before Christmas but Rebecca told him not to worry because Anthony, Kitty and the children all planned to stay.

When Henry returned from Australia, Rebecca was able to arrange a trip to the States which she had put on hold while he was away. Before her departure, the Wells estate was dispersed, and Rebecca, angry that she wasn't given anything as a keepsake, bought a carpet that Wells had loved very much, as an heirloom for her grandchildren.

Emanie and Dorothy Thompson, the American journalist whom Rebecca had known since 1924, met her when she docked in New York, and John Gunther was waiting for her at her hotel. Rebecca was delighted by how well Emanie looked, as well as how beautiful her small apartment was. Far nicer, she wrote to Henry, than Emanie's ex-husband had ever allowed. She spent a weekend in New Haven with Professor Evelyn Hutchison from Yale and his wife, establishing the beginnings of what would be a lifelong friendship. She was enchanted by both of them, and pleased to be in a 'decent cat-fearing household' with a Siamese and a black alley cat.[31]

On her return to New York, she was surprised, first by a telephone call, and then by a visit, from Max Beaverbrook. He seemed to have undergone a transformation. He was no longer a 'drunken, lying, cheating, little vagabond' but acted as if they were the dearest of friends.[32] Rebecca wasted no time in challenging him: why had he supported Tito? Max evaded her at first, then confessed that he had done so because 'Winston was so fond of him'.[33] He continued to be both charming and sweet but Rebecca was angry that he seemed to assume that all scars of their past relationship could be forgotten so easily.

Rebecca approached the *New Yorker* to see if she might report on a trial in South Carolina. Two days later, the editor, Harold Ross, agreed. On 17 May Rebecca arrived in Greenville. The heat overwhelmed her as did the voluptuous greenery, but the hotel was far more comfortable and cleaner than any she had stayed at in New York. The crime was described as a black lynching, although Rebecca pointed out that this was not a strictly accurate account of the reason for the proceedings. A white taxi driver had been murdered by a black passenger and a group of taxi drivers had sought to revenge his death by taking the perpetrator from the prison and shooting him. Thirty-one defendants were on trial, all taxi drivers. Rebecca carefully considered the nuances of the colour of the victim and the alleged perpetrators. While the taxi drivers no doubt believed that the law was unlikely to pursue them for killing a black man, it was equally likely, Rebecca wrote, that they would have killed the murderer of their friend if he had been white. The men were acquitted, but Rebecca felt the trial was a landmark and heralded a change: at least now there was the possibility of conviction for racially motivated murder. When she revised the piece for A Train of Powder, she noted 'by 1954 three years had gone by without a lynching in the United States'.[34]

Back in London, Rebecca received a commission from the Evening Standard to report on the fascist riots in North and East London. She attended public meetings and demonstrations in Dalston and Bethnal Green, as well as following the court cases that arose from the violent clashes. She felt that both the fascist threat and the Jewish retaliation were being exaggerated and said as much in her very first piece: 'For in fact it is not the Jews who are joining with the fascists to create disorder in North and East London. It is the Communists.'[35]

Rebecca believed that the communists were using the very small fascist threat to scare Jews into joining forces with them in order to gain their protection. The communists aimed to 'capture the Jewish vote' in forthcoming elections. She interviewed local residents and noted how one Jewish matron, whose street was plagued with fascist demonstrations, commented 'what nice people the Communists are', having attended a communist meeting to try to find support.[36]

Rebecca's position made her very unpopular and immediately set her at odds with Woodrow Wyatt, who reported on the riots for the *New Statesman*. Nonetheless she did not change her stance in subsequent articles. Fascists and communists alike loathed her pieces, and she found that when she turned up to report on an event they would join together to boo and hiss at her. Rebecca loved every minute of the attention, commenting that the bad people hated her and 'that's grand'.[37]

Henry's deafness and increased eccentricities continued to irritate her, and she wrote to Emanie that he was 'silly in the house, silly about the garden, silly about the farm and very selfish'.[38] *Time* magazine sent a team to Ibstone to interview Rebecca for a cover story, to appear at the end of the year. It was the day before Rebecca was due to leave for London to cover the wedding of Princess Elizabeth to Philip Mountbatten, and she was irritated that they followed her from room to room for the best part of a day. They interviewed her extensively, then before leaving asked for photos of her mother and father and, ominously from Rebecca's viewpoint, Wells. She immediately called A.D. Peters and told him to get an undertaking that Wells would not be mentioned anywhere in the piece.

The reporter ignored Peters' demand and the pre-publication article described both her relationship with Wells and the fact of Anthony's birth. The reunion in New York with Max had been fortuitous after all, and she now enlisted his help in having the offending section removed before the piece went to publication. Dorothy Thompson also intervened on her behalf, speaking to Henry Luce, the owner of *Time*. When Rebecca wrote to thank Dorothy, she explained why she had been so insistent. She had no desire to cash in on the kind of 'spurious glamour' the association with Wells might give her; the story of their relationship would be heavily edited until the Wells family were dead, and, perhaps most tellingly of all, Lettie would make her life unbearable as a consequence.[39]

At the end of 1949, the American edition of *The Meaning of Treason* was published. *Time* lauded Rebecca as 'one of the greatest of living journalists' and praised the 'three dimensional' nature of her reporting of the trials.[40] The book was a critical and commercial success; by Christmas it had sold 25,000 copies.

Included in the volume was an account of the trial of Dr Alun Nunn May. May was a Physics lecturer at the University of London and a member of the Communist Party. During the war, he had passed atomic secrets to Soviet Russia, then a British ally. After the war, he was tried for espionage. Rebecca was unequivocal in her condemnation, saying that if Russia ever dropped an atomic bomb on Britain or the United States, May would be to blame. Rebecca received letters from communists condemning her and started to worry more and more about plots against her. The abuse in the East End had made her feel that she was fighting a good cause, but this seemed a more insidious kind of hatred, and she wrote to Emanie of her unease.

The success of *The Meaning of Treason* heralded the end of a decade that had brought Rebecca more and more of the recognition she had worked so hard for. She now undertook major political journalism assignments in the States, covering the Democratic, Progressive and Republican Party conventions. She wrote openly against the Progressive Henry Wallace's candidacy, believing him to be a communist, and was inundated with letters of protest from left-wing Americans. She became convinced that she was a victim of a smear campaign launched by a CBS presenter called Don Hollenbeck, and she wrote to Doris Stevens to ask if she could get some background on him.[41] Doris enlisted her contacts and replied that they 'would see what could be done about him'.[42] Her next letter included a list of article references. Rebecca was intent on exposing communist infiltration wherever she saw it, but in doing so she was beginning to alienate many left-wing Americans who had previously championed her. When the British Institute for Political Research was formed to try to root out and quash communism, Rebecca agreed to sit on the board. The Federal Bureau of Investigation kept a dossier on

West, regarding her as well-informed on the matter of communist infiltration. Their legal attaché in London even met with her on a few occasions to interview her about particular leads. Much of what was discussed is blacked out in the remaining FBI file, but West did tell the FBI representative 'that she preferred furnishing the information to American authorities since she had little confidence in British Intelligence and the Director of Public Prosecutions in London'.[43]

Her achievement as a writer was also acknowledged when she was awarded a CBE in 1949. Greta Mortimer accompanied Rebecca and Henry to the investiture because Anthony was too busy. A delighted Rebecca wrote to Margaret Hodges about the splendour of the palace room where she was received, with its striped satin upholstery and shining parquet floors. The King murmured about 'having special pleasure' and an adoring Rebecca replied how wonderful it was to receive the award from him.[44] The only downside was a letter from Lettie, in which, with characteristic competitiveness, she pointed out that as her own CBE was a military one, it took precedence over Rebecca's.[45]

At home, things were less rosy. Anthony had finished a novel and wanted to include in his biography the fact that he was the son of Rebecca West and H.G. Wells. While she was happy to be named as Anthony's mother, she felt the association with Wells was not beneficial to anyone. Anthony felt that the decision should be his, not his mother's.

In the spring, a promotional trip to Germany, with Dorothy Thompson and Henry, brought disappointment too. The visit provided material for further pieces on Germany to add to *The Train of Powder*, but the dynamics of the trio were wrong. Rebecca resented the attention being focused on Dorothy Thompson and said so explicitly in a letter to Margaret Hodges. She wrote that Dorothy was 'very much on her way out in America as a writer', that she no longer wrote columns or was asked to speak on the radio, and yet 'the Germans had heard of her and not me'.[46] She was also rather peeved that the Germans rushed forward to present flowers to Dorothy, while neglecting even to shake hands with her. No doubt Rebecca's feelings of resentment were exacerbated too by Henry's newest crush, a thirty-eight-year-old German socialite who looked like a younger Rebecca. He described her as having a fine mind, and Rebecca christened her 'Fine Mind', but thought that, in spite of her charming manners, she had Nazi sympathies.[47]

The whole trip was further disturbed by the fact that Dorothy, as well as Henry, was becoming acutely deaf, and the two would rush on ahead, ignoring Rebecca as she trailed in their wake.

Rebecca returned to an escalation of her disagreement with Anthony. In September, Charles Curran, Rebecca's editor at the *Evening Standard*, called her. He had received an advertisement from Anthony for a forthcoming biography of H.G. Wells. Gip and Marjorie Wells were as upset by Anthony's announcement as Rebecca was. Anthony had discussed the fact that he was thinking about writing a biography of his father, but they had yet to give their approval to the project. Rebecca contacted his publisher, Eyre and Spottiswoode, who explained that Anthony had assured them that she had approved the advertisement. Henry now went to Dorset to speak to Anthony and Kitty directly.

The argument that transpired took place on the front steps of Anthony's house because Henry refused to enter until Anthony was fully aware of why he was there. He was uncharacteristically angry and attacked Anthony for the distress he was causing his mother. In a fit of temper, Anthony railed that he was furious with his mother because he had discovered that Wells had left one-ninth of his estate to Kitty rather than to him, and he was sure that it was Rebecca who had persuaded him to do so. Rebecca claimed that the main factor in Wells' decision was that he believed Henry would make Anthony his sole heir, in the event of his and Rebecca's death. Wells had thus felt no need to make any provision for Anthony. Henry retaliated by saying that if Anthony did not promise to stop advertising private matters he too would cut him out of his will. Kitty didn't speak but looked as if she disapproved of any interference on Rebecca's part.

When Henry returned with an account of the meeting, Rebecca called Marjorie to ask her if she knew any further details of this apparent change in Wells' will. Her account was a complete surprise to Rebecca. It transpired that when Wells had been very ill and Anthony had left his family, Kitty had come to Wells to ask him to leave her this money. Henry wrote to Anthony, without mentioning what Marjorie had told them, but stating categorically that Rebecca had nothing whatsoever to do with disinheriting him.

Anthony, however, was not mollified and responded immediately. He had proof of Rebecca's wish to diminish his inheritance in the form of an old letter he had found amongst Wells' effects. Anthony quoted from it in his reply. Rebecca had asked Wells to settle a capital sum on him rather than an income, with life interest on the sum going to her. Rebecca had argued that she found the idea of being dependent on Anthony for even the rent of her home, once he came of age, entirely unnatural. For his part, Anthony could not conceive of how any such provision might ever represent 'a possible source of humiliation and embarrassment' to her.[48]

Rebecca justified her position, agreeing that she had indeed asked Wells to make such a settlement, and reiterating the problems that could arise if she were dependent on Anthony should her work dry up or her health fail. Her solicitor had concurred; to do otherwise could lead to an impossibly difficult situation between them. Rebecca also pointed out that if Edmund had an income and Kitty did not, and was dependent on him, that, too, would be problematic.

Anthony found the whole idea ridiculous and said so. He also went on to ridicule her objections to it being known that he was Wells' son. It was, he said, the simple truth, which most people already knew anyway. He would not mention Rebecca's name, but he would write as H.G. Wells' son and that was final. He accused his mother of paranoia and mental instability. In a particularly cruel gesture he enclosed in his reply to Henry a copy of a letter Rebecca had sent him about Henry. He wanted to show his stepfather that Rebecca did not always represent those who loved her fairly or accurately; this letter was just one example.

The letter must have been tremendously hurtful to Henry. In it, Rebecca wrote about how difficult Henry was becoming, how incompetent he had been over various farming matters, and how silly he was, so much so that she worried about premature senility. The letter was a rant about her husband written by a tired and no doubt irritated woman in the midst of a terrible winter. Writing about the terrible saga to Emanie, Rebecca pointed out that when she wrote the letter, they had been stuck in the house with nine-foot snow drifts at the windows and no heating. For all that, Rebecca had still ended the letter to Anthony with a kind, mollifying statement: 'he [Henry] is very sweet and kind and sure he is doing his best for everyone'.[49] But Anthony had clearly intended to cause trouble between Henry and Rebecca. It failed. Henry good-naturedly conceded that he had given Rebecca a terrible time two years back and he didn't hold it against her. Rebecca feared, rightly, that this was the beginning of a much bigger feud between her and her son and confided to Emanie that she was afraid she would have no one 'to close my eyes, when I die'.[50]

Rebecca did not show the full force of her anger in her reply to Anthony but instead wrote that she felt that he had reinvented the story of his parents' relationship, so much so that he was 'living in a dreamland'. Yes, Wells was a great man, witty, humorous, but he had been unhappy, too, with a destructive streak that Anthony simply refused to acknowledge.[51] In closing, she suggested it might be better if they did not communicate with each other for some time. Wells, too, she reasoned, would have preferred Anthony to get on with his own life rather than keep dredging up, and living off, events long past.

Anthony spent the autumn in the United States and Emanie wrote to Rebecca with what little information she could glean, although Anthony did not contact her directly when he arrived.

A contact at the *New York Herald* and *Tribune* advised her that Anthony had said he had included the information about Wells in his biographical note to spite Rebecca, and that he intended to move to the States and become an American citizen. Emanie wondered how he thought he was going to earn a living; he would need a job beyond his writing, which simply didn't bring in enough to support the family.[52] Reports of Anthony's contempt also reached Rebecca by way of Pamela Frankau, who he had told, 'My father and mother's accounts of their relationship do not match. I must be loyal to him.'[53]

By December, Anthony was making plans to move to America early the following year, and for Kitty and their children to join him shortly afterwards. Echoing Emanie's concerns, Rebecca worried that the income from the settlement would also be greatly reduced when converted into dollars, and wondered how the family would manage. She dreaded Anthony setting Kitty and Edmund and Caro up in some isolated slum while he scraped a living by giving lectures about her relationship with Wells.[54] The memory of Christmas just a year before, when the whole family had been happily gathered at Ibstone, filled her with sorrow. This year she planned to travel to Amiens with Henry, Lettie, Winnie's son Norman and Anne Charles, but she wrote to friends wistfully of the intimate harmony of the previous year's festivities. Despite the usual friction with Lettie, the break made Rebecca happier, with its wonderful food and the haunting beauty of midnight mass at Amiens Cathedral.

But yet again Rebecca's homecoming was marred by new developments in the drama surrounding Anthony. In order to help him research the biography of his father, Wells' literary executors (Anthony's two half-brothers and Gip's wife, Marjorie) had loaned him four suitcases filled with Wells' papers. They were valuable, with an estimated worth of around £30,000, but uninsured. Without asking permission, which would have been refused, Anthony arranged his trip to the States and prepared to take the papers with him. Marjorie was furious; Rebecca was amazed at Marjorie's stupidity in allowing Anthony to have the papers when she had been warned that he was about to leave for the States.

After a row with Gip and Marjorie, Anthony did return the papers. While Marjorie checked through them, she realized that amongst them there were several copies of letters to Rebecca from Wells, which should have been returned to Rebecca on his death. Marjorie called Rebecca, and explained that while the letters weren't damning in any way, they were intimate and of a kind she might not have wished Anthony to see. She apologized and immediately returned them to Rebecca. For the most part, Rebecca was surprised at how well she came off in the letters, but there was one exception. It was a reply to a letter that Wells had written her, and it dated from the time when they were constantly arguing about Wells' lack of involvement in his son's life. In her letter, Rebecca referred to earlier letters, in which Wells had variously berated her for not letting Anthony be adopted, raged when she had Anthony at home with her because of an outbreak of mumps, preventing Wells from spending time with her alone. Finally, and worst of all, she mentioned his refusal to visit Anthony when Rebecca was delayed in America, because Wells said he had already seen him once and couldn't be bothered going again. Rebecca had ended her letter with the reassurance that Anthony would never see these letters unless Wells made trouble between them by blaming her for his separation from his son. Rebecca agonized over the effect this letter would have had on Anthony, who would now see all too clearly how little the father he adored had cared for him while he was growing up.[55]

Rebecca reasoned that publishing the facts of his birth would have achieved two kinds of revenge for Anthony. He could reject Rebecca totally, disregarding her as mad, while keeping some vestige of his idealized view of his father intact; and he could punish Wells posthumously by exposing his private life to all and sundry. Threatening to take the papers to America had been almost competitive, showing that he was the most important of

Wells' children and, as such, would take care of his father's memory.

The letters in the suitcase also reminded Rebecca of how she had managed to overcome all the difficulties in her relationship with Wells, and be friends with him in his old age. Sadly, she realized, she was not going to be able to achieve as much with Anthony. Anthony wrote to Marjorie saying that her actions over the papers, which he had never intended to take to the States, meant the end of any 'official' biography. He would still fulfil his contract to his two publishers, in Britain and the United States, but it would be a very different book, written completely without her cooperation.

Sometime in late January, Rebecca lost track of Anthony. He was supposed to have left for the States but Marjorie told Rebecca that she had heard he had not gone after all, and he didn't seem to be with Kitty and the children. Rebecca wrote to her friends in the States to see if they had heard news of him, or knew his whereabouts. Kitty wrote to Marjorie telling her that Anthony had been so upset by two or three of Rebecca's letters that he had in fact destroyed them. She defended her husband, saying that he had done so to spare his mother's embarrassment, but then added a plea that perhaps the 'intimate side' of Wells' nature didn't need to be included in any book, particularly a book by a stranger.[56]

Rebecca sympathized with Marjorie about the tone of Kitty's letter and dismissed any idea that there was any scandal to protect her from. She thought the whole matter symptomatic of the way that Anthony blamed her for causing a breach between him and his father in the months before his death. She had also made a decision: she would give her letters from Wells to Yale. The librarian was keen and the gift would be kept secret for whatever term she decided.

When news of Anthony did finally come from America, it wasn't favourable. Anthony had told Harold Ross at the *New Yorker* that he had been forced to drop the Wells biography because his mother was so against it. Anthony also seemed to be enlisting Dorothy Thompson's support and Rebecca resented the notion that she might be seen as a mother holding back her brilliant son.

The stress was beginning to affect Rebecca's work. She was reporting on the trial of the spy, Klaus Fuchs. The day after Ross's letter came she made a bad error in her reporting and wrote to her friend Peter Stern that she was afraid she was losing her ability to write. To her American friends, she confided that she had given up working on the 'Russian novel' for the time being because journalism was all she could cope with.

The 'continual lying and treachery' was making it difficult for her to be productive.[57] Kitty had again ceased to have any contact at all with Rebecca and she worried constantly about her grandchildren. She also learned that Anthony's finances were in bad shape because his salary from *Time*, for whom he was writing, was no more than he would have earned in England, where he would have had a higher private income.

Within a month even that salary was gone: Anthony quarrelled with the magazine and lost his job at *Time*. He wrote to Kitty that he no longer wished her to join him and wanted to separate. Unfortunately, by the time he did this, Kitty had already rented out their house and booked a passage for herself and the children who now would have to remain in England and find somewhere to live. Rebecca mused that it seemed to have been settled somehow that she would support her daughter-in-law and the grandchildren, who were once again on speaking terms with her. Anthony sent absolutely nothing back in terms of financial support, and she felt aggrieved. However, she conceded to Winnie, this annoyance was tempered with relief; she had had visions of him taking the children and Kitty over to lead a penniless existence, somewhere inaccessible in the American countryside.

But there were further rumours about Anthony's betrayal of her. A man at the BBC told her that Anthony had said she was bitter because Wells had not married her when Jane died and he was free to do so. Kitty arranged a meeting with Gip Wells to tell him that she wouldn't be joining Anthony, then added that she was going to model herself on Jane and wait for him to change his mind again.

By autumn Anthony had reconsidered and wrote lovingly to Kitty that after a deep depression he realized he was part of her, and that everything he did was pointless because he wasn't sharing it with her.[58] Money was a huge issue and he still didn't have enough to her and the children over, but he begged for their forgiveness and their patience, promising that he could give them a happy life in the States in time.

Rebecca sought solace in a visit from Winnie's son. Norman, now twenty-four, had grown into her favourite relative. In a gesture of appeasement, and given the new accord that seemed to exist between him and his family, Rebecca offered to book Anthony a trip home for Christmas. He refused, in part because his prospects had improved and he had been offered work with the *New Yorker*.

Anthony was not Rebecca's only cause for disquiet; her home life was far from harmonious. Henry so persistently flirted with the servants that many of them left, and the girls in Hatchards bookshop dreaded his visits and the bottom-pinching that accompanied them. Rebecca felt that Anne Charles, who was supposedly acting as a secretary for both of them, devoted most of her time to Henry and at times acted as if she wished to supplant Rebecca at Ibstone and take her place at Henry's side. Doris Stevens' brand of feminism, which regarded all men as awful, had long been regarded as a bit of a joke between Emanie and Rebecca. But in the early summer of 1951 Rebecca wrote to Emanie that she thought she might be starting to agree with Stevens. Anthony was nowhere near as hard working as she had been, and yet at the slightest whiff of trouble, other men in the writing business seemed to fall over themselves to help him. Max Beaverbrook had even offered him a job back in England on the *Evening Standard*, something he had never done for Rebecca, even when she was at her financial lowest. 'It's a closed shop and they hate us,' she lamented.[59]

Her rollercoaster relationship with Kitty and the grandchildren was blossoming again, but a visit from the family in August turned out to be a mixed blessing. Rebecca delighted absolutely in her grandchildren's talents, doting on Caro's drawings of horses and of worlds populated by cats, but found Kitty in a state of near collapse. They had successfully got their documentation together and were planning to sail out to Anthony soon. In anticipation of their visit, Anthony wrote that yes, he did want to see them all, but only because he felt he had to, for the children's sake. He didn't love her anymore and wanted to arrange a divorce. That same afternoon, a dying carrier pigeon found its way into Rebecca's study through an open window, and circled the room, out of reach, before falling down dead. It was, she thought, an omen of even worse to come. This time there was no reprieve. Kitty arrived in Stonnington, Connecticut, with the children, only to discover that Anthony was obviously living there with another woman. He acted as if nothing was wrong and the children were enchanted with their newfound American life, something that Rebecca worried would surely only make things more difficult for Kitty in the long run.

Rebecca continued to support Kitty on her return. Although Anthony was now making a good salary with the *New Yorker*, he still wasn't sending anything to his wife. Rebecca estimated that during the year she had given her almost £800. She had also paid for the family's fares to Connecticut, which meant in total she had to earn £1,500 to cover it. She was further hurt by the fact that Kitty did not invite her and Henry to spend Christmas with her and the children. December brought even more bad news; Harold Ross was dead. She was heartbroken; much more than an editor, he had been a dear and trusted friend, someone whom Rebecca felt was always 'warm, sympathetic and protective'.[60] Particularly upsetting was that she had not been to America for so long because of all the trouble with Anthony. It had been a terrible couple of years, with the arguments, the financial strain and interminable difficulties with the 'Russian novel', which she was afraid she might never complete. She went to a Mozart concert, trying to find consolation, as always, in music, but came back to a cable from William Shawn at the *New Yorker* offices, telling her that Ross had spoken of her at the end. The loss affected her anew, and with it came a realization: her son really was 'a monster'.[61]

Chapter Eleven

COMMUNISM AND KINDNESS

When King George VI died, on 6 February 1952, Rebecca was asked to cover the funeral for the *Evening Standard*. On a freezing day with wind and sleet, she stood and waited for the coffin to arrive at Westminster Hall. The event moved her, but she also despaired of the exhaustion that racked her at the end of fourteen hours, some of which time was spent balancing on kneeler cushions on the ambulatory step to see as much as she could. The surprise of the day, for her, was the commitment of her fellow journalists, some of whom she described as 'very hard-boiled', to supporting the new queen with a romantic fervour. As she wrote to Anne Charles, she felt very proud of her profession.[1]

Her piece on the King's funeral was not well received, however; some people felt that she had trivialized the event by observing that some of the people who filed past the King's coffin had brought sandwiches with them. She had not afforded the occasion the reverence it required. Rebecca thought their criticism was simply because there were different expectations for female journalists. Increasingly she noticed that one thing was good for men, but another for women. She complained to Emanie, 'If one is a woman writer there are certain things one must do – first, not be too good; second, die young, what an edge Katharine Mansfield has on all of us, third, commit suicide like Virginia Woolf. To go on writing and writing well just can't be forgiven.'[2]

When Kitty finally went to arrange her divorce from Anthony, who was still in the States, she asked Rebecca to accompany her. It was a terrible experience. Anthony's letters were read aloud in court; Rebecca thought them brutal, callous and idiotic and felt sorry for Kitty. Even the judge was horrified by the letters, calling them 'the most offensive' he had ever seen.[3] This led him to make a judgement whereby Kitty could not allow the children to visit Anthony in America, a fact that troubled Rebecca because she knew she would have to pay for an appeal so that the children could see their father.

She despaired that she had somehow managed to bring up a son who seemed to excel mainly in nastiness. Being childless, she now believed, would have been better than having a son who was no good for anything, except leaving a trail of misery. Worst of all, Rebecca felt that her writing was insufficient consolation for the sorrow with which her life was filled. She thought wistfully of her failed acting career and imagined how much easier it would have been to lose herself in different roles than to endure the troubles of her own life. For the rest, Rebecca saw her life as dull. Henry's deafness and slowness continued to irritate her. She was trapped in the country most of the time and unable to see a way out. The difficulties of her domestic life meant that too much work that she should have completed was left unfinished. Her writing progressed too slowly, and her secretary still attended to Henry far more than to her.

Henry's health appeared to deteriorate daily. Rebecca suspected cerebral arteriosclerosis, or hardening of the arteries in the brain, because the symptoms seemed to indicate that. His mind seemed disturbed, as if he were beginning a slow 'descent into nullity', his sight, hearing and handwriting were all worse than before, and at times his speech was slurred.[4] It would be another ten years before Rebecca's suspicions would be confirmed.[5] The gradual descent into irrationality, of which she had complained to friends since shortly after her marriage, was real: Henry's brain had been atrophying, probably for at least twenty years.

In what was to be a year of calamity, another tragedy befell

Rebecca. Her adored ginger cat, Pounce, her pet for thirteen years, died of liver cancer. She was distraught. She wrote to friends and family about how close her relationship with him had been. The house seemed dreary without him padding behind her as she walked around the garden, or curled up, purring in an armchair beside her, while she wrote.

Kitty and the children visited Ibstone far less frequently than Rebecca would have liked. Rebecca noted that although Kitty seemed well disposed to her, since she had provided her with emotional and financial support following the divorce, she now hated Henry with a passion. It seemed to have happened suddenly but Rebecca did not speculate about the possible reason with any of her friends.

Roberto Rossellini had approached Rebecca to see if she might write the dialogue for a new film he was proposing, based on Colette's *Duo*. Henry and Rebecca now travelled to Italy to meet Rossellini and his wife, Ingrid Bergman. The plan was to spend a week in Rome with Bergman and Rossellini, then Christmas in Florence. Before the couple left, they received a newspaper clipping from Emanie: Anthony was engaged to Lily Emmet, a nineteen-year-old Radcliffe student.

The Italian trip turned out to be disappointing for many reasons. Rebecca fell ill with colitis and bronchitis, Roberto Rossellini repulsed her and appeared to have no real talent or sense of direction. He was a 'show-off, very gabby, ignorant and pretentious'.[6] The idea of using *Duo* had been scrapped and a different film, based on an almost non-existent plot line, was to be written by Rebecca, but later presented as Rossellini's. She thought the idea, of a husband and wife travelling around Italy, getting jealous of each other, and falling in love all over again, was not enough to make a good film.[7] She refused the commission but dallied in Italy with Henry, 'to enjoy more veal and see more churches'.[8] In their last days in Italy, they met up with John and Jane Gunther who were about to embark on a tour of Africa. They dined with Charlie Chaplin, who Rebecca now found to be 'crazy beyond belief'.[9] Chaplin openly broadcast his communist sympathies, so incensing Rebecca that she informed the Federal Bureau of Investigation. They noted her contact but the details of her report to them and the investigation that followed are blacked out in her dossier and asterisked with a note that says they could not be substantiated.[10]

On their return, by way of Paris, she met a colleague from the *New Yorker*, Janet Flanner, who broke some news to her. Anthony had married Lily Emmet. Both Dorothy and Emanie wrote with descriptions of Lily when they met her early in the New Year. She was very tall and slender and dressed casually, just like the student she was.

When Rebecca arrived back home, she found a letter from Ingrid Bergman who had written to apologize for the wasted trip. Rebecca's reply was blunt. She accepted that Bergman might indeed love Rossellini very much, but asked that she also accept that he had no talent. Rebecca went on to write admiringly of Bergman's talent and to stress how it was being wasted by Rossellini. She finished her letter in prophetic fashion: 'But when your husband has made two more films for you, you remember this letter, and think about putting yourself in the hands of a competent director.'[11]

In fact, Bergman made only three more films for Rossellini, before making the acclaimed *Elena and Her Men* with Jean Renoir, and winning an Oscar for her role in *Anastasia*, directed by Anatole Litvak in 1956.

Ever since Yugoslavia, hating communism had been a passion for Rebecca. In March 1953, she began writing a series of articles for the *Sunday Times*. These would have a huge and long-lasting impact on her reputation, and would alienate her from many of the people who had been staunch supporters of her work throughout the decades. In Rebecca's opinion, the House Un-American Activities Committee, HUAC, could not possibly be perceived as a threat of the same magnitude as communism. The demonizing of McCarthy, and the States, by liberals, was hugely beneficial to communist infiltrators. For West, it was obvious that 'Anti-American propaganda has firmly convinced the rest of the world that there is one phase of "witch hunting" which cannot be excused on grounds of self defence. Most English educated people have been hypnotized into a firm belief that the investigating committee have killed academic freedom in the United States.'[12]

Yes, teachers and professors could be questioned by HUAC. But they should have nothing to fear; the reason that most of them were afraid was 'that they were not doing their job as teachers'. It was the 'abominable crisis of transatlantic life', but it was no more than propaganda with the 'slick coherence of a Goebbels' lie'. The American government was conducting investigations triggered by 'no more inquisitiveness' than would be shown by a society that was 'not manifestly insane'.[13]

McCarthy was not guilty of shooting his political enemies or of having organized gangs of thugs to intimidate and wreck shops or factories that did not meet his demands. This kind of extreme behaviour was the preserve of the American Communist Party. Rebecca received upwards of 150 letters for each of the four articles, some saying she was underestimating the evils of McCarthy. She remained resolute, believing that it was American liberals who were being wicked by exaggerating the McCarthy threat.

When the articles were reprinted in the US News and World Report, an established pro-McCarthy paper, they created a furore. Rebecca received another deluge of mail, some from supporters, but mainly what she described as 'really horrible letters from the liberal anti-McCarthyites'.[14] The American historian Arthur Schlesinger Jr, formerly a great admirer of her work, wrote Rebecca a long and detailed letter expressing his disappointment. It was unjustifiable of her to try to defend McCarthy. Rebecca cabled back that his letter was 'grossly offensive' and wrote to Emanie that his letter contained a 'vomit of insults'.[15] [16] She followed the cable with a long, vitriolic letter, where she went as far as to call Schlesinger 'a blood brother of Goebbels'.[17]

Rebecca was not actually a supporter of HUAC, but she did feel that American liberals were being fooled into concentrating too much of their attention on it, and away from what she perceived as the greatest danger of all, communism. However, the interpretation of her article and its appearance in the *US News and World Report* did much to alienate the American liberals who had previously formed the bulk of her admiring readership. For several months afterwards Rebecca felt that she was getting fewer and fewer offers of work from the British press. It wasn't until March the following year that she was able to write to Doris Stevens that the London ban seemed to have been lifted.

Domestic life too was on a downward spiral. Henry's odd behaviour now included losing quantities of money on the stock exchange. Worse still was the way he recovered from the resulting depression: by travelling to London alone and taking young actresses to dinner at the Savoy. 'Everything is much worse since the cat died,' Rebecca complained to Emanie.[18] She decided to try to find two new pets to make the house seem cosier. A tabby called Mr Briggs and a blue Persian wild-cat cross called Zadok the Priest, moved into Ibstone. Zadok seemed to take Pounce's place well, affectionately playing with Rebecca and following her around.

There was to be no family reunion that Christmas; Kitty was not bringing the children to Ibstone. They were going skiing in Switzerland instead. Rebecca dreaded the 'unspeakable desolation' that Christmas had become since her quarrels with Anthony. Alison's communist leanings had caused a strain in Rebecca's usually good relationship with Winnie, so even spending the holiday with her favourite sister seemed unlikely. But the difficulties with Winnie were quickly forgotten when she was taken to hospital, seriously ill, apparently suffering from cancer of the liver. Winnie had always been Rebecca's favourite and she immediately set about caring for her sister. Christmas came with thick fog and the precipitous death of Zadok, who was hit by a car. A few visitors stayed at Ibstone but Rebecca felt there was 'no geniality, no amiability, no goodwill'.[19] Even a last minute visit from Kitty and the grandchildren, on their return from holiday, did not lighten the atmosphere, with Rebecca finding Caro to be an increasingly moody and withdrawn child.

The following autumn, Rebecca went, at the behest of her old friend Vyvyan Holland, to the unveiling of a blue plaque at Oscar Wilde's former home, followed by lunch at the Savoy. Vyvyan brought his only son, nine-year-old Merlin, noting in his diary that he had been in two minds about doing so. His son was going to learn about his grandfather eventually and Vyvyan thought he might as well be prepared by eulogistic speeches from one of his own idols, Monty Mackenzie. Vyvyan didn't enjoy the speeches and Rebecca noticed how depressed he looked. Realizing that their financial status might be precarious, she turned to Vyvyan and asked bluntly, 'Are you perhaps worried about that child's schooling? Because, if so, I can help.'[20]

Vyvyan almost wept. He told Rebecca that, yes indeed, things were dire. The Treasury had made him hand over the whole amount he had received from a Gielgud revival of a Wilde play, under a scheme called the capital levy. Then he was also required to pay income tax on the sum they'd just taken. Furthermore he had just lost his job, could not pay the tax and was now bankrupt. 'I have got more money than I need,' Rebecca replied, 'and if you will let me do so, I will undertake the responsibility.'[21]

Vyvyan was overwhelmed by Rebecca's spontaneous generosity. Three days later, he wrote to her saying that he felt it was impossible to give her adequate thanks for the kindness she had offered. Of all the people they knew, both he and his wife, Thelma, were moved beyond words that it was Rebecca who had offered to help their son. Vyvyan hoped that in time Merlin's gratitude might be some reward. Rebecca immediately enlisted her friends into the scheme to help Merlin. It was a complicated enterprise; if Rebecca just gave the money to Vyvyan then he would be obliged to pay tax on it. Instead, Rebecca enlisted a small group of her friends, including John van Druten and Margaret Rawlings, who, with Henry and herself, would each make contributions and receive tax rebates on them, which meant they cleared the school fees easily. They called it the

'Merlin Holland Education Racket'. Initially there were some communication difficulties in setting it up. Margaret Rawlings, an actress friend of both Henry and Rebecca, was enthusiastic about the project but too disorganized to deal with the paper-work. Rebecca teasingly told Vyvyan that she had explained in monosyllables a foot high, in red ink on thick card, before Rawlings complied as directed, and Vyvyan joked by reply 'that actresses, like cats, think that their status absolves them from any form of active participation in real life'.[22]

Rebecca proved to be a loyal and supportive friend to the Hollands in other ways, inviting the family to Ibstone the fol-lowing Easter, just after Vyvyan had faced his creditors. She openly condemned mutual acquaintances whose attitude to the family had drastically altered and scorned the social stigma that was attached to bankruptcy.

The Hollands were not the only friends Rebecca was busy rescuing. Milan Gavrilovic was in America while supporting his wife and five children in London. The family were having accommodation and money problems and Rebecca wrote to Doris Stevens to see if she could help them to settle in the US.

Rebecca frequently bewailed the fact that her many friend-ships far surpassed her relationship with her son, on all counts. An article in the *Sunday Express* brought new trepidation. Anthony had written an almost hagiographic article to celebrate Winston Churchill's eightieth birthday. She found it ironic that Anthony, a staunch Labour voter, could produce such a piece, and was worried that he was alluded to as a 'famous biographer'. She assumed this meant the Wells' biography was once again in progress. Actually, something much, much worse was about to transpire.

That year, 1955, was the beginning of an all-too-public drama that would haunt Rebecca for all the years that remained to her. In mid September, a letter from Emanie spoke portentously of Anthony's new novel, the first part of which had appeared in *Harper's Bazaar*. *Heritage* was a barely disguised autobiographical account of his upbringing as he saw it. The lead character was a dark-haired actress called Naomi Savage. The existence of her son, Richard, prevents her from enjoying the full social and artistic possibilities that are available to her and he is consequently sent from her Kensington flat to a farm, and later to a boarding school. While a pupil there he learns of his illegitimacy. His celebrity father, Max Town, and his exotic mistress take him from the school and introduce him to their glamorous Riviera lifestyle. Richard seems to be no more than a pawn, and at times an inconvenient one, shuttled between the twin worlds of his self-centred parents.

A month after Emanie's first warning, Rebecca declared that the book must have had a co-writer because it was too spiteful even for Anthony. Most hurtful of all was the suggestion that Rebecca had had a relationship with Wells because 'it was a short cut to the top of the tree'.[23] To add insult to injury, Rebecca's French agent, Odette Arnaud, informed her that she had been approached by the publisher Sidgwick & Jackson. A partner of the firm had suggested that, as she was a friend of Rebecca, she might ask her if she would write a preface for a proposed British edition of *Heritage*. The request also hinted at a subtle blackmail: if Rebecca agreed, certain more malicious passages of the book might be suppressed; if she did not, it would be published in full.

Rebecca retaliated; if they published, she would sue. One consequence of this was that Rebecca was forced to read the book in its entirety. It was a 'screaming book of hate', yet, reading it, Rebecca found its preposterousness was almost cathartic.[24] Anthony had gone beyond anything that could be construed as 'normal, or even decently abnormal'.[25] He was a person she had to protect herself from. The book was no more than the end product of a long series of horrific chapters; Anthony was 'hopelessly, irredeemably bad'.[26] It was a heartrending realization and possibly the worst thing that had happened to her in her entire life, but there was simply nothing to be done. There was also, Rebecca felt, implicit in Anthony's resentment, something of the general male antipathy to women who work. She drew a comparison between her own situation and those of Ellen Terry and Sarah Bernhardt, who both had terrible experiences with their sons.

The whole debacle was highlighted because it had followed something of a brief hiatus in the difficulties between mother and son. In the summer just past, Lily and Anthony had visited Henry and Rebecca, but had given no inkling of the book that was about to appear. Rebecca had thought the visit a mitigated success and, although she thought the twenty-two-year-old Lily seemed only as mature as a fourteen year old, she did find Anthony's new wife charming and very well mannered. While Rebecca had some doubts, Henry had none and had delighted in the visit. The two couples had gone to watch Caro ride in a local gymkhana then picnicked with her and Edmund afterwards, and at the end of the stay Rebecca and Henry had taken the couple to dinner at the Ritz. Henry had even given Anthony £200 as a belated wedding present.

Now that *Heritage* had been published, in America at least, Lily wrote to Rebecca that she wanted to reassure her that the book had not been written with 'any feeling of animosity'. Its form was as much by accident as by design, and Anthony still spoke of her as 'a magnificent, passionate, gifted woman'.[27] In reply, Rebecca railed against Lily's hypocrisy and despaired that her son seemed to have found someone as vile as himself to settle down with. To Doris Stevens, she wrote that the immediate feeling was strange: 'I feel as if I were dead but were going on settling my affairs.'[28] Kitty took Rebecca's side. She was sent a copy of the book and, as soon as she had finished reading it, she phoned Rebecca in tears. She seemed frantic with worry as to how she would explain Anthony's behaviour to the children.[29]

However, many of the reviews were far from negative. The *New York Times* praised the book for avoiding the 'autobiographical whine' and for its distinct style, a literary union of Wells and James.[30] Friends wrote sympathetic and consoling letters. The editor of the *Ladies' Home Journal* had been sent a copy to consider for serialization and wrote to reassure Rebecca that he thought it too abominable to do her any great harm. Most surprisingly to Rebecca, Max Beaverbrook surfaced as her champion, too, and wrote a letter of extreme kindness and support. G.B. Stern amused her with a phone call in which she was initially compassionate, but ended by saying that the book wasn't as bad as Rebecca made out, because Anthony had called her beautiful in several passages. Vyvyan Holland wrote to reassure Rebecca that he and Thelma always knew she was 'a most proud and devoted mother and made all kinds of sacrifice' for Anthony.[31] Merlin, unlike Anthony, Vyvyan added, loved Ibstone with 'the pigs and shooting arrows on the lawn'.[32]

Rebecca worried more now about the possibility of the Wells biography that Anthony had mooted and took a precautionary measure; she contacted the American academic Gordon Ray to discuss the idea of a volume of her correspondence with Wells. Ray had established a Wells archive at Illinois and been chosen by the family to act as the authorized biographer. He had begun working on the Wells papers and Rebecca enjoyed meeting him when he was in London, finding him to be good company as well as a careful scholar.

When Anthony finally did write to his mother about *Heritage*, he defended himself. He thought she was wrong to describe him as malicious. He had not intended to settle old scores but rather to write about the area of life where he felt he had most experience. It was not through a desire to be famous but rather to write well about his reality, rather than produce 'flawed books'.[33] Rebecca was not mollified, going so far as to annotate the letter she had received with her displeasure. Years later, immediately following Rebecca's death, when Anthony finally did publish the book in Britain, he was more honest about the reason he had written *Heritage*: he was angry with his mother.

Only her marriage seemed to offer some respite: Henry and Rebecca celebrated their twenty-fifth wedding anniversary on 1 November 1955, at the Dorchester. Vyvyan Holland was one of the forty-two guests, and one of only seven who had actually attended the wedding in the country church at Newland's

Corner. Vera Brittain and Barbara Bach, Douglas Woodruff and Lady Bonham Carter all attended the dinner party, and Rebecca found she was able to set her troubles aside briefly.

In addition to working, albeit slowly and sporadically, on the still-growing 'Russian novel', Rebecca had written the first book of what she intended to be a trilogy. It was a novel titled *The Fountain Overflows*, and seemingly autobiographical. Set in Victorian times, it examined the married life of a couple who bore many similarities to Rebecca's parents, seen through the eyes of their children.

The following May, Rebecca sailed to the States and was able to write to Lettie, in great excitement, that *The Fountain Overflows* had been bought as a separate novel by an American publisher for the immense sum of $35,000. The main purpose of the Ameri can trip was to deliver a series of lectures on literary criticism at Yale. These lectures would later be published as *The Court and the Castle* and the glowing reviews the volume received from renowned literary critics, among them Frank Kermode, did much to cement Rebecca's literary reputation. The prospect of the lectures themselves terrified Rebecca, but despite all her misgivings they went well, and by the third she was moved to a larger hall to accommodate her ever-growing audience. Perhaps because of her acting training, she was particularly astute at interpreting female characters' motivations. In one of her lectures, she analysed *Hamlet*, writing later to Emanie: 'I didn't understand why Ophelia was supposed to have killed herself for love, because she was obviously scared, she had had a hell of a time being mauled about by Hamlet and then left by him and she didn't like her father being murdered, who would, and went mad from fright.'[34]

The US excursion was, as usual, extremely convivial and she visited John Gunther and his wife, meeting Greta Garbo, whom she thought to be 'a darling', while she was at their home. However, the spectre of her difficulties with Anthony seemed to follow her, and she now discovered that Anthony had told John Gunther that his life in England had been impoverished and isolated. Rebecca now set about reassuring him. Anthony's house had been large and comfortable; Kitty and he had entertained many friends; his career at the BBC had been fairly successful.

While she was there, Anthony tried to make contact with Rebecca directly, ostensibly to make amends, insisting through mutual friends that he really had not meant to cause offence with *Heritage*. Wary, Rebecca believed that he was surprised at how well-received she still was in the States, despite his attempts to blacken her character. She was disturbed by his weight gain and thought that his apologetic overtures were just an attempt to avoid any difficulties with the influential friends who showed such loyalty to her.

Back in London, the publisher Secker & Warburg was now deliberating over a British issue of *Heritage*, but a letter from Marjorie, and later Frank Wells, assured Rebecca she need take no action this time. If the publication went ahead, they themselves were going to sue.[35] Ironically, when *The Fountain Overflows* appeared in print, Anthony took umbrage. It seemed to him that Rebecca had done exactly what she was accusing him of. She defended herself to Emanie, pointing out that the plot of her book was significantly different from any of the events that had befallen her as a child. Cordelia and Mary, the two sisters in the novel, were not in fact like Winnie and Lettie, she had no brother, and her family hadn't even lived in London at the equivalent period of their lives.[36]

Rebecca saw Max Beaverbrook who gave the impression that he was defending Anthony, in spite of his supportive letter the year before. They met in a room in which a Gainsborough, a Turner and a Constable were all propped against a white wall. Max was in the process of buying the last two for the art gallery at his Brunswick University. Max confronted her; he thought Anthony was 'the most gifted writer of his time'. Surely Rebecca was not going to prevent him from publishing *Heritage* in the UK. Max, she thought, still hated her. Doris Stevens had suggested that her problems with Max in the past might have to do with impotence. It was ironic that he had now made an alliance with her son, whose antagonism, she thought, stemmed from anger at her own potency.[37] Max also seemed very interested in her correspondence with Wells, and when she told him she had given them to an American University, he expressed concern that she had sold them to get some security for herself and Henry. Anthony, it transpired, had suggested that she was having financial difficulties.

A new edition of *The Meaning of Treason* led to legal difficulties when Evelyn Waugh threatened a libel action against her publisher. Rebecca had mentioned him in a sentence that dealt with Burgess, MacLean and Korean prisoners of war. In it, she stated that 'the people who have upset admiration for the classic virtues are not all on the left but that Graham Greene and Mauriac and Evelyn Waugh have done their share'.[38] The result of Waugh's action was that rather than risk losing even more money, the publisher suppressed the whole edition. Because Waugh had not sued Rebecca directly, she was unable to defend herself, and found that she was left with three months' work wasted. She was shocked that one writer would treat another in this way, but also wrote to Emanie that she was afraid of Waugh, and thought him 'a snake'.[39]

The end of the 1950s brought Rebecca some very welcome professional recognition when she was made a Chevalier of the French Legion of Honour. But this literary success was not matched by any improvement in her private life. First of all, the publication of *The Fountain Overflows* turned her relationship with Lettie, always difficult at best, into one of squabbling letters. Lettie was unhappy at the way she felt Rebecca had portrayed her in the character of Cordelia. Rebecca tried to mollify her by saying that there was no resemblance intended, and indeed the only similarity between Cordelia and Lettie was their affection for a horrible aunt. To Emanie, Rebecca admitted that, although she hadn't actually intended to model Cordelia on her sister, she had ended up by portraying her. Old grievances surfaced and Rebecca complained about the way she felt Lettie continued to interfere in her affairs as if she had 'in some strange way been put in authority over me'.[40]

Winnie's illness was a constant concern and her health continued to fluctuate wildly. Rebecca was by turns exasperated by the change in personality wrought by her condition, and deeply saddened as she found it more and more difficult to communicate with her. On good days, Rebecca was buoyed up by the hope that Winnie might live for 'as much as two years'; on bad days, she was sure she was about to lose her 'angel protector' sister.[41]

Anthony and Lily's behaviour towards everyone around them was a source of complaint. On a visit to Kitty and the children they treated Kitty like an unpaid servant, which disgusted Rebecca. They strewed their clothes on the floor, Lily did no housework at all, and when they left, Kitty wept over a pile of used sanitary towels that Lily had left in the bedroom.

Henry was as kind as ever, but also just as irritating. He was dull and his friendships with young women made Rebecca feel inadequate and old. She was still fond of him and told Emanie she'd be lost without him, although she also confessed to being 'damned bored by my marriage, not only bored but frustrated and irritated'.[42] It was a quandary, she admitted: while she would never have found happiness with anyone she had been in love with, she did love Henry, and that was something.[43]

In January 1958 the woman that Rebecca thought of as one of her closest friends in England died. Ruth Lowinsky was sixty-five, and Rebecca wrote to Doris Stevens of the loss. It was strange, she began, but she realized she'd never actually mentioned Ruth to Doris in the past, perhaps because she was so different in interests and background from her other women friends. It had been a kind of 'schoolgirl friendship' of going to galleries and the theatre and shopping. They had an outing planned, to see the opening night of Poulenc's *Les Carmelites*, an opera that would remain one of Rebecca's favourite pieces of music till her death. Ruth had put down the phone after a long gossip with Rebecca, had a coronary thrombosis and died. Before her death, Ruth asked her son to give her tickets to Rebecca so she would go to the opera no matter what. The opera was a masterpiece, but as she sat through the performance Rebecca ached 'with hunger for her funny loving personality'.[44]

Ruth's death seemed to act as a trigger for Rebecca to start recording the events of her life, and within weeks, at the age of sixty-five, she began compiling notes for an autobiography.[45] It was clear from her opening words that the pain of Anthony's treachery was still acute. 'Nothing that my son tells in his book *Heritage* is true.'[46] His hatred ate into her 'flesh and soul'.[47]

Her only hope was that after death some reconciliation might be possible: 'I cannot bear to think that there is not another life in which I can learn the explanation of what he has done to me.'[48] Her greatest comfort remained in her relationships with her closest women friends: Greta Mortimer, Doris Stevens and, above all, Emanie Arling.[49] However, recently even Emanie had become a focus of anxiety. She had visited Rebecca and Henry with her new man, Victor Wolfson. Both Rebecca and Henry were far from impressed by him. While Rebecca admitted he was lively and amusing, she felt that there was an air of insincerity and outright cruelty which worried her greatly. He also seemed very tight with money, expecting Emanie to pay for everything, and dropping hints to Henry and Rebecca about gifts he would appreciate. Emanie it seemed was desperate to find a man; Rebecca thought she might be better to cultivate some new women friends and slowly widen her social circle.[50] Perhaps as a consequence of her reflective mood Rebecca also commissioned a portrait of herself, by an Australian artist named Louis James. She was delighted with the result, and thought it 'a beautiful picture'.[51]

To Rebecca's dismay, Anthony secured a French publisher for *Heritage*. Gallimard in Paris issued a translation of the book and Rebecca was understandably upset, seeing it as a direct, malevolent consequence of her recent honour from the French. Obviously Anthony was also benefitting financially from Rebecca's current fame in France, but, to Rebecca, this seemed secondary to his wish to discredit her.

In her correspondence with Gordon Ray over his proposed

work on the letters between Wells and Arnold Bennett Rebecca attempted to stamp out what she saw as misrepresentations of her relationship with Wells. She refused to allow Ray to use a letter from Wells where he stated: 'I shall go alone because RW is having the time of her life in America and I don't want to interrupt it', remembering that this was actually written in the aftermath of the Gattenrigg incident.[52] Particularly maddening for Rebecca was the way in which Jane seemed to be portrayed as the woman who looked after Wells and tended to him when he was ill, when most of the time she felt it had been her.

The closure of *Time and Tide* magazine, of which Rebecca was still officially, after all these years, a director, was 'a heart-break' for her. But she conceded that the magazine's losses were so overwhelming that no other course of action was possible.[53] Within three months of the journal's demise, its founder, Lady Margaret Rhonda, was dead and Rebecca felt that she, too, had come to the end of an era.

In 1959, Rebecca was made a Dame. Before the investiture at Buckingham Palace, Rebecca confessed to Emanie that she was nervous, like a schoolgirl moved to an upper form with older girls who was worried about being able to keep up with them. She also worried that the honour might trigger some new spiteful activity from Anthony and from Max Beaverbrook. Numerous women writers wrote to congratulate her, but from men she had only a very few letters. T.S. Eliot and Noel Coward both wrote, but the dearth of recognition from male writers made her ponder again the sexism that seemed to run through the literary estab-lishment. The FBI had not forgotten her assistance, however, and J. Edgar Hoover sent a letter of congratulation. West replied, 'It was most kind of you to send me your congratulations on my Damehood or Dameship, I haven't myself yet grasped what it should be called. I am proud of my honour and proud too that the FBI should have sent me their good wishes. Long may they live to establish law and order.'[54]

Rebecca thought that the formal presentation was less inter-esting than the one for her CBE had been, but the Queen invited her to a lunch the following day, which was much more enjoyable. Terence Rattigan also attended, as did Princess Margaret, who bewitched Rebecca with her pale, perfect skin and violet eyes. Rebecca declared the Queen herself to be 'lovely, beyond belief, in this incredible way'.[55]

Just before New Year, Rebecca had a shocking revelation, which brought into question the area of her life in which she had always sought security, her marriage. Her problems with secretaries had continued, most recently with a young woman called Lorna Yendoll, who seemed to suffer from some mental-health issues. Lorna was given to hysteria and to periods of amnesia and Rebecca tried to find medical help for her. Henry was adamant that Lorna remain at Ibstone until a residential place was found for her treatment, and indeed that she should return to their employ immediately after she was released from hospital. Rebecca had her doubts that Lorna would ever regain complete health and was particularly worried by Henry's idea that Lorna might look after the estate when they made a planned trip to America together in the coming year.

A place was found at a hospital in Richmond, but when Henry took Lorna there she refused to be admitted. Instead she checked into a hotel in Richmond and wrote a letter to Henry, almost a love letter, but also announcing her resignation, which he dutifully showed to Rebecca. However, just a few days later, Rebecca overheard Henry speaking to her on the phone. The conversation was intimate. It was clear, Rebecca thought, that if they weren't actually making love it was only because they hadn't got round to it yet. He ended the conversation by asking her to write to him, not at home, but to his club, Brooks, in London. Worst of all for Rebecca was that her husband was apparently cheating on her with someone plain, without any real charm or education.

Rebecca did not tell Henry about the conversation she had overheard, but she did tell her lawyer. Unaware that Rebecca knew about the sentimental bond that existed between him and Lorna, Henry again begged her to allow Lorna to return to Ibstone. Rebecca refused and rang up her former secretary, Margaret Hodges, for moral support. Margaret surprised Rebecca by saying that rather than speak about this on the telephone she thought she had better pay a visit. She arrived in Ibstone the following Sunday and stunned Rebecca into silence.

Henry, it transpired, had always been chasing her secretaries. There had been endless attempts to snatch a kiss, countless declarations of love. Margaret Hodges herself had been pursued, as had Anne Charles. Rebecca's fears that Anne was plotting to usurp her from Ibstone were only a tiny part of the story. In fact, Henry had been pursuing her since she arrived. Other servants had warned her but Rebecca had dismissed their suggestions. Anne Charles might have reciprocated, but one poor girl from New Zealand had fled at short notice to escape his advances. What Rebecca had regarded as Henry's harmless flirtations with young women now seemed to be indicative of something far more threatening.

Rebecca consulted her lawyer again. She was unsure if she could go on living at Ibstone with a husband who constantly harassed her secretaries. She broached the issue with Henry but he was absolutely determined to bring Lorna back to Ibstone. Her lawyer was adamant; if Lorna did return, Rebecca would need to leave.[56] For her part, Rebecca felt that she would have to leave Henry 'sooner or later'. Anything, even loneliness, would be better than the humiliation he was heaping upon her.

In January 1960, Rebecca travelled to South Africa to write about apartheid for the *Sunday Times*. She was undecided if, at the end of her trip, she would return to Henry or not. As soon as she arrived, she wrote him a long letter chatting about her first impressions, carefully avoiding any mention of the tension that existed between them. Henry's reply shocked her out of her attempts at reconciliation. It seemed to reflect on various small incidents where he thought Rebecca had behaved badly in their marriage, ending with a defence of Lorna. Henry had suggested that perhaps she might have helped Lorna through her illness by giving her some of *This Real Night*, the second part of the trilogy that had begun with *The Fountain Overflows*, to type up. Rebecca was livid that he had even suggested using her book 'as a medicine for a highly undesirable lunatic'.[57]

Furious, Rebecca sent both Henry's letter and her reply to her lawyer. While she waited for legal advice, she wrote to Lettie, confiding her marital difficulties, but adding that her work was proving a great distraction from the problems at home.

She spent the first month in Johannesburg looking at the economy, largely based on mining. From there she visited Cape Town and the Transkei, before spending some days in Durban. Rebecca was outspoken in her criticism of apartheid. In both Cape Town and Johannesburg it was as if 'They were living in a Shakespeare play where the King's brother had stolen the throne and the people were living in a state of indignation, not only against what he did but against an unjustifiable transfer of power'.[58]

It was a terrible prospect. Johannesburg would be destroyed by withdrawing the black labour on which it depended. If Afrikaners took over the gold mines, using solely white labour, and sent the Africans to the land to eke out a living from agriculture, the white working population would be reduced by 40 per cent. The nine million Africans, starving because there would not be enough agriculture to support them, would rise up against the whites and 'drive them into the sea'.[59]

Rebecca's penultimate article was an account of the partial proceedings of a treason trial.[60] The trial had been going on for more than three years by the time she arrived and there were more defendants than there were seats for them to sit in. Most of them were members of the African National Congress; all were eventually acquitted, but Rebecca criticized the way that one of the judges addressed an African witness, naming the judge as Mr Justice Kennedy.

By March, in Durban, Rebecca had resolved to return to Henry, but was firm in the resolution that she would have to leave him if there was ever any kind of repetition of his behaviour. But her return to Ibstone, a few weeks later, confirmed her worst fears: she no longer felt secure in her own home.

Chapter Twelve

LEAVE-TAKINGS AND REGRETS

In June 1960, Rebecca's beloved sister Winnie died. Rebecca hadn't seen her since her return from South Africa, but her death brought consolation as well as sorrow, because the last years of her illness had been so awful. Winnie had been Rebecca's 'guardian angel' and it was only years later that the thought of Winnie would allow her 'to retreat into days at Pollock* or in Richmond Park with her and feel joy in her all over again'.[1] While comforting their nephew, Norman, Rebecca and Henry worked to rebuild their own relationship and achieve some semblance of the contentment they had known before. Henry was very supportive over Winnie's death, taking care of Norman and helping with the funeral arrangements, but Rebecca was frequently confronted by mementoes of the time when Lorna had been working for them. Piles of monogrammed sheets, expensive and unused, that Lorna had ordered, lay stacked in the linen cupboard; seven thermometers were found hidden in a drawer, signs of Lorna's mental illness. Rebecca felt 'ice cold'. Lorna had damaged her relationship with Henry in exactly the same way that *Heritage* had ruined her love for her son. Both represented a betrayal by those closest to her, and both involved other people being witness to her perceived humiliation. Above all she felt physically disgusted by the thought of Henry's relationship with

---

* Pollok Park in Glasgow, where they took childhood walks together.

a woman who had obviously been ill. She felt as if 'Edgar Allen Poe has invaded this house'.[2]

Not long after Winnie's death, a letter arrived on behalf of Mr Justice Kennedy, threatening legal action over her article in the *Sunday Times*. Rebecca insisted on the trial records being consulted. They were, and it was found that the remark was actually attributable to Justice Bekker. Justice Kennedy sued for damages, but finally settled, out of court, for an apology from both the *Sunday Times* and Rebecca, and a much smaller sum than the £16,000 he had initially asked for. Rebecca fretted over her mistake, telling friends that her hearing seemed to be getting worse, but writing in her diary that she had relied on a companion, the writer Lulu Friedman, to identify the speaker.

Henry went into hospital in the summer to have an operation for his deafness, and while he was in hospital Rebecca received more bad news. Kitty informed her that Anthony had sold *Heritage* to a London publisher and that it would be published in Britain as soon as she died. As always her friends and her work were Rebecca's sanctuary. Vyvyan Holland consulted Rebecca about a new edition of Wilde's letters. The volume included various letters to his homosexual friends. While he thought it best they be published and dealt with in a sympathetic way, with explanatory notes, his wife, Thelma, wanted to censor them. He sent Rebecca samples of the texts and she recommended leaving them in, feeling that they were now too old fashioned to be shocking. She thought it infinitely better that the 'nameless wolves and jackals' be prevented from using them in the future and, while sympathetic to Thelma, felt that it would be impossible to keep Wilde's homosexuality a secret from Merlin. Indeed, Rebecca predicted, Merlin might in fact 'be wearied of the subject by the very excess of attention which is given it'. It seemed to her to generate more interest than Wilde's actual work. 'Your poor father. He *also* wrote, didn't he?' she commented in her reply.[3] In gratitude, Vyvyan dedicated a pictorial biography of Wilde to Rebecca. She thanked him, and having looked over the galley proofs for the volume of letters, noted wryly that 'what your father did to little boys is not so criminal as what little boys did to your father's prose'.[4]

The death of Dorothy Thompson, Rebecca's friend of forty-one years, in May 1961 was horribly reminiscent of that of her sister, Winnie. Rebecca chose to remember her as that young, bright, composed girl in her twenties, not as the confused and disorientated invalid she became towards the end. To John Gunther, she confided, 'When I think of how calm and happy she was when I first met her I could weep – but we all start as grazing land and end up as ploughed fields.'[5]

The metaphor was particularly poignant because it echoed the sentiment of the young and beautiful heroine of her novel *Sunflower*: 'how it would feel to be a meadow, to have a body of smooth wet earth pricked upwards with a million blades of growing grass'.[6]

A new, unwelcome revelation about Henry distracted her from work on her 'Russian novel'. In addition to his frequent flirtations with the secretaries, he had taken to sending fan mail to young girls he saw on television. If they replied, he became embroiled in long correspondences with them, championing them if they fell into trouble. One girl was fired from her position and Henry wrote long letters to the BBC, demanding her reinstatement. Rebecca was humiliated. Everyone at the BBC knew that Henry was her husband; the mixture of pity and scorn his behaviour would generate was too much to bear.

But they stayed together. When she mourned for Dorothy, Henry supported her. He was given to moments of extreme kindness and generosity, at times buying her extravagant gifts which Rebecca treasured, and she continually questioned how much of his aberrant behaviour was due to illness. The couple bought a Labrador, which Rebecca named Albert, and she found great respite in long walks across the countryside surrounding Ibstone, although she constantly complained to friends in letters that she was sick of country life and longed to return to London. There seemed a never-ending demand on her time from the house and its surroundings, and even small projects, like establishing a garden for spring bulbs, seemed thwarted at the outset by Henry's incompetence and intransigence when he was in one of his difficult moods. Henry's odd behaviour was now becoming apparent to visitors. Gwenda David, the Viking Press representative in London, stayed at Ibstone and noticed the difference in the way that Henry treated Rebecca as opposed to his interaction with guests. Gwenda and Henry took Albert for a walk, leaving Rebecca working at home. Henry told her that he planned to go to London for a few weeks to allow Rebecca to write. Gwenda remonstrated with him. He would be leaving Rebecca alone to cope with the farm and the isolation of the country, which she hated, while he was free to enjoy himself. If he wanted to do something good for Rebecca, he could take her on holiday to the West Indies. Rebecca was touched by Gwenda's intervention and the two became good friends. Henry did take her to Barbados for a holiday and she described their time there as 'heavenly'. T.S. Eliot and his wife Valerie were staying at the same hotel. Rebecca and Henry watched them from their balcony, noticing the obvious disparity in age between them. The couples dined together at the Colony Club, Eliot huddled in a raincoat at the barely sheltered table, complaining bitterly about the volume of the music from the orchestra.[7]

Most importantly for Rebecca, after the Barbados trip she journeyed back alone by way of New York, where she was able to spend time with Emanie Arling, who pampered and advised her, helping her to recover from her losses and to reconcile with Henry.

Rebecca was invited as a guest participant to a conference on censorship as part of the Edinburgh International Festival of 1962. She had given evidence in D.H. Lawrence's favour at the *Lady Chatterley's Lover* trial but despised the book's original publisher, Maurice Girodias. Other Girodias authors, including Laurence Durrell and William Burroughs, attended the conference. Rebecca thought their output was 'filth' and pointed out to the audience that pornography was closely linked to sadism. Norman Mailer, whom she dismissed as a 'stupid lout', argued that pornography was needed so that we could 'liberate ourselves'. Rebecca riposted that there had been more than enough pornography for any amount of liberation, had that indeed been the way that freedom came about. Mailer and many other male writers reminded Rebecca of Wells in the way that they advocated sexual freedom for themselves, without considering the true consequences for their female partners.

That same year brought a meeting in New York with Anthony and Lily and their new baby, Sophie. The meeting was stilted and formal and brought no reconciliation. The grievances they had with each other seemed to hang in the air between them, unspoken but impossible to ignore. Anthony was now forty-seven and though Rebecca hoped that age might have settled him, he seemed more distracted than ever, refusing to prearrange meetings with her, dashing off suddenly, trying to hide the fact that he had an apartment in New York. In England, Rebecca asked Kitty about the peculiarities of Anthony and Lily's situation. They seemed to be living well beyond their means, with the apartment in New York and a house with cattle in Connecticut and the expense of putting Anthony's son Edmund through medical school. Thinking of how reckless with money Anthony had always seemed to her, Rebecca discreetly intervened. She earmarked part of the capital she was leaving to Kitty, Caro and Edmund so that it could be used to get Anthony out of any financial difficulties he might get himself into after her death. She didn't tell Anthony or Kitty, only their lawyer. She was certain, though, that her action was necessary, and simply that of a mother trying to secure her son's future after she was no longer there.[8]

Henry's deafness was somewhat relieved by the surgery he had undergone, but his behaviour was still erratic and he had developed a propensity to fall asleep suddenly. This latter was to prove his undoing when he slumbered at the wheel on the drive between London and Ibstone. He awoke to find himself on the wrong side of the road, facing an oncoming truck, which fortunately swerved. Miraculously, no one was hurt, but Rebecca worried that the ensuing prosecution for dangerous driving might lead either to a ban, or to a restriction such that he might only be able to drive when accompanied by another driver. Although Henry was chastened by the experience and consented to a new barrage of tests, he still insisted on driving at every opportunity. Often this was without Rebecca's knowledge, and his mishaps became a source of village gossip.

Rebecca wrote to Vyvyan and Thelma Holland about Henry's accident, urging them to be discreet, and then going on to say how much she had enjoyed the advance copy of *The Letters of Oscar Wilde*. At last, Rebecca wrote, Wilde was being presented as so much more than his sexuality. She was sure that Merlin would appreciate this view of his grandfather in the years to follow.

Henry went to trial in June. The barrister gave a splendid speech, stressing, truthfully, that Henry had not drunk any alcohol, and that the bill from his club that afternoon proved that he had only had lemon barley water with his lunch. The court appeared to be sympathetic and Henry kept his licence, but was fined and given an endorsement. Ironically, a visit to an eye specialist the following day led to the discovery that the arteries of his eyes were hardening, and a recommendation by the specialist that he stop driving.

A few days later, Rebecca had yet another meeting with Anthony and Lily. They were in England, staying at a cottage in Wiltshire, and arranged to meet Henry and Rebecca with Caro and Edmund. Anthony had grown even fatter since she had seen him in America. He looked obese and smug and on the return drive to Ibstone spoke again of his time at Stowe, inventing more reasons why he had been expelled, which Rebecca dismissed as fantasy. He seemed oblivious to the difficulties of his own children. Caro was studying English Literature at Cambridge but hated it; Edmund was worried that his American degree would be useless in Europe; although he liked the States, he had decided he didn't want to live there permanently. When Anthony returned to the States, he surprised Rebecca with a request. His letter began in a friendly and conciliatory way, and ended with his wish that Rebecca should take care of their newest baby for a few weeks, during the summer, while they were in Hungary. Rebecca dreaded the prospect and, to put them off, said that she did not plan to be in England over the summer. To Emanie she wrote that she found that any enthusiasm she was meant to feel at being a grandmother was being pushed upon her. She did not find the role to be in any way instinctive and while she loved Edmund dearly, she found Caro difficult. She dreaded the idea of developing a close relationship with Anthony and Lily's offspring because she found both of them so unpleasant to deal with.[9]

It was at this point that their GP suggested that Henry was probably suffering from cerebral arteriosclerosis, as Rebecca had suspected for some time. The diagnosis was confirmed and the doctors felt that he should not be driving, but Henry seemed oblivious, immediately offering to drive Rebecca to Bath. Rebecca wrote to Emanie darkly, and only half-jokingly, that on bad days she thought he had hopes of killing her off in a driving accident. Henry appeared to have a new girlfriend, one with whom he dined mysteriously, and who seemed to have made him start regretting afresh that he had no children. Rebecca was hurt, but resigned. She had come to the realization that although Henry was a destructive force in her life, she had done well to marry him, 'because nothing can be worse than the lot of a woman without a man'.[10] Later in her diary she expanded on this: it was not that being man-less made her feel that her worth was diminished, but rather 'that society disapproved of me in that state'.[11]

The disruption caused by Henry's condition, as well as by the anguish following the revelations about his dalliances, meant that Rebecca's work was going very slowly. The 'Russian novel' was not complete, and work on *This Real Night*, the second book of her trilogy, had barely begun. Henry seemed to chide her constantly for her inability to finish work that she had begun, which only added to her own worries and insecurity. The sole ray of light which Rebecca declared made her happier than she had been for years was news of Emanie's forthcoming wedding. She had been seeing a man called August Philips, whom Rebecca thought to be glorious, and he had finally proposed.

Rebecca had a regular reviewing spot, every three weeks, with the *Sunday Telegraph*, who paid her thirty-five guineas for each review. She also continued sporadically producing reviews for various publications, including the *Times Literary Supplement*. In 1963 she finished an article about the trial of John Vassall, a spy who claimed he had been blackmailed into espionage while working in Moscow at the British Embassy. On the day she completed her account, the Prime Minister, Harold Macmillan, defended himself in the House of Commons for the way he had handled the Profumo affair. It was a scandal that rocked Westminster, irreparably damaging the Conservative government, and indirectly leading to Macmillan's resignation on the grounds of ill health, months after the story broke.

John Profumo, the Secretary of State for War, was charged with having an affair with Christine Keeler, a prostitute believed to be the mistress of a Russian spy. Profumo met Keeler through an osteopath named Stephen Ward and her various lovers included a Russian naval attaché, Yevgeni Ivanov. Profumo and Keeler became lovers. When the friendship between Ward and Profumo was discovered, Profumo was advised to cut his ties. He did so, but when suspicion arose that he had been in a sexual relationship with Keeler, and he was questioned in the House of Commons, he denied it. When evidence of the affair came to light, he was forced to resign.

Rebecca was critical of the way reports of the drama focused on the sexual elements of the case and demonized the two girls involved: Christine Keeler and her friend Mandy Rice Davies. She was disgusted by the middle-aged women who waited outside the courtroom to hurl abuse at the two girls when they arrived and when they left. She thought them largely envious of a glamorous facade that belied the true difficulties of the girls' lives. The fact that they were flagellant prostitutes troubled Rebecca and she shuddered, not with disapproval of the nature of the girls' work, but at the far more troubling discovery that there were obviously men who derived pleasure from whipping, or being whipped by, young women.[12]

In November John F. Kennedy's assassination brought tears to Ibstone. Rebecca remarked to Emanie that it was odd to see how the people in Britain 'take the death of your president as hard as we do the death of our King or Queen'.[13] The household at Ibstone gathered round the television to watch when the housekeeper heard the news on the radio just thirty-five minutes after it happened. Rebecca's sorrow was combined with indignation that the Americans interviewed assumed that the assassin would be a Southern segregationist. As always, she suspected communist motivation.

✿

Christmas at Ibstone was awful that year. At best Ibstone was a cold house; its east-facing aspect did not afford much direct sunshine, even in fine weather. But then Henry announced to the household that the oil tank was empty and the radiators needed to be shut off. The damp cold blew through the long corridor that joined the library to the main body of the house and Rebecca was exasperated almost to the point of weeping when the oil men arrived and announced that actually there were fifty gallons in the tank. In the run-up to Christmas, Rebecca held a small but successful drinks party. But on Christmas Day itself the house was empty except for Henry, Lettie and Rebecca's old friend Greta Wood, accompanied by her husband, Charles Mortimer. Charles suffered from Parkinson's disease, which was very advanced and which Rebecca felt would make having other guests difficult. This was no hardship: she found Charles to be a lively and amusing conversationalist and his dignity in dealing with his illness she declared inspirational.

Henry's eccentricities, of which the incident with the oil was only the most recent example, had begun to take a more serious turn. Rebecca now dreaded their frequent trips to see plays in the West End. Henry's deafness prevented him from hearing the dialogue clearly and he often fell asleep, sloughing over in the seat beside her. In a moment of inspiration, she thought she would introduce him to classical ballet, to see if the visual appeal might compensate for his limited perception of the music. It was a success; Henry absolutely loved the ballet. More precisely, Henry loved the dancers. He pursued his favourites with letters, finally devoting his attentions to Gerd Larsen. She was a Norwegian soloist and ballet mistress with the Royal Ballet, who danced roles such as the Queen in *Swan Lake* and the Dancer in *The Rake's Progress*, the latter role, Rebecca noted wryly, requiring her to wear red stockings and calling for almost acrobatic gifts. Rebecca described her as an edgy personality, highly intelligent, like a character from an Ibsen play. Gerd was in her early forties, a widow with one child. Rebecca, friendly at first, invited her to join them for supper following a performance of *Swan Lake*. Henry insisted on driving Gerd home, although he took a route that ensured he could first drop Rebecca off at their club en route. He hastily left Rebecca at the club door but took their room key with him. Rebecca was forced to camp out in the corridor waiting for him to come back. This was embarrassing enough, but her distress was compounded when, on Henry's return, he brightly told her that he had invited Gerd to a Goya exhibition; she had accepted, but said that she would go only if Rebecca accompanied them.

Initially Rebecca surmised that Gerd hated Henry's attentions, regarding him as a 'crazy old man'.[14] But only two months after that first dinner she began to revise her opinion. She now thought that Gerd was a 'cold and calculating little body' who 'no doubt will profit' from Henry's doting.[15] There was a bill of over £50 for wine for her, and a new lawnmower which Rebecca wryly commented she 'would like to have seen handed over the Covent Garden footlights wrapped in cellophane'.[16] Worst of all was that Henry seemed to make no attempt to hide his feelings. Rebecca, humiliated, felt as if everyone in their social circle was aware that her husband was pursuing yet another much younger woman.

Furthermore this infatuation threatened to be more damaging than the others. Henry refused to take a planned holiday to Rhodes and Crete, deciding instead to accompany Rebecca only as far as Athens for a Byzantine exhibition and then fly straight home. Rebecca was forced to fly back too rather than remain alone. There would be no swimming in the warm sea – her favourite holiday activity; a much-needed escape from a particularly cold and grey winter was to be abandoned, all so that Henry could return quickly to pursue his ballerina. The only respite, she quipped to Emanie, was that while Gerd might be a ballet mistress, she was not Henry's mistress as yet.[17]

Rebecca completed a revised version of *The Meaning of Treason* for Viking. Time–Life would follow up with a paperback edition. *The New Meaning of Treason* contained all of the trial accounts of the first volume but had been updated to include her accounts of the Vassall case and the Profumo scandal. In the autumn it was chosen by the Book of the Month Club, which brought her a sum of $30,000.

Work stalled temporarily when Rebecca suffered from vomiting and pain in her abdomen. Gall-bladder problems were diagnosed and she underwent an operation to remove it. She found it impossible to relax either before or after the surgery. Henry was quarrelling constantly with their latest secretary, whom she found to be perfectly competent. The radio played far too much modern music, when it was clear to Rebecca that the best stuff had been written more than 150 years ago.[18] For the most part, Henry looked after her well during her convalescence, with the exception of one occasion when he disappeared to spend the day with Gerd, and left her alone, without visitors. Emanie, in an attempt to bring her friend's musical taste up to date, sent her an LP by the Beatles; Rebecca thought it 'wonderful' because it helped her fall asleep.

A week after the operation, Rebecca took a turn for the worse with constant vomiting and a high fever. Doped up with morphine, she lay listening to a radio soap opera about a family of farmers called *The Archers* which, she recalled later, seemed to be all about dogs, followed by another called Mrs Dale's Diary, which seemed to be all about cats.[19] But it was a temporary relapse and she was released from the hospital. She arranged to spend a week at the Ritz, rather than return straightaway to Henry's complaints and the organizational chaos of Ibstone. But even in London Henry's behaviour upset her. When her nephew, Norman, came to visit to talk to her and Henry about his father who was now unable to live alone, Henry absented himself abruptly, in the middle of tea, to go to see Gerd.

When she eventually returned to Ibstone she found it languishing in May sunshine, lovelier than she had ever known it, with its wonderful expanses of green. But even that pleasure was tinged with worry; a neighbouring millionaire had bought much of the surrounding land and turned it into a game reserve. From now on, every Saturday Ibstone would ring with the sound of shooting, disturbing the countryside and upsetting the ramblers. She could no longer enjoy her peaceful weekend walks with Albert.

That summer, Max Beaverbrook passed away. Rebecca was amazed by her own reaction; she felt very little at his death. He could, she felt, have tried to build a better friendship with her after their calamitous affair. Tommy Kilner's death shortly after was a different matter entirely. She was filled with sorrow that she had not seen him again, despite the fact that he lived nearby. She thought of Tommy as a lost opportunity. Had they met when they were both young, they might have been happy together. Reading their obituaries, something odd suddenly struck her. Max and Tommy had both married twice. Their first wives had been exceptional women, Tommy's a nursing sister and a talented musician, Max's one of the most beautiful women of her time. Yet in the obituaries no mention was made at all of these first wives. 'Women are dependent on men in such odd ways,' Rebecca wrote to Emanie, 'if your husband marries again after your death, well, you're wiped out.'[20]

Henry's deteriorating health thwarted several of Rebecca's attempts to travel, and his doctors stressed that he should not be left alone. Rebecca fumed at being trapped in Ibstone, now freezing because Henry's condition seemed to make him impervious to the cold, with the effect that he went around turning all the radiators off. He was also obsessed by how little money was coming in. Now seventy, he was no longer able to take up lucrative non-executive directorships. But the drop in income had been more than compensated for by the Book of the Month Club deal for *The Meaning of Treason*. Rebecca started to worry about how much money he might be spending on his ballet mistress.

Rebecca tried to resume work on her 'Russian novel' and, in the autumn of 1965, sent it off to Gwenda David at Viking Press. Gwenda didn't think much of it, but hesitated about breaking the news to Rebecca. When she did, Rebecca rewrote it. The book's title, *The Birds Fall Down*, ostensibly came from a poem by Conway Power, and on the title page four lines of poetry appeared. 'Conway Power' was in fact Rebecca West, and after the book was published she had some amusement from replying to written enquiries about the poet with snippets of fictitious biography.

This little act of trickery was a tiny hint at the deceit and treachery that are the main themes of the novel. Like *The Meaning of Treason*, this was a book about deception, but personal as well as political. The protagonist Laura's longing for her father was reminiscent of Rebecca's own paternal relationship; Laura's father's affair with his wife's best friend makes him oblivious to her needs. The political convictions and fanaticisms of the characters, mostly developed through their dialogue with each other, paint a picture of the inevitability of the Russian Revolution. In 1966 *The Birds Fall Down* was released in America by Viking and in England by Macmillan. It was critically acclaimed and also chosen as a *Yorkshire Post* Book of the Year, and as a Book of the Month Club selection in the United States, giving Rebecca $37,500, in addition to her royalties.

An author tour of the States followed, giving Rebecca time for a much-needed break with Emanie. Afterwards, Rebecca did not return to England, embarking instead on a trip to Mexico with Henry. She wanted to see the Mayan ruins before she died. Mexico captured her imagination just as Yugoslavia had. The racial and cultural intermingling, the sheer intensity and colour of street life, seemed to awaken her from torpor.

When Rebecca did return to Ibstone she felt revitalized. She was obsessed with Mexico, planning at first a short article on Trotsky's time there, but later giving in to the same kind of need she had felt when writing *Black Lamb*. She planned to write an epic historical and political account of the country; she was seventy-four, but her age was incidental. Her book on Mexico was never completed, but the disjointed notes she compiled offer an expansive portrait of a country caught in ambivalence about its past.[21]

An uneasy truce continued with Anthony and Lily, who visited from time to time. Rebecca worried over her son, still thinking that he looked 'terribly old and harried'.[22] She was acutely disturbed that their newest baby, born in 1965, would not be twenty-one until its father was seventy-two. Easier and far more pleasurable for Rebecca were her visits from her grandson Edmund and his wife, Vita.

In September 1966, Albert, Rebecca's beloved Labrador, died. He had been diagnosed with cancer and when his condition deteriorated to such a state that he was in constant discomfort Rebecca had him put to sleep. To Lettie she wrote that she was 'dreadfully lost' without him. He had been her constant companion and she missed him quite as much as she missed Pounce.[23] Months later, Justin Lowinsky, the son of her late friend Ruth, gave her a West Highland terrier called Annie, but Rebecca continued to write about Albert in journals until her death. The lack of her beloved old dog to accompany her on long walks in the countryside meant that Rebecca felt even more keenly the desire to return to London. She entreated Henry, arguing that there would be advantages for them both; she would be less isolated, he would be closer to good medical care if he needed it.

In a decade of loss, Rebecca was hit by yet another death,

that of Vyvyan Holland. She had been close friends with Vyvyan since the 1920s. His son Merlin, Rebecca's protégé, was now an undergraduate at Oxford, and she and Henry tried to support him. One night, when Henry and Rebecca planned a theatre trip in Oxford, he resolved to show his gratitude by inviting them both to supper at his tiny and very dingy bedsit. Only at the last minute did he start to worry about how suitable his surroundings were for entertaining two rather grand old people in their seventies who were used to a certain amount of luxury. But he made chicken-liver pâté, and poached some salmon, and the three sat together convivially. Rebecca was gracious in her thanks, telling Merlin how beautifully cooked the salmon had been.

Just before Merlin's finals, Rebecca returned the favour, inviting him to Ibstone to relax for a weekend before the exams started. Merlin was fed and watered and wined and got to know Rebecca much better than he had before. For the first time, the slight feeling of awe coupled with intimidation was gone, and he told her so. She replied that she had found it wonderful too, because, for once, she hadn't needed to be on her best behaviour. So much of what Rebecca presented to the outside world was a protective mask. But in her letters to Emanie and other friends the mask was dropped. Merlin was not a threat; he had joined the small group of people with whom Rebecca could be herself, without any pretence. Perhaps Merlin, her nephew Norman and Justin Lowinsky, all young men she came increasingly to depend upon, were as she might have wished Anthony to be, before *Heritage* fractured the delicate bond between them.

Rebecca and Henry spent the festive season with Norman and his wife Marion. But when they returned to Ibstone they found their home had been burgled. Most distressing of all, they realized that Henry's precious collection of jade pieces, put together over thirty years and worth around £4,000, was gone. Rebecca's friends suspected an inside job, questioning who else but an employee of the house would have known where they kept the collection. For Rebecca, it was another warning of how vulnerable and isolated she was at Ibstone, especially in the light of Henry's illness. Reluctantly, he agreed that it might be better to sell the house and the farm and move back to the city. The farm had been losing money for years, which had been useful for reducing their tax bills, but Rebecca never grudged paying her taxes, conceding:

> I approve of heavy taxes, I know I ought to pay the State a lot of money, because at my age I can remember the time when a baby whose parents were not fortunate was likely to have scabs on its face, might be bow-legged, when sickness meant to many people, it could be said to most people, not only pain and weakness and the risk of death but utter ruin, when unemployment meant starvation, when the old who were also so poor were often so wasted and frenzied by the extremity of their want that it could be understood how the ignorant had believed in witches.[24]

However, with Henry's investments at Lloyds doing less well, the farm began to seem more of a liability than an asset. They set about trying to put the estate in order and hired a new farm manager. The farm was tidied up for prospective buyers, and Rebecca looked for a firm of professional cleaners to set to work on the granaries and cowsheds, thinking that in its current state it would be impossible to sell. She hoped too that once Henry was settled in London, he might stop dashing around so much, which she felt was exacerbating his poor health.[25]

The decision to sell Ibstone brought Rebecca considerable relief from the stress she had been under. She was joyfully reunited with Emanie and her husband, who were en route to Holland, for a 'perfect evening' at the Savoy.[26] And then, in July 1968, Rebecca was feted with yet another professional honour. She was made a Companion of Literature at the Royal Society of Literature, an award that had been inaugurated just seven years earlier. Rebecca travelled up to Aviemore for a week's conference but was stricken with a viral infection that left her suffering from vomiting and diarrhoea. Within days of her return, Henry too was suffering from stomach pains and the local doctor assumed he had caught Rebecca's virus. Henry's reason seemed even more disturbed than usual and he became obsessed by the fact that Ibstone was in Rebecca's sole name and that she had not bequeathed it to him in the event of her death. She had, she assured him, as well as leaving an allowance to enable him to afford the upkeep. But he would not be calmed and Rebecca set up a meeting with her solicitor so they could all go over it together until Henry was comforted.

While Rebecca's symptoms of the virus eased, Henry's seemed only to worsen. So much so that their doctor recommended that Henry be admitted to hospital the following day. An X-ray revealed an obstruction in the stomach and the follow-up operation to remove it suggested that it was an inflammation rather than the cancer Rebecca had feared.

The stress she was under seemed to herald a new flare-up of the virus and, with her frequent visits to the bathroom, Rebecca was confined to the house. While she was at home, Henry took a turn for the worse. She could not visit him for three days and when she was finally able to visit, she was shocked by the state he was in. Shaken by hiccoughs, feeling utterly helpless and consequently very distressed, Henry seemed like a ghost of himself. His operation wound was infected, and he was suffering from anaemia. Soon they would discover that he also had cancer of the colon. He returned to his worry over whether or not he would inherit Ibstone, having completely forgotten the meeting with their lawyer. Rebecca, unable to reassure him that all was in place, resorted to the ruse of telling him that she would alter her will so it was so. He was reassured and relieved, saying 'That will make all the difference'.[27] Rebecca saw, then, that in his madness he believed that not he, but she, was dying, and that he wanted to live at Ibstone with Gerd after she had passed away.

When Rebecca visited him in the ward, he would raise his hand in greeting as she approached his bed. Nurses were scarce and Rebecca helped out with many of the small tasks necessary to keep his wound clean. But it was not a peaceful bedside; the stench from Henry's colostomy bag forced her to escape to the corridor at regular intervals lest she vomit. When Gerd visited Henry, she found the atmosphere more than she could bear. Rebecca recalled that the smell from Henry's suppurating wound made Gerd nauseous and faint; the ward itself Gerd thought 'was sordid and terrifying'.[28] She stopped visiting. Towards the end, Rebecca sat beside him as he lay comatose. He briefly regained consciousness and, with his eyes still closed, reached for her hand and kissed it. When his lips brushed Rebecca's aquamarine ring, he made a sound like a sigh. 'Your ring,' he said. Rebecca replied that yes, it was the ring he had given her. But he turned away, shutting her out with a last look of distaste. For Rebecca, the truth was quite plain; he had believed, for a minute, that it was Gerd's hand he was kissing. Nothing would ever sweeten that moment. That final betrayal would stay with her, conveying Henry's weariness of her more than any recriminating word ever could. She had been 'wholly dispossessed' by Henry's lover. Henry died the following day, on 3 November, at seven in the morning, while Rebecca was asleep at Ibstone.

Rebecca returned to the hospital and was taken out to the mortuary. When she saw Henry's corpse she was amazed by how, in death, he seemed to have regained the beauty of his youth. It was a beauty she had all but forgotten, for it had been lost to the physical signs of his deteriorating health, 'the glaze on his eyes, the gaping mouth, the stoop and the torn shuffling feet'.[29] After thirty-eight years of marriage, Rebecca was a widow.

Henry was buried at Fingest church, just down the hill from Ibstone. The vicar conducted the service but Rebecca asked a Russian Orthodox Priest to deliver the blessing of the dead. Her grandson Edmund and his wife, Vita, accompanied her, and everyone went back to Ibstone after the burial for a meal. The funeral brought Rebecca the first of a series of revelations about Henry. Much to her consternation, a woman whom Rebecca described as a bogus psychoanalyst appeared in the church and demanded to sit with Henry's family through the service. She nicknamed her Mrs Sludge the Medium, after the fake spiritualist in the Robert Browning poem

After the service, when the guests had gone, and Rebecca sifted through Henry's papers, she found letters that showed that 'Mrs Sludge' had been yet another object of Henry's affections. More than that, it was clear that they had actually made love. Rebecca wrote to Emanie that this was a shock; she knew of Henry's various infatuations but it had never occurred to her that he was 'actually sleeping with all these women'.[30] She also discovered that he had discussed marriage both with Gerd, who had rejected him, and 'Mrs Sludge', who had not.

Most painful of all was a photograph she found in one of Henry's drawers, bundled with numerous others, taken long ago. It was of a woman called Irene Ravensdale, whom Rebecca had thought of as a friend, standing on the steps of Amiens Cathedral. It was clear that Henry had taken the photo, but she knew that the three of them had never travelled there together. Henry had taken her there alone. It was the worst betrayal of all. She and Henry had been to Amiens when they were still lovers; they had lain together on their bed, listening to the nightingales in the garden below them. Rebecca had seen that Henry was infatuated with Irene, but had been reassured when Irene told her she could never do anything that might hurt her. Rebecca had invited her to Ibstone, had listened to her criticizing Gerd and worrying about Henry's affairs without knowing that she and Henry had been together: 'It was the utmost treachery for him to take Irene Ravensdale, and it was the utmost treachery for her to go with him.'[31]

Henry left everything he had to Rebecca with the exception of two small bequests to his cousins, and £5,000 to Gerd Larsen. The strain of his illness and the cruel surprises inflicted after his death weakened Rebecca and, as her seventy-sixth birthday approached, she fell ill with whooping cough. She took comfort in the many letters and telegrams she received. Henry was greatly missed by many who had benefitted from his kindness. Merlin

Holland wrote to Rebecca: 'I shall miss an ear to listen to my inexperience and guide me now – real gentleness seems to come only later in life when the masks are down and the rough edges smoothed: I think it was that which made me devoted to Henry.'[32]

And although Anthony did not pretend that his troubled relationship with his mother would suddenly be resolved he did write consolingly: 'I wish things were other than they are between us so that I could have been some comfort and help to you. I wish I could be some comfort and help now – all I can say is, that in spite of all the reasons I have given you to make you feel the contrary, you are very dear to me and it gives me great pain to feel that I am useless to you now.'[33]

Rebecca told her sister that she saw Henry's death as a relief from the physical and mental torture of his last year. He was at peace and, ultimately, his had been a good life. She could not say that of her own. She wrote to Emanie: 'Hell, how many men of seventy-four have a mistress demanding to sit with the family at the funeral, whom he hadn't known for more than eighteen months?'[34]

Even from the other side of the Atlantic, Emanie was a comfort to Rebecca, and to her alone she confided the resentment she still felt against Henry. The breaking off of their sexual relationship when seen in the light of his promiscuity was 'planned cruelty'. Rebecca found, to her astonishment, 'that an unhappy marriage goes on being unhappy when it is over'.[35]

Rebecca spent Christmas with Kitty and Caro, who did everything they could to make it as happy as possible. Dorset seemed bright, with blue skies and crisp cold weather, compared with the grey skies and deep snow of Ibstone awaiting her on her return. It hastened her resolve. She would sell up and move back to London immediately.

Chapter Thirteen

LAST JOURNEYS

Henry had left his affairs in chaos. He left a substantial sum in securities, much of which Rebecca immediately had to pay out in death duties. She struggled to deal with solicitors while packing up her home, finding that leaving Ibstone affected her far more than she had expected, despite the fact that she was looking forward to a return to the city. The furniture had to be moved in three lots and the new flat, although huge by London standards, could not contain everything that had been in Ibstone. Some pieces simply didn't fit, and Rebecca found herself weeping over her drawing-room bookcases which were too tall to move to the new flat.

In the midst of the turmoil, Rebecca found scant time to read and comment on a manuscript that had arrived: it was a bio-graphy of Wells, written and sent to her by Lovat Dickson. She did, however, manage to rewrite the passages about her youth and correct some errors about her relationship with Wells. Above all, she wanted to protect people who were still alive from painful memories. Accounts of her life that were untrue, she wrote to Lovat, made her feel she was 'being dissolved into mist'.[1]

Rebecca's new, and last, home was at Kingston House North. It was part of a very grand building facing Hyde Park, just a short walk from the Royal Albert Hall. The entrance hall carpet was thick and dark green and the doorman wore matching green livery. There was even a restaurant for the residents if they wished to use it. Best of all for Rebecca was that as you descended down from the reception area you came to wide glass doors leading out onto a garden, a tranquil place with magnificent trees and, in the summer, a tangle of flowers. This residents' garden was the view from one of her windows and in the evening she would sit eating yoghurt by the window, watching the light fade, enjoying the peace which was only minutes from the bustle of town.

The flat was convenient for the Harrods Library, where she could send secretaries to buy general reading books, and for the main store from which she ordered a weekly delivery of all of her food, even her cans of Heinz tomato soup. It was also just a short taxi ride from the London Library in St James's Square, which she relied upon for research.

Anthony wrote dutifully to Rebecca to ask how she was coping. But he then went on bluntly to say that he was concerned at his lack of a bequest from Henry, again reiterating his belief that he had been left out of Wells' will only on the understanding that he would inherit from Henry. Rebecca set him straight on both counts: Jane was the main reason he didn't have more from Wells, and while Henry had thought of making Anthony his heir, quite apart from their many difficulties, Henry had 'got less companionship' out of Anthony than he had hoped for.[2] The money from Ibstone had been enough to secure her flat, with very little over. However, Rebecca offered to send Anthony either various items from Ibstone – some first editions, drawings by Wyndham Lewis, including one of her, and a wonderful Aubusson rug – or, if Anthony preferred, the proceeds from selling them.

Rebecca's old acquaintance, the dancer and choreographer Agnes George de Mille, shared a 'glorious moment' with her in a letter. After a Royal Ballet premiere at Covent Garden, Agnes was approached by a comely middle-aged woman, who enquired if she remembered when Henry Andrews had introduced them. Agnes did not, but politely avoided saying so. They chatted politely about Henry and Rebecca and then the woman said to Agnes that what had distressed Rebecca the most during Henry's last years was the reduction in his income. Agnes furiously defended her friend, pointing out that no, what had upset her was Gerd. The woman stormed off, and Agnes suddenly realized that the woman she had been speaking to was Gerd herself. She wrote to Rebecca worrying about what she had done. Agnes stressed that she minded being so unwittingly insulting: if she was going to 'cut someone down to the roots' she ought to know she was doing it.[3]

Rebecca replied pragmatically. In one way she was grateful to Gerd for dealing with Henry when he had become so difficult, but she also felt that she had taken advantage of an ailing old man. That said, Gerd had only been one of many women in Henry's last ten years, a period in which he seemed to believe that he had no duty to be faithful and that it was his right to sleep with anyone who was willing.

Setting up the new flat proved to be a protracted business. Rebecca felt like Mariana in Tennyson's 'moated grange', the only character who perhaps had waited even longer than her. Mariana, she joked to Emanie, was only waiting for a lover, very unimportant when compared with waiting for a carpet-layer. Her jewellery and silver were so valuable that special locks had to be fitted on the flat before the insurers would agree to cover them. Rebecca was amused by the insurance company's elaborate preparations, noting drily that when she accidentally locked herself out of the flat, and feared she would never enter again, it took Fred, the ex-navy 'main entrance man', thirty seconds flat to climb up the fire escape and get in through a bathroom window.

Once Rebecca had moved in properly, the flat became little more than a base; in the remaining six months of the year that Henry died, Rebecca began travelling again. In July she went to Poitiers, visiting the lovely Loire chateaux, then travelled on to Switzerland, where her enjoyment was somewhat spoilt by the thick grey fog; she didn't catch so much as a glimpse of a mountain. Invigorated by the trip, Rebecca concluded that she would ideally spend only the spring and autumn in London, summering and wintering abroad, but her income as a writer, while substantial, was not enough to sustain that kind of lifestyle.

Rebecca was often unwell – viral infections, a bad bout of flu, rheumatic aches and pains – but nevertheless she planned a longer trip to America, to see Emanie and to meet a cousin of Henry's, a woman who had survived the concentration camps and to whom Henry had bequeathed a little money. Rebecca hoped that she would be able to help her, because she was a 'good and loving' person whose terrible experiences had led to fits of depression.[4] This she would precede with another visit to Mexico. Henry had disapproved of her Mexican project. Now, with his death, Rebecca prepared to grapple with the immense book she had first contemplated after their visit in 1966.

Rebecca's granddaughter Caro was making plans of her own, to marry a 'Ghanaian negro'. Rebecca seemed to welcome the prospect of her new husband far more warmly than she had greeted her niece Alison's West Indian lover, years before. Kitty was less enthusiastic; a position that puzzled Rebecca, because she thought of her as a 'professed liberal'.[5] Rebecca's relationship with Caro had never been altogether happy, and she was particularly taken with the way Caro's intended husband seemed to put Caro in her place. She hoped that she might go out to Ghana and get a mother-in-law who could 'put the fear of God into her'.[6]

The return trip to Mexico was hard work, unsurprising, perhaps, given that she was now approaching her seventy-seventh birthday. Getting around was 'utter hell'. She visited Frida Kahlo's house and was unimpressed, judging her work to be mediocre, and raging against her communist sympathies, and her busts of Stalin and Lenin. The house and grounds, with their bright colours and miniature Aztec temple in the garden, were, she declared, in appalling taste. The day was saved only by a wonderful lunch with the celebrated Mexican film star Dolores del Rio; Rebecca was stunned by how beautiful she was, even at sixty-eight.[7] Rebecca loved Yucatan, with its 'lovely pie-crust colour' ruins; she even managed to climb the smaller Aztec pyramids, but was too afraid of breaking a hip to venture up the higher ones.[8]

Following her Mexico travels, Rebecca settled in for a cosy ten-day break with Emanie and August. The flight home did not seem too bad at the time, but within days of her return, she found herself very badly affected by jet lag. The symptoms were so bad, including headaches, exhaustion and vice-like chest pain, that both she and her doctor thought she had developed heart problems. As a precaution Rebecca had a cardiogram, which was thankfully clear, but she was nonetheless slow to recover. During her convalescence, Rebecca saw old friends and enjoyed visits to the theatre, including one to see the musical *Hair*, which was then both hugely popular and enjoying critical acclaim. She, however, dismissed it as 'a very poor version of the kind of thing one saw in Berlin night-clubs just before the Weimar Republic collapsed – but the Germans did it far, far better'.[9]

The beginnings of the industrial disruption that would characterize much of the seventies came to Rebecca's home when a play she was enjoying on the BBC halted abruptly. Colour technology was available but many television technicians refused to work with it, and strike action intermittently affected broadcasts like this. In January 1971, the tense truce that had existed with Anthony since Henry's death ended abruptly when Rebecca caught sight of a review of his new book. *David Rees Among Others* was yet another loosely autobiographical novel. The review, in the *Daily Telegraph*, discussed a passage in which the protagonist remembers his maternal grandmother calling out to a nurse to 'take away the bastard out of sight'. Rebecca was horrified; it was the 'most loathsome lie', the 'most hideous of this horrible creature's fantasies', and disrespectful to the memory of her mother.[10] In her diary, she recalled how kind her mother had been to Anthony and how she had only refused to see them at the end because she had thought the hideous disfigurement caused by her illness would be too much for such a small child.

The day after the review appeared Rebecca instructed her solicitor to redraft her will, disinheriting Anthony once more.

To Emanie, Rebecca confided that she was really worried about how Anthony's book would affect Lettie, who was now eighty-six and was bound to be hurt by her nephew's attitude towards his grandmother; had there ever been anyone 'so hopelessly nasty, foul, stupidly cruel, as Anthony'?[11] Rebecca went to see Lettie so she could warn her before other reviews appeared in the Sunday papers, which she would undoubtedly see. On hearing the news, Lettie immediately burst into tears and told Rebecca that, as the eldest, she could even remember their mother dictating a letter to the other relatives telling them to be kind to Anthony because she loved him so. Both sisters agreed that he should indeed be cut out of Rebecca's will and both were distraught. Rebecca found that she woke in the night crying, with grief for the loss of her mother, and for the hateful thing that Anthony had done. It was fifteen years since Anthony had written Heritage and now, it seemed, it was all to begin again. Rebecca was seventy-seven; this was not the way she wanted to spend the little time she had left.

When her initial rage had dissipated somewhat, Rebecca's self-confidence seemed to have dissipated too; the new drama with Anthony had destroyed it.[12] She worried about the amount of weight she had put on, wishing she could get thin so she didn't look 'so repulsive', and she thought that her age made her less interesting company. She found a new secretary, Ann de Haviland, cousin of the actress Olivia, who suited her tremendously well. The postal strike in February cut her off from letters from Emanie and other dear friends but it also brought respite from her usual barrage of professional mail, making it seem a bit like a holiday.

Merlin Holland was working in Lebanon and, in the spring, Rebecca offered to accompany his mother, Thelma, on a visit to him. It was, in part, an act of generosity, because Rebecca knew that, while Thelma was desperate to see her son, her finances would not be sufficient for a trip to the Middle East. Perhaps because so many of the friends to whom she had written long letters on her previous travels were now gone, she kept a diary, a mix of traveller's observations, amusing anecdotes and occasional grumbles about Thelma.

Rebecca loved the Lebanese food, the unleavened bread, the dips made of aubergine and cheese with mysterious blends of herbs and spices. Thelma was less enthusiastic. They travelled from Beirut to Baalbeck and Rebecca marvelled at the Roman ruins, the majesty of the columns rising among the poplar trees, the absolute beauty of this place, perched on the edge of an agricultural plateau when Rebecca had expected only desert. First confirming that it was safe to do so, they drove out to the ruins of Palmyra on the Syrian border. She declared the site one of the most magnificent she had ever seen, but deplored the state of the Syrian lavatories. Musing on the great Syrian queen Zenobia, who had ruled Palmyra until she was defeated by the Romans, and who, like Cleopatra, was most often depicted as a conquered ruler, Rebecca lamented that the focus seemed to lie on the voluptuous breasts of both queens when they were pictured beside their subjugators, as if the flat, broad chest of the dominant man made their breasts more desirable in contrast. In notes for an unfinished essay on Lebanon, she wrote wryly, 'We see the two great queens at moments when they are not throwing their bras away but their bras are throwing them away, and leave them bulging and unprotected.'[13] Leaving Palmyra, conscious of her age, she was moved, and lamented, 'Sadly I shall never see it again.'[14] Overall, however, her impressions of Lebanon were disjointed: she despaired of the Balfour convention, acknowledging that it had ignored the rights of the Palestinian people, but seemed unable to relate it directly to the kind of suffering it caused. Her own experience of war crowded in; she had seen so many other conflicts that she found it almost impossible to rationalize any more.

Merlin took her to visit the grave of Lady Hester Stanhope, one of Rebecca's heroines. Lady Hester was an eccentric eighteenth-century aristocrat, the niece of William Pitt, who had lived in the East for many years, taking a much younger lover, dressing in male attire and becoming a heroine of the Druse. Her tomb was situated on a hill in the village of Sidon, in the midst of the ruins among which Lady Hester had built an immense fortress-like home, in which she spent her final years in virtual isolation, surrounded only by squalling cats. Rebecca thought the site 'quite a find' and on her return to London, immediately immersed herself in every book she could find about the woman, whom she thought had been badly maligned by history.

That summer, Rebecca fell in love with London again. The weather was exceptional and despite her painful joints, she walked most days in Hyde Park. She was amazed by the beauty of nature, the play of light and shade on the avenues of Kensington Gardens, the glorious flowers, and happy dogs splashing in the pool in Hyde Park. But she also contrasted this beauty with new 'hideous' abstract art she saw in the recently opened Serpentine Gallery just bits of wood set in planks at unusual angles, or a pile of string.[15] Rebecca's health had not been good since her return from Lebanon, and a constant pain in her ears led to acute deafness. She was recommended to a specialist in Edinburgh, whom she visited in July, and the treatment he prescribed did improve matters a little.

Caro's wedding to her Ghanaian fiancé, Osei Duah, went ahead – principally, Caro told Rebecca, so that she could join him in Africa without entry problems. Rebecca remained unperturbed; she would far rather Caro married Osei, whom she thought of as dull but nice, than an unpleasant white man.

After the wedding, Rebecca took a trip to Ireland with Lettie. She loved Ireland, feeling an empathy with the country of her ancestors. She was amazed by the ignorance of American tourists who seemed puzzled by the presence of British troops in Ulster. They were all, she sniffed, 'Liberals', and wasn't liberalism 'the greatest factory of misinformation in the world'.[16] Her attitude to the Irish, however, was equally robust: Dublin was a lovely city, but its people seemed curiously insensible to the deaths on both sides of the Northern Irish Troubles, as if it was all some kind of lark. She was exasperated that her ancestors had spent so much money on such 'ungrateful people'.[17]

On her return, Rebecca's health took another serious downturn; she was suffering from 'queer aches and pains and contractions' which were, this time, ominously diagnosed as heart trouble.[18] Nevertheless she continued to work, slowly but meticulously, drafting and redrafting her memoirs, and adding to the Mexican notes. She had occasion to revisit her past, too, when Gordon Ray asked her to send him memoranda for his book on her relationship with Wells. Rebecca granted him access to the papers at Yale, reasoning that she would rather a distinguished academic like Ray had a go at the book than anyone else. Norman and Jeanne Mackenzie were also mailing her questions for their biography of Wells. When she received a copy of the finished book she was shocked that they had turned the charismatic and clever Wells into someone dull, as well as being concerned by what she saw as an account based on very limited sources.

The coal miners' strike of 1972 disturbed Rebecca, chiefly because she thought that the government had handled it all so badly. She was convinced that the Conservative prime minister, Edward Heath, should resign, wondering how he had fallen into the miners' trap. A pay rise was overdue, but the miners had pressed home their advantage and now sought to exploit it even further.

One evening in April, a telephone call from Anthony brought back all the misery of the previous year. He was in London, ostensibly to see Caro before she went to Africa, a fact that Rebecca found both surprising and rather suspicious given that he had not come over for her wedding or even made any enquiries about her. He asked if he might visit. Rebecca replied honestly that she doubted it would be a good idea, given that visits between them, even those that seemed to go well, were generally followed by slanderous books and lawsuits. Anthony assured her that this time it would be different, although he also stressed that he had no regrets about anything he had written.

Rebecca had 'said far worse things' about him than he had about her.[19] The conversation left Rebecca shaky and afraid. She called Kitty to see if she knew how long Anthony intended to stay. She suspected, rightly as it turned out, that he was intending to move back to England, and that that, rather than his visit to Caro, was the real reason for him being in England.

～∞～

Caro settled in Ghana. Her situation was far from what she had anticipated. She was living in a jungle village with her in-laws who spoke no English. Suffering from both the isolation and the climate, Caro contracted malaria, developed an acute form of anaemia and then had a nervous breakdown.[20] At the beginning of December, Caro's condition was so severe that Osei brought her back to England and she was admitted to Maudsley Hospital, celebrated for its pioneering work with patients who were mentally ill. Rebecca described her as being 'desperately physically ill at first and manic depressive, hallucinated [sic] and suicidal, varying between violence and catatonia'.[21]

She wrote gentle letters to Rebecca. She and Caro had never been close but now Rebecca found herself 'sickeningly concerned' with her. 'Oh dear,' she lamented, 'what the tie of blood is – what a pain it gives and one can do nothing.'[22] She was gratified, however, that Anthony seemed to be a devoted father, coming over again so that he could visit often and tending to his daughter. Rebecca's own health was also deteriorating. She had cataracts in both eyes, leaving her partially blind, and acute pain in her legs prevented her walking anything but the shortest distances. The worry, coupled with her already poor health, weakened Rebecca further and she was admitted to St John and Queen Elizabeth Hospital with pleurisy and pneumonia. After two weeks she was released and was invited to recuperate with Margaret Hodges and her husband till she could better look after herself.

When finally Rebecca was well enough to return to London, she resumed work on a novel she had begun in the late sixties: *The Only Poet*. The heroine, Leonora, is over eighty, and she catches sight of the woman who destroyed the most important love affair of her life. The story of the lovers and Leonora's regrets for what might have been end with Leonora realizing that she is going to die. Throughout there are hints of Rebecca's own failed love affairs, what might have been with Tommy, and an overarching sense of the futility of a life lived without true love.

While she worked on the novel, the Mackenzies' biography of Wells finally appeared. The finished book infuriated her and she wrote angrily to Gip Wells, asking for his support in refuting the book. She dismissed it as merely 'an attempt' at biography, stressing that only Gordon Ray had access, granted by her, to the letters deposited at Yale. Worse still, a serialization of the book had been sold to the *Sunday Times* with the lurid title 'The Sexual Torment of H.G. Wells'.[23] Rebecca had given permission, for the publication initially, on the understanding that the book was to be a work of literary criticism; she would ask that they change the title and omit some passages about her.

For Rebecca's eighty-first birthday on 21 December 1973, the *Times Literary Supplement* ran an article about her body of work, expressing surprise that she had not 'gained a following among the partisans of women's liberation'. The piece went on to celebrate the 'fine, strong androgynous mind' that allowed her to express herself outside of the expectations and restrictions imposed by gender definition. She was driven by the need to express reality; she wrote 'to discover what she knew'. The eclecticism of her output, 'the interstices between her books' were too wide: 'Dame Rebecca's work has not fused in the minds of critics, and she has no secure literary status ... she is too difficult to define.'[24]

'Quite tearful with gratitude' Rebecca wrote to the editor, Arthur Cook. She praised the astuteness of the writer of the anonymous article.* She did indeed strive for reality, and that motivation was detrimental in a literary world that had been

---

* The piece was by Samuel Hynes and would be shortened as an introduction to Rebecca's collected works.

shaped by T.S. Eliot. Eliot was more concerned with ambition and Rebecca believed that the culture he had created was represented by Centre Point, the empty tower block at the junction of Tottenham Court Road and Charing Cross Road. Tax issues meant that the building was impossible to rent out and so it stood vacant; it should have been 'sheltering the homeless and shelters no one'. This was a prophetic remark. Just two months later, a charity for the homeless occupied the building, demanding that it be used to help alleviate homelessness in London.

Gordon Ray's *H.G. Wells and Rebecca West* was finally published in 1974. Shortly before publication, Gip Wells, angered by the portrayal of his mother in the draft he had been sent, complained that Ray had gone too far in following Rebecca's demands, which had been precise and insistent. Despite her increasingly poor sight – her cataracts had worsened and she could barely see at all – she had made detailed comments on each of his drafts and refuted many of his suggestions. But as a result of Gip's remarks, Ray now immediately agreed to amend the text. Nonetheless, Rebecca defended the book to those friends, among them Evelyn Hutchison, who thought she was taking a risk in allowing intimate details of her life with Wells to appear in print. She argued that it was her only chance of controlling how it would be represented to posterity before she died. Indeed, Ray commented in his preface that Rebecca 'set down with accustomed force' this chapter of her life, and added that Rebecca had described the project to him as 'a long essay in self analysis'.[25]

Unsurprisingly, *H.G. Wells and Rebecca West* received a huge amount of publicity. One of the most savage reviews was by Anthony in the January issue of *Harper's Magazine*.[26] Rebecca's upbringing was 'genteel, middle class' not virtual poverty. Her situation, according to Anthony, even when she was bringing him up alone, was comfortable, with an array of servants. Ray's account of Anthony's conception, in which Wells did not use birth control, in order to bind Rebecca to him, was ludicrous.

Anthony's attack on the book came across as a very extreme defence of his father. Where Ray sees Wells' affair with Amber Reeves as justification for the Webbs' vilification of Wells and his views on free love, it was, for Anthony, more about the working-class Wells having been sexually successful with 'the daughter of upstairs people'.[27]

Rebecca was particularly disconcerted by Anthony's defence of Jane. He argued that Jane had agreed to Rebecca being her husband's mistress on the understanding that she would remain no more than that. When Rebecca started demanding more of the relationship, she was breaking the rules of their agreement. Rebecca wrote to the editor of *Harper's Magazine* complaining about Anthony's misrepresentations. She finished her letter by pointing out that she did not think that Anthony had ever even met Jane Wells, but that if he had he could 'hardly have gained much enlightenment about her emotional life', given that he was only thirteen when she died.[28]

As her eighty-second birthday approached, given her precarious health, Rebecca thought increasingly about her own death. She hunted for a grave and finally, accompanied by Gwenda David, bought a plot in Brookwood Cemetery in Surrey. In her diary she wrote enthusiastically about the site: the bluebells were supposed to be beautiful in the springtime and her plot was close to a pink hawthorn. In the years that remained, Rebecca visited her intended grave from time to time, on one occasion discomfiting the very young secretary who accompanied her, by this apparent show of morbidity.

Rebecca's closest friend, Emanie, was also suffering from serious health conditions related to her age. Emanie's husband, August, kept Rebecca informed as his wife was admitted to hospital with heart trouble and a pacemaker was fitted. While terrifying, he said, this was still less of a concern than the periods of dementia that had begun to afflict her. August resolved to keep Emanie at home with him as long as possible and eventually Emanie herself was able to reassure Rebecca, in a brief letter, that 'with enough rubber and straps' she was almost as good as new.[29]

A year later, Rebecca went into the London Clinic to have her cataracts removed. In a letter she dictated to Emanie after her surgery, Rebecca told her old friend that the private clinic was luxurious. She was the only white patient, the others all being Arabs, and it felt as if 'there were camels padding up and down the corridors'.[30] [31] The operation restored her vision, but she could no longer type. Spectacles, which allowed her to see the paper at the back of the typewriter, made the front appear as a blur. Bifocals were out of the question. They made her 'like a distracted hen' with the constant looking up and down: 'I can't do it. Hens must wear bifocals, if one looks closely. It explains it all.'[32]

Her relationship with her grandson Edmund had become more difficult since he had announced his separation from his wife, Vita, two years previously. At the end of the year Edmund brought his new partner, Cheryl, to meet his grandmother. Rebecca, still loyal to Vita, did not take to her and, remembering Anthony's affair with the woman from the BBC, worried that Edmund took after his father more than she had realized. When Edmund invited Rebecca to his wedding to Cheryl the following year she 'declined with the single monosyllable "no"'.[33]

January 1976 brought fresh familial horrors from Anthony, with the publication of two articles by him in the *Observer*. 'Life with Aunty Panther and H.G. Wells' appeared on 4 January, and 'My Father's Unpaid Debts of Love' followed a week later. Rebecca wrote to Gip Wells as if to try and enlist his support for a putative libel action. The articles were 'packed full of lies'. Anthony's allegation that he was sent away to boarding school by a neglectful mother was libellous to begin with. It had been 1917, the Germans had begun to demonstrate their bombing power from the skies; Rebecca had been trying to keep him out of harm's way. Gip was unperturbed by the *Observer* pieces, reasoning that he thought it 'only fair that he [Anthony] should be allowed to tell his story as he sees it'.[34] He would not be joining with Rebecca in any lawsuits because he was not personally 'defamed or damaged'.[35] Rebecca replied at once that she hadn't meant Gip to take any action. Furthermore she had been advised by a *Sunday Telegraph* lawyer that she couldn't take Anthony and the *Observer* to court successfully either. She had hoped that Gip would have been as upset as her about the slur on Wells' character implied by Anthony's suggestion that his father had deliberately ignored the headmaster's alcoholism and left him at St Piran's.

The success of the cataract operation meant Rebecca could again seek solace from the disharmony in work, and she employed a new secretary.[36] Elizabeth Leyshon had been suggested by a mutual friend of her mother and Rebecca. She was just twenty and was employed to work at the flat for four hours each day. In practice her work frequently extended outside of this time, a fact that Rebecca had made explicit right from the outset with a letter asking for a 'sliding boundary' with regard to her working hours. Elizabeth joined Rebecca's other staff: Mary, a devout Irish Catholic and a superb cook; John, Rebecca's driver with his Daimler limousine; and not one but two cleaners. But only she, much to her amusement, was invited to have lunch with her employer every day, seated at the formal dining table, suitable for at least eight people.

One of the new secretary's jobs was keeping track of the many accoutrements that Rebecca now needed: her wig, her hearing aid and various pairs of spectacles; Elizabeth soon became known as 'the keeper of the spare parts'.[37] But the most important part of her job was typing up revised and corrected drafts and redrafts of Rebecca's reviews for the *Daily Telegraph*. Elizabeth marvelled at how Rebecca never missed a deadline, although sometimes writing the reviews so exhausted her that after completing one she would collapse in bed.

In September, Rebecca received an invitation from the BBC to be interviewed by Ludovic Kennedy, then a highly regarded television presenter. It was not a success. Kennedy kept trying to steer the conversation back to Anthony and Wells. Rebecca had been adamant in her refusal to discuss this area of her life, but found herself trapped by microphone cables and unable to escape. Mary, the cook, suggested to Elizabeth that the media's obsessive interest in Rebecca's past love affair had been triggered by the Ray book. Rebecca herself thought that Kennedy was wicked and 'drank like a fish and ate like a pig'.[38] She called her agent to complain both about the tone of Kennedy's questions, and the fee, a ludicrously low £50. Her limited income and the ever-increasing cost of living were, by this point, having a real impact. Rebecca lamented that she could no longer attend the theatre as often as she once had, and trips to the ballet and opera were out of the question because the tickets were just too expensive.[39]

Solicitors were frequent visitors to the flat, as Rebecca continued to revise her will, although she kept the principal beneficiaries and executors the same. Anthony was completely excluded from all bequests, and Rebecca's slowness in actually completing a will, coupled with her constant minor revisions, caused both amusement and impatience. At one lunch meeting with a solicitor to discuss the most recent version, she gained the smiles of the entire restaurant by declaring loudly 'sex always gets a better press than it deserves!'[40]

In the autumn of 1976 Lettie's health deteriorated and she was admitted to St Stephen's Hospital in the Fulham Road. It was a cheerless place with grim grey corridors. Lettie, now ninety-one and recovering from a mild stroke, greeted Rebecca warmly, waving her left arm, her yellow wig slipping over one eye. Her mind was sharp, but the loss of power in her right arm and right leg meant that on her release from hospital Lettie would need full-time care. The task of finding a suitable nursing home fell to Rebecca. Fortunately she remembered Lettie's First World War service in the air force and Lettie was welcomed into an RAF care facility, with what Rebecca was pleased to describe as 'some fanfare'. Lettie was, by now, 'a romantic relic'.[41]

Emanie's health, too, was deteriorating rapidly. Her dementia had progressed to the point that she experienced only occasional bouts of lucidity and in his letters to Rebecca, August seemed resigned to her condition being incurable. On good days she still enjoyed listening to Rebecca's letters being read to her, and she was settled into a care home where the atmosphere was relaxed and sociable. August worried only that with further decline she would have to leave and be moved to a more traditional nursing home.

When Rebecca received a letter from August explaining his wife's position, she bundled up copies of the letters she had written to Emanie in a packet and, mindful of future biographers, attached a covering note. The contents of the letters, especially her distress over Henry's behaviour in later years, now seemed to her to have been written in moments of grief and despair. They did not accurately reflect the full story of her marriage, so she explained how her feelings had changed in the years since his death. She was reconciled at last to the pain of his final decade and had once again regained her 'deep affection' for Henry, remembering him as he had been in those very first happy years of their marriage. His 'kindness and sweetness and sympathy' were all the more remarkable for the cruelty he had suffered both in the internment camp, and from his uncle's bullying. It was true that he had been cruel in the years that followed, but this was, she now believed, due to his illness, the slow, steady atrophy of his central nervous system. Henry had been essentially a good man, whose 'madness set [her] an insoluble problem'. Above all, Rebecca 'would give anything for things to be right for us again in another life'.[42]

Elizabeth occasionally slept over at the flat and one night she heard Rebecca calling out, 'Ric, Ric', her pet name for Henry, in her sleep. Her memories, it seemed, were filled with regret for what should have been. Ibstone, too, was haunting her and she realized that it 'was more than its ravaged garden and the line of light under Henry's bedroom door'.[43]

Once, on an impulse, when Merlin Holland visited, she asked him to drive her to Ibstone. He duly did, and she peered over the wall at the house that had been so much part of her and

Henry's life. She remained quiet, but then on the journey home she turned to Merlin and said, 'As you get older you learn it isn't people but places that break your heart.'[44]

In the autumn of 1977, Rebecca agreed to a BBC television adaptation of *The Birds Fall Down*. The people involved were charming and she thought the prospect 'might cheer up the winter'. That autumn too came the publication of *Rebecca West: A Celebration*, an anthology of Rebecca's work. The introduction was largely adapted from the anonymous piece in the *Times Literary Supplement* that had celebrated her eighty-first birthday. It was in fact written by Samuel Hynes and he now put his name to the piece. The publishers, Macmillan, gave a lavish launch party and Rebecca commissioned the Japanese couturier Yuki to make her a new dress. Rebecca enjoyed the party but felt that she did not entirely merit the attention. The book was principally a reissue of her earlier work and the critical response was, in fact, mixed, with the *Observer* acknowledging her talent but worrying about her vehement anti-communism, while the *New Yorker* thought the non-fiction work was far more successful than the novels.

Lettie died in February 1978. Rebecca recorded her sister's last words to her in her diary. Lettie had told her that she had always loved her. With her death it seemed Rebecca was finally reconciled to the difficulties that had dogged their relationship since childhood. She had felt bullied by her sister, and patronized, but she was also immensely proud of what she had achieved. At Lettie's funeral, Rebecca broke down weeping for the loss of her last sister, and Elizabeth had to support her to keep her steady as they stood by the open grave. Alison, Rebecca's niece, however, did not see Rebecca's sorrow and was aggrieved at what she thought was Rebecca's indifference, going so far as to think that Rebecca seemed angry – not at Lettie's passing, but at the praise given in her memory.[45]

Lettie's death brought some respite from the hostilities with Anthony, who wrote a short letter of sympathy. Rebecca was briefly hopeful that they, too, might at last be reconciled, but a difficult meeting with him and his family dispelled any optimism she might have harboured.

In the early summer, Rebecca, accompanied by Elizabeth and vast amounts of luggage, set off for Paris, where some of the filming for *The Birds Fall Down* was taking place, to observe. Rebecca relished being back in France, and spent happy hours visiting galleries between the shoots and enjoying long, elaborate lunches in traditional French restaurants.

Although relations with Anthony were poor, Rebecca remained anxious about her granddaughter Caro's health. Caro was pregnant and her mental health was still precarious. In the months leading up to the birth, Rebecca wrote many concerned letters to Kitty, but when Caro and Osei had a baby boy, Barnabas, all seemed well. Rebecca was utterly enchanted by the baby, in contrast to her feelings towards so many of the other children born into the family. He was her 'ravishing creature', with his perfect 'bronzed' colouring, and, most importantly, a truly happy child.[46] [47] Other family members saw how Rebecca doted on this new great-grandchild. Alison noticed that she lit up when she spoke about him, and that doing so seemed to dissipate even the blackest of her moods.[48] But immediately following the birth, Caro sank into a deep depression. She was given electroshock therapy and was monitored by a Scottish midwife whenever she held Barnabas.[49]

After Barnabas' christening, Caro was hospitalized and prescribed the drug Tryptizol.[50] But living in London, rather than at home in Ghana, was proving a financial drain, and as soon as Caro was able, the couple returned there. Heartbreak swiftly followed.

Rebecca found out when she received a letter from Kitty. Kitty wrote that she had received terrible news. While she had been sitting in the garden, enjoying some early sunshine, a police car had driven up. The police told her simply, 'Your grandchild is dead and your daughter in hospital'.[51] The police had come to warn her lest she read the news in the papers. On hearing the terrible news, Rebecca sat up all through the night, comforted by Justin Lowinsky, the son of her dear friend Ruth.

At the inquest in Ghana in March 1979, Barnabas' death was found to be a cot death: 'no identifiable cause of death' to be recorded.[52] Caro was free to return to England for the care that she needed.

Rebecca was heartbroken at the loss of the 'marvellous baby' but also filled with pity for her poor granddaughter, and immediately spoke to her solicitor to arrange some money to be transferred so that Anthony could stay by his daughter's side in Ghana for as long as was necessary. She suggested some names of people who might be able to advise him. Yet rather than herald a breakthrough in their relationship, Rebecca's offer triggered a renewal of active hostility between her and Anthony. Anthony resented what he saw as Rebecca's interference; he was furious that Rebecca seemed to suggest he needed advisors to tell him how to care for his own daughter. Their acrimonious telephone exchange shook Rebecca, who felt she was being vomited on. When she rang off, she ended by saying, 'This is the last time I will ever speak to you.'[53]

The combined shock of the tragedy and the ensuing row with Anthony heralded a real mental and physical decline that was noted both by Rebecca's secretary, Liz, and by her niece, Alison; she never really recovered. Rebecca had taken to Barnabas in a way that she had failed to with her other grandchildren or great-grandchildren. She was haunted by 'the liveliness and intelligence of the baby', the 'extraordinary sound' of his almost 'melodious' crying. He had been so 'beautifully finished in every respect'.[54]

Soon after this, Rebecca was upset still further when a riding accident forced Elizabeth Leyshon to return to her family home and a new secretary, Diana Stainforth, was appointed. Diana's main task was working on 1900, a picture book with reminiscences about the turn of the last century. It required a huge amount of fact-checking and Diana would sit on the floor by the huge horseshoe-shaped desk that Rebecca had brought from Ibstone, and look things up in a vast selection of encyclopaedias. Rebecca herself usually settled in a white plastic armchair with a vivid turquoise cushion, a decorative touch that was completely incongruous with the exquisite furnishings in the rest of the flat.[55]

Rebecca had also been invited to appear as 'a witness to history' in Warren Beatty's film *Reds*. Her friendship with Emma Goldman made her ideally suited, and she appeared alongside Dora Russell, with characteristic spirit. Beatty was caught in her spell and remarked that the longer he interviewed her, the lovelier she became.[56] She enjoyed the filming, although had doubts about Diane Keaton being cast as Louise Bryant, saying she was far too plain to be convincing as Louise, who had been a real beauty.

Shortly afterwards, Rebecca found herself a witness to yet more history. Six armed men stormed the Iranian embassy, which was subsequently under siege for six days. The back of the building was clearly visible from the picture window of Rebecca's flat and she eagerly watched the events unfolding. On the telephone to Alison she sounded as if she was enjoying all the excitement, but later admitted that she had been afraid of what might have happened if a bomb had gone off in a building so close to her own.[57] She subsequently wrote an article for the *Daily Telegraph* about the siege. Her only acknowledged regret was that the evacuation of Kingston House had meant she couldn't watch the end of the drama live. Rebecca had always admired Margaret Thatcher's ability to succeed in a male-dominated profession; the prime minister's handling of the siege seemed further proof of her strength and ability.

On 13 June 1981, Rebecca's most enduring friendship ended with the death of Emanie Arling Philips. Rebecca was far too frail to even contemplate a trip across the Atlantic, so August sent her details of the memorial service and transcripts of the various speeches, some of which bore testimony to the incredible friendship that had existed between them for more than fifty years.

෧෯෯෨

In anticipation of Rebecca's ninetieth birthday on 21 December 1982 she had been commissioned to write a piece for the *Sunday Telegraph*. She was mostly confined to bed and dictated or wrote from there. Her eyesight had deteriorated still further and work on her reviews was painfully slow. The stress of trying to write and to keep track of her work overwhelmed her at times, even on one occasion reducing her to tears, which shocked Diana, who had never seen her cry before.[58] When the birthday article was finally completed, Justin Lowinsky, to whom Rebecca had given power of attorney, and Diana decided that, for a while at least, she should not accept any more commissions. Together with Tessa Munro, the housekeeper,* Diana and Justin worked to ensure that visitors were now restricted to an even smaller group of close friends.

In addition to Mrs Munro, Rebecca was now cared for by a nurse who visited every morning to bathe her. But just weeks before her birthday, she had a bad fall that necessitated hospitalization. She stayed there for three weeks; the doctors were uncertain whether or not she would recover. She rallied and was allowed to return home, where she lived, fading gradually, for three more months. She vacillated in these last weeks between being confused and angry, showing a characteristically lively sense of humour. Diana remembered her joking to her, 'I'm not going to need you for much longer, dear. I'm going to die. Mind

---

* Tessa Munro, a widow and qualified lawyer, was only meant to work for Rebecca for six weeks. In fact she didn't leave, remaining with Rebecca until her death, and took on responsibility far beyond that of her job description, protecting Rebecca in those last years, especially from visiting journalists. Rebecca would boast to interviewers about how unusual it was to have a qualified lawyer, whose late husband had been head of the British Presbyterian congregation in South Africa, working as her housekeeper.

you, I might need a secretary in the afterlife so perhaps you'd better come with me.'[59]

Her nurse, Philippa Thorpe, said that at times they were so busy laughing together it was almost impossible to wash her.

On 15 March at 11.35 a.m. Rebecca died in her sleep, while Philippa, the ever-present Tessa Munro and Diana kept vigil around her bed. Justin and Alison were due to visit her that afternoon. Philippa had dreaded the moment of her death; she had never seen 'such fight in a person', but when it actually happened it was peaceful and serene.[60] Anthony had not visited or spoken to his mother for weeks. Alison had wanted to tell him that his mother was dying but Rebecca had been adamant that she should not. When Alison phoned to tell him his mother had died, he hung up as soon as he heard her voice.

Dame Rebecca West was buried, according to her wishes, at Brookwood Cemetery in Surrey. In the spring, there was a memorial service at St Martin-in-the-Fields in Trafalgar Square. Michael Dennison read from Rebecca's own writing, as well as work by Robert Louis Stevenson, John Donne and D.H. Lawrence. Bernard Levin gave the eulogy, remembering her diverse talents. Her reporting, he said, was 'unequalled in our time, perhaps in any time'; *Black Lamb and Grey Falcon* was 'one of the bare handful of undoubted, and undoubtedly ageless, masterpieces of our century'.[61] That she would be remembered because her work would go on being read, was her greatest legacy.

EPILOGUE

Sadly, her work was not the only reason that Dame Rebecca West would be remembered after her death. Many times over the years, Rebecca had written to friends that she was sure Anthony would find a way to plague her, even after she was dead. It proved to be a prophetic remark. Within a year, Anthony published *H.G. Wells: Aspects of a Life*, a very personal account of his relationship with his father, a book which *Time* magazine referred to as 'a new permutation of *Rashomon*'; *Heritage*, the novel that had haunted Rebecca's later years, was released in Britain for the first time.[1] The introduction to the British edition left absolutely no doubt as to its purpose. It was a book written in revenge against a mother whom Anthony felt was 'minded to do me what hurt she could'.[2]

Rebecca had left behind many papers, a partially completed book on Mexico, countless drafts and revisions of her family memoirs, even an early novel, *The Sentinel*, which only came to light because an astute graduate student found it catalogued under yet another pseudonym, 'Isabel Lancashire'. Rebecca's last secretary, Diana Stainforth, meticulously catalogued and annotated many of the papers. Several books appeared posthumously, painstakingly pieced together from her manuscripts. The novels *This Real Night*, *Cousin Rosamund* and *Sunflower* were all published in the five years immediately following Rebecca's death. *Family Memories* was published in 1987; a collection of short fiction, including *The Only Poet*, in 1992; and *Survivors in Mexico*, a brilliant attempt by the American academic Bernard Schweizer to reconstruct as much as possible of her Mexican epic, in 2004. Her work has been discussed in both academic studies and newspaper articles. She began writing in the nineteenth century, and unpublished work written by her was still appearing in the twenty-first, and still being well-received. When, in 1972, Bernard Levin wrote an article in *The Times* entitled 'Rebecca West: The Light that Never Failed' he could not have foreseen how true his description would be.

Acknowledgements

While writing this book my husband and I managed to live and work in four different countries. Because of this there is rather a long list of people whose support and encouragement, and in some cases professional advice, were fundamental to my ever finishing it.

My agent, Peter Straus of RCW Lit Agency, has been a real protector. In the early stages of the project I was amazed by his continual support and delighted when he found George Morley at Macmillan, who shared the enthusiasm we both had. Rebecca firmly believed that 'great editors are rarer than great writers'; I am lucky enough to have found one.[1] Will Atkins was a meticulous and tactful copy-editor who really did an excellent job of helping to get the book into shape. Thanks too to everyone at Pan Macmillan for producing such a lovely book.

The staff at the Beinecke Rare Book and Manuscript Library, Yale University, and at the Lilly Library, Indiana University, have been unfailingly patient with my requests for copies and scans and information. A particularly large debt of gratitude is owed to Marc Carlson, Head of Special Collections at the University of Tulsa, who was so very helpful to me during my stay in Tulsa and after I returned. Samantha Extance, a very talented graduate student at TU, went out of her way to search for obscure letters and send them to me on the few occasions I asked her. She did this out of the kindness of her heart and refused any payment that I offered. I heartily recommend her as a paid researcher to anyone who might like some long-distance help with the vast and glorious archives in Tulsa. Laura Stevens of the English Department at Tulsa was a fabulous host to me during my visit, arranging lovely accommodation for me on campus and making sure that I could have everything I might need or even just want! An earlier Rebecca West biographer, Carl Rollyson, generously allowed me to use his own collection at Tulsa, which included valuable recorded interviews with people who are no longer with us.

Julian Moore provided me with a copy of the research he had conducted on Rebecca's father, as well-giving me his blessing to include it in this book.

Norman and Marion Macleod made me welcome in their Oxford home and happily let me record them while enjoying old papers, cards and letters from and to Aunt Cissie. Alison Selford made me cups of tea in her room at Highgate's wonderful Mary Ward Centre and told me all the stories she could think of. Alison's daughter Cathy, Rebecca's great-niece, was also kind enough to share her memories and review some chapters of the book.

Liz Leyshon, Rebecca's former secretary, shared not only her correspondence with me, but all of her contacts and, most precious of all, her own diaries from when she worked at Kingston House. Liz also read several draft chapters at various stages and gave me excellent comments and notes. Now that I no longer need to dredge her mind for every passing remembrance, we remain good friends and I am grateful that Rebecca, who had so many great women friends herself, afforded me this pleasure.

Merlin Holland invited me to spend a few days at his home in France and acted as a fabulous host, allowing me access to many private papers, letters and diaries, as well as sharing his memories, both poignant and joyous.

Raymond and Orme Olliver shared their reminiscences of Rebecca and Henry's days at Ibstone. Ariadne Getty generously allowed me access to the grounds of Ibstone and my husband and I enjoyed an educational and lovely walk with the Ibstone gardener, Ian Edwards, and the incomparable Chilli.

As always, old friends played their part. Dr Michael Newton cast a critical eye over various chapters. I'm not sure what I would have done without his advice and his gentle encouragement. Charles Palliser offered his usual kind support. Richard Allen looked after me in Serbia, not only by sharing his home, but by giving me the benefit of his expert knowledge on the region. I am grateful too to Jasminka, now Richard's wife, who eagerly wandered around Serbian bookshops with Richard, after I'd gone, to track down the Gavrilovic volume of letters. Jim Moody had long Rebecca-esque conversations with me during our breaks at Qatar University. Alessia Bianchardia in Ventimiglia kept me cheerful while my oldest friend, Duglas Stewart, and his son Colvin helped out with everything from music to Glasgow libraries. I also benefitted from that most essential of friendships for any writer, an IT specialist! I am truly fortunate to have not one but two dear friends to rely on in this respect, Jim Burns and Chris Burkinshaw. *Un grazie a Dr Pierluigi Conte per tutto il suo aiuto – Vedi? Hai potuto leggere qualcosa dei miei libri anche se scritti in inglese.*

Thanks are also due to the University of Chicago Library Manuscripts Division, Library of Congress, New York Public Library, Pierpont Morgan Library, Glasgow's Mitchell Library, Wellcome Library, Edinburgh University Library, National Library of Scotland, UCL Library, University of Birmingham Library, University of Sussex Library, House of Lords Library, King's College, University of Warwick Library, University of Reading, University of Exeter and the Public Records Office. As always, the British Library staff made it an ideal place to work and do research, and I am again indebted to Marcus Langley White for all his help.

I am grateful to the Society of Authors, who awarded me a grant which made the Tulsa research for this book possible. Qatar University also gave me a very-much-appreciated small-research award, which paid for many of my copies from the United States.

The International Rebecca West Society provided me with an invaluable forum to make many contacts and to enjoy listening to West experts. Thanks are also due to Rebecca's last secretary, Diana Stainforth, Chrystal Brassfield, for horses, hospitality and being such a good friend, Stuart Bannerman and Professor Rainer Schulze at the University of Essex, Dr Siham Alqaradhawi, the late Professor Hassan Altamman, Dr Dawish Al Emadi, Dr Haifa Al Buainain, Dr Moneera Ghadeer, Dr Eiman Mustafawi and Professor Jalal Udin at Qatar University, for their academic support and encouragement.

My late friend, Paul Coombs, was still with us when I first began this project. He immediately started reading West and planning trips to everywhere relevant he could think of. My beloved dad, too, died before this book was finished. As she has always done, my mum supported me, loved me and believed the book would be good in the end. Alan

Wesselson, my husband, has seen me through all the difficulties and sadness, gone for long walks with me in London, Ibstone, Serbia and the Riviera coast, read drafts over and over, commented and corrected and just 'been there'. I owe him another dinner at the Ivy, the restaurant that was the scene of so many of Rebecca's little dramas, to celebrate the publication, and to say thank you for so many things.

Endnotes

Abbreviations

Research Resources

Beinecke: Beinecke Rare Book and Manuscript Library, Yale University Library

BL: British Library

Lilly: Lilly Library, Indiana University

MS: Manuscript

NYPL: New York Public Library

Tulsa: The Rebecca West Papers, Special Collections, McFarlin Library, University of Tulsa

Correspondents

AM: Alison Macleod   AW: Anthony West

CF: Cissie Fairfield   DS: Doris Stevens

DT: Dorothy Thompson   EA: Emanie Arling

EG: Emma Goldman   EH: Evelyn Hutchison

HA: Henry Andrews   JG: John Gunther

KW: Kitty West   LF: Letitia Fairfield

RW: Rebecca West   SM: Sally Melville

VB: Venessa Ball   VH: Vyvyan Holland

VW: Virginia Woolf   WF: Winnie Fiarfield

WM: Winifred Macleod

Prologue

1 'Dame Rebecca West at 80', BBC Radio interview with Anthony Curtiss, 21 December 1972.
2 Marcus, p. 38.
3 Ibid., p. 17.
4 RW to the editor, *Freewoman*, 1 August 1912.
5 RW to A.L. Rowse, 27 February 1961, Tulsa.
6 'Dame Rebecca West at 80', BBC Radio interview with Anthony Curtiss, 21 December 1972.
7 West, Anthony, *Heritage* (Introduction).
8 RW to Emanie Philips, 15 December 1968, Tulsa.
9 Diary, 24 June 1971, Tulsa.
10 Entry in Journal D, 2–51–6, Tulsa.

Chapter One

1 *Family Memories*, p. 197.
2 Radio 4 recording of RW, *Recollections of an Edwardian Childhood*, 1963, BL.
3 See McKay, Thomas (ed.), *A Plea for Liberty* (London: John Murray, 1891), pp. 145–201.
4 *Melbourne Argus*, quoted in Glendinning, p. 18.
5 *Family Memories*, p. 203.
6 Cathy Selford, personal communication, recalling a story told to her by her mother, Alison (Winnie's daughter).
7 'I Regard Marriage with Fear and Horror', *Hearst's International*, November 1925.
8 'My Father', *Sunday Telegraph*, 30 December 1962.
9 'Dame Rebecca West at 80', BBC Radio interview with Anthony Curtiss, 21 December 1972.
10 Ibid.
11 RW to Hugh Walpole, 19 September 1928, and *Family Memories*, p. 207.
12 Ibid.

13 Interview with Alison Selford, 3 October 2010, personal
    communication.
14 I am indebted to the scholarly and methodical research of Julian K.
    Moore. He very generously allowed me free access to his written
    draft and I enjoyed many pleasant and informative discussions about
    Charles Fairfield with him.
15 Moore, 'Damned Precursors': Charles Fairfield is listed on the
    Immigrant Ships Transcribers Guild website: http:
    immigrantships.net/v6/1800v6/baltimoreco18680217.html
16 Ibid.
17 The information on Charles' admission comes from the National
    Archives, PCOM3/333/ No25392. See also Moore (2010).
18 Ibid. Also cited in Moore (2010), p. 18.
19 Will of Arabella Margaret Fairfield, proved 3 July 1875, the
    National Archives, IR26/2892/1031.
20 The Paris Review Interviews: 1, p. 222.
21 Ibid.
22 Interview with Alison Selford; she recollects her mother telling her
    about this 3 October, 2010.
23 RW, notebook 19, Tulsa.
24 Brian Harrison's interview with LF, 17 February 1977, Wellcome
    Foundation, GC/193 A17.
25 Memoirs, 2/51/9, p. 44, Tulsa.
26 Wellcome Foundation, GC 193/A17.
27 The Maharani of Baroda and S. M. Mitra, 'The Position of Women in
    Indian Life', Freewoman, 30 November 1911. See also Marcus, p. 12.
28 The Paris Review Interviews: 1, p. 241.
29 Linda Walker, interview with Letitia Fairfield, 28 March 1976,
    transcript, Tulsa.
30 Memoirs 2/51/9, p. 46, Tulsa
31 To HA, quoted in Rollyson (2005), p. 7. See Yale 29-5-50
32 Family Memories, p. 201.
33 Personal papers, box 38, Beinecke.
34 RW to Norman Macleod, 25 November 1958, private collection.
35 Family Memories, p. 207.
36 Interview with LF, 28 March 1976, Wellcome Foundation, GC/193/
    A17.

37 Glendinning, p. 21.
38 Memoirs, notebook 2/51/7, p. 24, Tulsa.
39 Glendinning, p. 22.
40 Memoirs, notebook 2/51/7, Tulsa.
41 See Memoirs D, 2/51/7, Tulsa.
42 *Family Memories*, pp. 216–217.
43 Ibid.
44 *Family Memories*, pp. 216–217.

Chapter Two

1 Family Strains (notes), 2/52/4, Tulsa.
2 RW to Norman Macleod, 25 November 1958. Private Collection.
3 See RW to EA, undated 1956, Beinecke.
4 Interview with Alison Selford, 2010.
5 RW to Dachine Rainer, undated. Cited in Rollyson (2005), p. 11.
6 Radio 4 recording of RW, *Recollections of an Edwardian Childhood*, 1963, BL.
7 Lang, 2002.
8 CF to LF, 15 September 1907, Lilly.
9 CF to LF, 5 December 1909, Lilly.
10 'Suffragette and Votes for Women', 7 February 1913 Pamphlet, and *Edinburgh Evening Dispatch*, 31 January 1913.
11 CF to Lettie Fairfield, 5 December 1909, Lilly.
12 Ibid.
13 Ibid.
14 *Time and Tide*, 16 July 1926.
15 Marcus, p. 5 (quoting West's article in *Time and Tide*, 1926).
16 See Laing, Kathryn, ed., *The Sentinel: An Incomplete Early Novel by Rebecca West* (Oxford: Legenda, EHRC, University of Oxford, 2002).
17 Ibid., p. xxi.
18 *The Judge* p. 229.
19 Glendinning, p. 32.
20 CF to LF, undated, 1909, Lilly.
21 CF to LF, undated 1909, Lilly.
22 CF to LF, December 1908, Lilly.
23 CF to LF, 18 April (u/d), Indiana University.

24 Rollyson (1995), p. 16.

25 Ibid.

26 Personal papers, box 38, Beinecke.

Chapter Three

1 Fremantle, p. 149.

2 Cole, p. 7.

3 Mackenzie (1979), p. 379.

4 Fremantle, p. 153.

5 Ibid.

6 Interview with LF, 17 February 1977, GC 194/A17, Wellcome Foundation.

7 Interview with LF, 28 March 1976, GC 193/A17, Wellcome Foundation.

8 RW to Jean Overton Fuller, 27 March 1962, Tulsa.

9 Marcus, p. 12, quoting from the *Freewoman*, 30 November 1911.

10 Humphrey Ward in letter to *The Times* quoted in B. Clarke, *Dora Marsden and Early Modernism* (University of Michigan Press, 1996) p. 219.

11 Garner, p. 77.

12 Wells, H.G, *Joan and Peter* (London: Macmillan, 1935).

13 Marcus, p. 6.

14 *Freewoman*, 14 March 1912.

15 Interview with Anthony Curtiss, *Listener*, 15 February 1973, pp. 211–213.

16 *Clarion*, 27 September 1912.

17 *Clarion*, 28 November 1913.

18 *Clarion*, 20 December 1912.

19 *Daily Herald*, 5 September 1912.

20 Marcus, p. 11.

21 Hardwick, p. 60.

22 Hunt, *I Have This To Say*, p. 203.

23 Ibid.

24 Ibid.

25 Ibid.

26 Ibid. p. 205.

Chapter Four

1 West's review of *Marriage* in the *Freewoman*, 19 September 1912.
2 See Sherbourne p. 171.
3 Wells, H.G., *The Book of Catherine Wells* (New York: DoubleDay, Doran and Co., 1928, pp. 26–27.
4 West, *H.G. Wells: Aspects of a Life*, p. 25.
5 Meyer, *H.G. Wells and His Family*, p. 48.
6 Ibid. p. 112.
7 Anthony West, *H.G. Wells in Love*, pp. 94–95.
8 RW to Harold Rubinstein, 2 October 1912, Beinecke. See also Scott, p. 17.
9 RW on Wells, 1CDR 0019053, BL.
10 Ibid.
11 RW to Harold Rubinstein, 2 October 1912, Beinecke. See also Scott, p. 17.
12 RW to Charles Sarolea, 12 October 1912, Glasgow University.
13 Anthony West, *H.G. Wells in Love*, p. 95.
14 Ibid.
15 See Ray, p. 17, and the accompanying footnote.
16 Ibid., p. 93.
17 RW to Wells, March 1913, Beinecke. See also Scott, p. 20.
18 Wells to RW, June 1913, Beinecke. Also quoted in Ray, p. 23.
19 *New Freewoman*, 15 June 1913, pp. 5–7.
20 *New Freewoman*, 1 August 1913, p. 67.
21 *New Freewoman*, 1 July 1913, p. 26.
22 Wells to RW, early July 1913, quoted in Ray, p. 24 (Yale).
23 *New Freewoman*, 1 October 1913. See also Anthony West, *H.G. Wells: Aspects of a Life*, pp. 22–23.
24 Usborne, p. 167.
25 Wells to RW, 14 January 1914, quoted in Ray, p. 35.
26 Quoted in Lidderdale and Nicholson, p. 77.
27 Anthony West, *H.G. Wells in Love*, p. 95.
28 I am grateful to Alison Selford for discussing her mother Winnie's memories of this.
29 Wells, *H.G. Wells In Love*, p. 96.

30 Personal papers, box 38, Beinecke.
31 Usborne, p. 168.
32 Translated in Usborne, p. 168.
33 See David C. Smith, *The Correspondence of H.G. Wells*, vol. 2, p. 363.
34 Ray, p. 47.
35 Wells to RW, late January 1914, Pierpont Morgan Library, quoted in Ray p. 46.
36 Ibid.
37 Anthony West, *H.G. Wells: Aspects of a Life*, p. 25.
38 From 'Women of England', *Atlantic Monthly*, January 1916, quoted in Ray, p. 50.
39 Wells to RW, 23 August 1914, The Morgan Library and Museum, New York.
40 Wells correspondence, vol. 2, p. 367, 14 April 1914.
41 Wells to Robert Ross, 1914. See Ray, p. 51.
42 See also Hammond, p. 85.
43 Anthony West, *H.G. Wells: Aspects of a Life*, p. 27
44 Mackenzie, p. 297.

Chapter Five

1 Jane Wells to Wells, 4 August 1914, Beinecke.
2 Ray, p. 54.
3 See 'Women of England', *Atlantic Monthly*, January 1916.
4 Mrs Townshend to Wells, 18 August 1914, quoted in Ray, p. 58 (Beinecke).
5 RW to Sylvia Lind, autumn 1915. See Scott, p. 24.
6 RW to Violet Hunt, Berg Collection, NYPL, 64B7087.
7 Ibid.
8 Wells to RW, autumn 1914, Tulsa.
9 Ibid. See also Smith, *The Correspondence of H.G. Wells*, vol. 2, p. 372: Wells to Catherine Wells, August 1914.
10 RW to Sally Melville Winfield, undated, RP71613, BL.
11 Ibid.
12 Ray, p. 61.

13　RW to Sylvia Lind, undated, Mugar Memorial Library, Boston University. Quoted in Marcus, pp. 26–27.

14　Ibid.

15　RW to S.K. Ratcliffe, 4 February 1916, quoted in Ray, pp. 68–69 (Beinecke).

16　Lowndes, S. (ed.), *Diaries and Letters of Marie Belloc Lowndes* (London: Chatto & Windus, 1971), p. 217.

17　'The World's Worst Failure', *New Republic* (1916), reprinted in Dickinson, Ellen Key (ed.), *The Woman Question* (New York: Boni and Liverwright, 1918), pp. 213–214.

18　RW to Sylvia Lynd, undated, RP 7613, BL.

19　Quoted in Ray, pp. 79–80.

20　RW to Sylvia Lynd, undated, RP 71613, BL.

21　Ibid.

22　RW to Sally Melville undated, RP2821, BL.

23　Wells to RW quoted in Ray, p. 94, Pierpont Morgan.

24　Anthony West, *H.G. Wells: Aspects of a Life*, p. 59.

25　Diary, 1918, Beinecke.

26　RW to SL, 28 July 1918. Tulsa. See Scott, p. 40.

27　Ibid.

28　See Sherbourne, *H.G. Wells: Another Kind of Life*, p. 258.

29　Ibid, p. 259.

30　Mackenzie (1979), p. 186.

31　RW to SM, late 1920, cited in Marcus, p. 44 (Beinecke).

32　RW to LF, late autumn or winter 1920, Lilly.

33　Wells to RW, late October 1920, cited in Ray, p. 104.

34　Cited in Ray, p. 106.

35　See Hastings, p. 294.

36　'Elegy', *The Essential Rebecca West*, pp. 388–390.

37　'A Letter From Abroad', *Bookman*, May 1930.

38　Ibid.

39　'Elegy', *The Essential Rebecca West*, pp. 388–390.

40　D.H. Lawrence to RW, 7 October 1929, R3186 (ii), BL.

41　RW to Isabella Fairfield, Firenze, April 1921, Lilly.

42　Wells to RW, 17 April 1921, Beinecke. See also Ray, p. 109.

43　Wells to RW, 30 April 1921, Beinecke.

44　Wells to Marie Stopes, Easton Glebe, 16 Aug 1921, Pierpont Morgan.

45 RW to Reginald Turner, 6 October 1921, Beinecke. See also Glendinning, p. 94.
46 Diary entry, January 1922, Beinecke.
47 Ibid., February.
48 Virginia Woolf to Ottoline Morrell, 18 July 1922, quoted in Nicolson and Trautman, vol. 2, p. 76.
49 Somerset Maugham to RW, undated 1922, Tulsa.

Chapter Six

1 Nicolson and Trautman, p. xi.
2 Ibid., p. xiii.
3 Wells to RW, 21 March 1923, Beinecke. See also Ray, p. 130.
4 Biographical note by RW, dated 28 January 1958, Beinecke.
5 Ibid.
6 RW to Winnie Macleod, undated, Lilly.
7 *Westminster Gazette*, 23 June 1923.
8 H.V. Gattenrigg to Catherine Wells, 8 July 1923, from Smith, *The Correspondence of H.G. Wells*, vol. 3, p. 147.
9 Alison Selford, personal communication, 10 February 2010.
10 RW to Sally Melville, undated, but 1923, RP2821, BL.
11 RW to Sally Melville, summer 1923, RP 2821, BL.
12 RW to Winnie Macleod, 24 August 1923, Lilly.
13 RW to Winnie Macleod, 2 November 1923, Lilly.
14 Ibid.
15 Memoirs, notebook, 1970, Tulsa.
16 EA to RW, 1924, Tulsa. Also quoted in Glendinning, p. 96.
17 RW to GR, Pierpont Morgan, undated. Cited in Ray, p. 156 and Rollyson (1995), p. 76.
18 Zelda to Scott Fitzgerald, September 1930, Fitzgerald and Fitzgerald, p. 68.

Chapter Seven

1 RW to LF, 7 March 1924, Lilly.
2 Ibid.

3 Ibid.
4 Anthony West, 'Life With Aunty Panther and H.G. Wells', *Observer*, 4 January 1976.
5 Ibid.
6 Ibid.
7 Wells to RW, 4 June 1924. See Ray, p. 158.
8 Wells to RW, 28 June 1924. See Ray, p. 158.
9 RW to Fannie Hurst, 12 June 1924, University of Texas. See also Scott, p. 74.
10 Ibid.
11 Ibid.
12 Wells to RW, 3 August 1924, Pierpont Morgan Library. Also cited in Ray, p. 159.
13 RW to EG, 2 October 1924, Emma Goldman Collection, International Institute of Social History, Amsterdam.
14 Goldman, p. xi.
15 EG to Stella Ballantyne, 25 October 1924, International Institute of Social History, Amsterdam.
16 RW to WF, 17 November 1924, Lilly.
17 RW to Lord Beaverbrook, autumn 1924, cited in Scott, p. 78.
18 Goldman, p. ix.
19 Quoted in Newton, p. 327.
20 Goldman, p. v.
21 Ibid., p. vi.
22 RW, 'Foreword', in Causton B. and Young, G.G., *Keeping It Dark or The Censor's Handbook* (London: Mandrake Press, 1930), p. 7.
23 RW to WF, 17 November 1924, Lilly.
24 Goldman, p. v.
25 EG to Wells, 1 December 1924, Institute of Social History, Amsterdam.
26 Glendinning, p. 100.
27 RW to Harold Ross, 25 August 1947, Berg Collection, NYPL.
28 'Autobiography' box, 19 December 1924, John Gunther Collection, Chicago University.
29 Ibid.
30 Ibid., 21 December 1924.
31 Ibid., 11 March 1925.
32 Ibid.

33 John Guntner to RW, 18 August 1961, Tulsa.

34 RW to WF, 17 November 1924, Lilly.

35 Anthony West, 'Life With Aunty Panther and H.G. Wells', *Observer*, 4 January 1976.

36 Cited in Ray, p. 168.

37 RW to VH, 17 August 1925, private collection.

38 Scott, p. 84.

39 Ibid.

40 Ibid.

41 Scott, p. 85.

42 Sherbourne, p. 275.

43 Ibid., p. 276.

44 Ibid.

45 RW to JG, December 1926. Cited in Scott p. 88.

46 Ibid.

47 Ibid., p. 89.

48 Notes for *Sunflower*, 2/62/1, Tulsa.

49 *Sunflower*, p. 145.

50 RW to LF, 1927, undated, Lilly.

51 *The Strange Necessity*. Also cited in Glendinning, p. 113.

52 RW to EA, 4 May 1962, Beinecke.

53 Ibid.

54 Anthony West, H.G. *Wells: Aspects of a Life*, p. 118.

55 Sherbourne, p. 279.

56 Scott, p. 97.

57 RW to Wells, 1927, Beinecke. Also cited in Scott, p. 100.

58 Ray, p. 171.

59 Parental memoirs, MS 2/51/6, p. 62, Tulsa.

60 Ray, p. 172.

61 Conrad Aitken, the *Bookman*, August 1929.

62 Wells to RW, 2 May 1928, cited in Ray p. 173 (Pierpont Morgan Library).

63 Anthony West, H.G. *Wells: Aspects of a Life*, p. 351.

64 For a fuller account of Anthony's view of events see H.G. *Wells: Aspects of a Life*, p. 146.

65 *The Strange Necessity*, p. 199.

66 Ibid.

67 Ibid., p. 200.

68 Ibid., p. 204.
69 Wells to RW, July 1928. Cited in Ray, p. 177 (Pierpont Morgan Library).
70 RW to WF, 23 August 1928, Lilly.
71 RW to Fannie Hurst, 27 August 1928. Cited in Scott, p. 104.
72 RW to WM, 23 August 1928, Lilly.
73 RW to Mr Medley, 11 December 1928, Tulsa.
74 RW to LF, 1928, undated, Lilly.
75 *War Nurse*, p. 92.
76 RW to LF, 1928, undated, Lilly.
77 RW to WM, January 1929. Cited in Scott, p. 110 (Indiana University, Bloomington).
78 RW to Sylvia Lynd, 31 August 1929. Cited in Scott, p. 112 (BL).
79 Ray, p. 180.
80 RW to LF, 11.9.29 (postmark), Lilly.
81 AW to Victoria Glendinning, 1984. See Glendinning, p. 125.
82 Nicolson and Trautman, vol. iv. Quoted in Rollyson (1995), p. 111.
83 RW to A.D. Peters, 1929. Cited in Scott, p. 113 (Tulsa).
84 RW to Bertrand Russell, September 1929. Cited in Scott, p. 115 (Beinecke).
85 See Scott, p. 118.
86 *Selected Letters of Winifred Holtby and Vera Brittain*, p. 177.
87 Memoirs, unnumbered notebook, 1973, Tulsa.
88 RW to Mr Andrews, 15 November 1929, Beinecke.
89 Gourevitch, *Paris Review Interviews I*, p. 247.
90 *Chronicle of Friendship*, p. 68.
91 Ibid.
92 Scott. p. 123.
93 See Glendinning, p. 135.
94 *Family Memories*, p. 231.
95 *Family Memories*, p. 237.
96 Sladen, *In Ruhleben*, p. 169.
97 Quoted in Rollyson (1995), p. 119.
98 Memoirs, notebook D, p. 9, Tulsa.
99 Ibid., p. 10.
100 RW to HA, January 1930 (postmark), Beinecke.
101 Ibid.
102 www.editions-fayard.fr/Site/fayard/fayardinfos/fayard-historique.jsp

103 RW to WM, 29 March 1930, Beinecke.

104 Reprinted in *The Essential Rebecca West*, p. 387.

105 RW to HA, 30 May (postmark) 1930, Beinecke.

106 HA to RW, 13 August 1930, Beinecke.

107 EA to RW, 12 August 1930, Beinecke.

108 Telegraph, RW to LF, 2 November 1930, Lilly.

109 *Family Memories*, p. 223.

Chapter Eight

1 RW to WM, undated, Lilly.

2 See Rollyson (1995), p. 123.

3 RW to WM, undated, Lilly.

4 RW to HA, Monday 1931, Lilly.

5 See Rebecca West, *Arnold Bennett Himself* (Norwood Editions, 1978), p. 6.

6 Ibid., p. 13.

7 Ibid., p. 21.

8 HA to RW, 2 July 1931. Quoted in Glendinning, p. 137 (Tulsa).

9 RW to WM, undated (circa 1931), Lilly.

10 Ibid.

11 See Rollyson (1995), p. 124.

12 Biographical note, box 38, folder 1402, Beinecke.

13 Anthony West, *H.G. Wells: Aspects of a Life*, p. 108.

14 Biographical note, box 38, folder 1402, Beinecke.

15 RW to HA, undated, 1931, Beinecke.

16 Ibid.

17 Ibid.

18 Ibid.

19 Postcard, RW to HA, undated, 1931.

20 *St Augustine*, p. 161.

21 *St Augustine*, p. 160.

22 Postcard, private collection, RW to HA, 1931.

23 Glendinning, p. 140.

24 Memoirs, MS 2/51/6, p. 69, Tulsa.

25 *Daily Telegraph*, 24 June 1932.

26 Nin, *Incest*, p. 323.

27 Ibid., p. 326.

28 Nin, *Fire*, p. 132.

29 *The Diary of Virginia Woolf*, vol. 4, 27 June 1935, p. 326.

30 Ibid., 10 July 1933, p. 167.

31 VW to VB, 25 May 1928, in *The Letters of Virginia Woolf*, vol. 3.

32 *The Diary of Virginia Woolf*, vol. 4, 27 June 1935, p. 326.

33 Ibid.

34 RW to HA.

35 Biographical note, box 38, folder 1402, Beinecke.

36 RW to HA, 28 March 1935, Beinecke.

37 Ibid.

38 Ibid.

39 Nin, *Fire*, p. 89. Journal entry for 14 May 1935.

40 Ibid., p. 119. Journal entry for 29 July 1935.

41 Ibid., pp. 131–133. Journal entry for 12 August 1935.

42 RW to DS, 1936, undated, Beinecke.

43 Memoir draft, series 2, box S1, folder 4, Tulsa.

44 RW to Stanislav Vinaver, 14 December 1936, Tulsa.

45 RW to HA, May 1936, Beinecke. Also in Scott, pp. 146–153.

46 RW to HA, May 1936. Quoted in Scott, p. 152.

47 RW to HA, May 1936. Quoted in Scott, p. 151.

48 RW to Doris Stevens, September 1936, Beinecke.

49 Ibid.

50 RW to EA, undated, 1937, Beinecke.

51 RW to WM, undated,1936, Lilly.

52 Autobiographical note, box 38, folder 1402, Beinecke.

53 RW to EA, 8 December 1936, Beinecke.

54 RW to EA, 30 June 1937, Benecke.

55 Ibid.

56 RW to WF, undated, 1938, Lilly.

57 See Glenny, *The Balkans 1804–1999: Nationalism, War and the Great Powers*, p. 442.

58 See Glendinning, p. 152.

59 RW in *Spain and Us* (London: Holborn and West Central London Committee for Spanish Medical Aid, 1936).

60 See also Scott, p. 164.

61 RW to SV, 14 December 1936.

62 In *That Woman*, Wallis' biographer, Anne Sebba, cites many letters,

only now made public, which show Wallis' deep and lasting love for her husband.

63 *Black Lamb and Grey Falcon*, p. 23.
64 Ibid., p. 1089.
65 Ibid., p. 1126.
66 Ibid., p. 1074.
67 'Last Months in Al Hamra', *Spectator*, 24 January 1987.
68 Now in the Beinecke.
69 RW to EA, 1938, Beinecke.
70 Ibid.
71 *Black Lamb and Grey Falcon*, p. 914.
72 Ibid., p. 915.
73 Ibid., p. 912.
74 Ibid., p. 911.
75 RW to EA, 4 May 1962, Beinecke.
76 Series of cards dated 1938 sent from Belgrade, Beinecke.

Chapter Nine

1   *Nash's* magazine, 25 June 1936, quoted in Glendinning, p. 152.
2   RW to Ben Haubsch, 22 December 1938, Library of Congress.
3   RW to WM, 6 July 1939, Lilly.
4   Ibid. and interviews with Alison Selford, 2010 and 2011.
5   RW to Mary Andrews, 21 October 1939, Beinecke.
6   RW to EA, 20 July 1944. Beinecke.
7   RW to Irita van Doren, December 1940, Library of Congress. See Scott, p. 168.
8   Ibid.
9   RW to G.B. Stern, undated, Tulsa.
10 *New Yorker*, 8 December 1940.
11 Memoirs, D 2/51/7, Tulsa.
12 RW, 'A Reporter At Large: Housewives' Nightmare', *New Yorker*, 14 December 1940.
13 RW to Mary Andrews, 10 February 1940, Beinecke.
14 RW to EA, 29 February 1940, Beinecke.
15 Ibid.
16 Ibid.

17 Diana Stainforth, personal communication at the International Rebecca West Society Conference, 2009. See also Rollyson (1995), p. 371.

18 RW to EA, 2 August 1940, Beinecke.

19 RW to EA, undated, but can be dated as April 1941 by the mention of the fall of Salonica, Beinecke.

20 Ibid.

21 Ibid.

22 Ibid.

23 Quoted in Glenny, *The Balkans 1804–1999: Nationalism, War and the Great Powers*, p. 475.

24 *Black Lamb and Grey Falcon*, p. 1149.

25 Ibid.

26 Ibid., p. 1145.

27 In a letter to Alexander Woolcott (April 1941), she writes 'the best part of the book is the last part'. See Scott, p. 169.

28 See Rollyson, p. 176.

29 Clifton Fadiman reviewed *Black Lamb and Grey Falcon* for the *New Yorker* on 25 October 1941.

30 See Blythe, *Private Words* (1993), p. 32.

31 RW to EA, December 1941, Beinecke.

32 Ibid.

33 Ibid

34 Ibid.

35 RW to MA, undated, but datable to 1943, Beinecke.

36 Ibid.

37 Gavrilovic, p. 16.

38 For a much more detailed history of the Balkans in this period see Glenny, *The Balkans 1804–1999: Nationalism, War and the Great Powers*, pp. 485–495. I am also indebted to my dear friend and Balkans expert, Richard Allen, for his patient, explanatory emails and conversations.

39 See Glenny, *The Balkans 1804–1999: Nationalism, War and the Great Powers*, p. 488.

40 Ibid., p. 489.

41 Alison Selford, personal communication, 10 February 2010.

42 RW to EA, 16 June 1945, Beinecke.

43 RW to EA, 6 January 1944, Beinecke.

44 Diary entry, June 1944, Tulsa.

45 RW to EA, 29 May 1944, Beinecke.

46 RW to DS, 10 February 1945, Beinecke.

47 RW to Marjorie Wells, 11 July 1944, Tulsa.

48 RW to EA, 29 May 1944, Beinecke.

49 RW to EA, 20 July 1944, Beinecke.

50 RW to WM, 22 September 1944, Lilly.

51 RW to EA, 29 May 1944, Beinecke.

52 RW to EA, 20 July 1944, Beinecke.

53 RW to EA, 20 July 1944, Beinecke.

54 Ibid.

55 RW to Marjorie Wells, 11 July 1944, Tulsa.

56 RW to EA, 20 July 1944, Beinecke.

57 RW to AM, 22 September 1944, Lilly.

58 RW to Doris Stevens, 10 February 1945, Beinecke.

59 RW to AM, 15 December 1944, Lilly.

60 RW to EA, 6 June 1945, Beinecke.

61 RW to DS, 10 February 1945, Beinecke.

Chapter Ten

1 RW to EA, 16 September 1945, Beinecke.

2 Ibid.

3 RW to MA, undated, but can be dated to 1946 because RW mentions the appeal, which was in January of that year, Beinecke.

4 RW to EA, 25 September 1945, Beinecke.

5 Ibid.

6 'The Crown Versus William Joyce', *New Yorker*, 29 September 1945.

7 RW to Max Beaverbrook, 4 December 1947. See Scott, p. 219.

8 RW to EA, 25 September 1945, Beinecke.

9 RW to EA, 14 Jauary 1946, Beinecke.

10 Ibid.

11 Ibid.

12 Ibid.

13 Elma Dangerfield *Beyond the Urals* (Thomas Lyster, 1946), p. 10.

14 RW to EA, 13 August 1946, Beinecke.

15 Ibid.
16 'Dame Rebecca West at 80', BBC Radio interview with Anthony Curtiss, 21 December 1972.
17 Ibid.
18 Much of the information contained in the description of Wells' last days is taken from two sources: Michael Sherbourne's excellent biography of Wells, H.G. *Wells: Another Kind of Life*, and also from Anthony West's *H.G. Wells: Aspects of a Life*.
19 RW to EA, 13 August 1946, Beinecke.
20 RW to DS, 26 October 1947, Beinecke.
21 RW to Monica Sterling, 1946, Tulsa.
22 Francis Biddle to RW, 1946, Beinecke.
23 *A Train of Powder*, p. 66.
24 RW to Winnie Macleod, 3 May 1950, Lilly.
25 RW to EA, 1946, Beinecke.
26 Ibid.
27 RW to EA, 18 August 1946, Beinecke.
28 RW to EA, undated, Beinecke.
29 *A Train of Powder*, pp. 5–6.
30 'Dame Rebecca West at 80', BBC Radio interview with Anthony Curtiss, 21 December 1972.
31 RW to Henry Andrews, 21 April 1947, Beinecke.
32 RW to Henry Adams, undated, Beinecke.
33 Ibid.
34 RW, *A Train of Powder*, p. 123.
35 *Evening Standard*, 29 September 1947.
36 Ibid.
37 RW to EA, 9 October 1947, Beinecke.
38 RW to EA, 11 December 1947, Beinecke.
39 RW to Dorothy Thompson, 26 November 1947, Syracuse University.
40 'Circles of Perdition', *Time*, 8 December 1947.
41 RW to DS, 29 August 1948, Beinecke.
42 DS to RW, 10 September 1948, Beinecke.
43 See Rollyson, 'Rebecca West and the FBI', in *Rebecca West and the God that Failed*, p. 68.
44 RW to Hodges, 30 July 1949, Rollyson Archive, 4/11, Tulsa.
45 Ibid.

46 Ibid.

47 RW to Anne Charles, 28–29 May 1949. Cited in Scott, pp. 234–237.

48 Letter Anthony West to Henry Andrews, undated, Beinecke.

49 Copy of the letter Anthony sent to Henry enclosed with RW to EA 19 September 1949, Beinecke.

50 RW to EA, 19 September 1949, Beinecke.

51 RW to AW, 16 September 1949. Cited in Scott, pp. 239–242.

52 EA to RW, 23 October 1949, Beinecke.

53 RW to Winnie Macleod, 30 November 1949, Lilly.

54 Ibid.

55 RW to EA, 31 January 1950, Beinecke.

56 Marjorie Wells to Kitty West, 10 February 1950, Tulsa.

57 RW to EA, 6 March 1950, Beinecke.

58 AW to Kitty West, 24 September 1950, Tulsa.

59 RW to EA, 25 May 1951, Beinecke.

60 RW to EA, 8 December 1951, Beinecke.

61 Ibid.

Chapter Eleven

1   RW to Anne McBurney, 17 February 1952. See Scott, pp. 252–253.

2   RW to EA, 11 March 1952, Beinecke.

3   RW to WM, 8 May 1952, Lilly.

4   RW to EA, 14 September 1952, Beinecke.

5   RW to Evelyn and Margaret Hutchison, 25 September 1962, Beinecke.

6   RW to Doris Stevens, 17 January 1953, Beinecke.

7   The film was eventually made as *Journey in Italy*.

8   RW to Doris Stevens, 17 January 1953, Beinecke.

9   Ibid.

10 See Rollyson, 'Rebecca West and the FBI', in *Rebecca West and the God that Failed*, p. 70.

11 RW to Ingrid Bergman, 10 March 1953. See Scott, p. 268.

12 'The Terrified Teacher', *Sunday Times*, 5 March 1953.

13 Ibid.

14 RW to EA, 16 June 1953, Beinecke.

15 RW to Arthur Schlesinger Jr, 7 June 1953. See Scott, pp. 270–275.

16 RW to EA, 16 June 1953, Beinecke.

17 Ibid.

18 RW to EA, 17 October 1953, Beinecke.

19 RW to EA, 29 December 1953, Beinecke.

20 RW to John Van Druten, 31 December 1954, private collection. Courtesy of Merlin Holland.

21 VH to his solicitor, 19 October 1954, private collection. Courtesy of Merlin Holland.

22 VH to RW, 23 May 1955, courtesy of Merlin Holland.

23 RW to EA, 29 October 1955, Beinecke.

24 Ibid.

25 RW to EA, 15 November 1955, Beinecke.

26 Ibid.

27 RW to EA, undated, 1955, Beinecke.

28 RW to DS, 31 October 1955, Beinecke.

29 RW to LF, 11 October 1955, Lilly.

30 *New York Times*, 2 October 1955.

31 VH to RW, 20 January 1956, courtesy of Merlin Holland.

32 Ibid.

33 AW to RW, mentioned in Scott, p. 306.

34 RW to EA, 13 March 1956, Beinecke.

35 RW to LF, 6 May 1956, Lilly.

36 RW to EA, undated, 1956, Beinecke.

37 RW to DS, 22 June 1956, Beinecke.

38 RW to Harold Guinzberg, November 1956, Viking Press Archive. See Scott, p. 317.

39 RW to EA, undated, 1956, Beinecke.

40 RW to LF, 1957, Lilly.

41 RW to EA, 3 July 1958, Beinecke.

42 RW to EA, undated, 1957, Beinecke.

43 See RW to EA, 1958, 'You're probably right . . .', Beinecke.

44 RW to DS, 21 January 1958, Beinecke.

45 Autobiographical note, 28 January 1958, Beinecke.

46 Ibid.

47 Ibid.

48 Ibid.

49 Ibid.

50 RW to DS, 28 August 1958, Beinecke.

51 RW to DS, 23 June 1958, Beinecke.

52 Discussed in RW to DS, 28 March 1958, Beinecke.

53 RW to DS, undated but marked recd., 12 March 1958, Beinecke.

54 See Rollyson, 'Rebecca West and the FBI', in *Rebecca West and the God that Failed.*

55 RW to Margaret Hutchison, 14 February 1959. See Scott, p. 341.

56 RW to EA, undated, 'You often have showed . . .', Beinecke.

57 RW to HA, 30 January 1960. See Scott p. 351 (Beinecke).

58 RW to Lulu Friedman, 21 February 1960, Tulsa.

59 RW to VH, 7 May 1960, private collection. Courtesy of Merlin Holland.

60 'In the Cauldron of South Africa', *Sunday Times*, 24 April 1960.

Chapter Twelve

1 RW to Norman Macleod, 18 October 1977, private collection.

2 RW to EA, 9 June 1960, Beinecke.

3 RW to VH, 25 June 1960, private collection. Courtesy of Merlin Holland.

4 RW to VH, 30 June 1960, private collection. Courtesy of Merlin Holland.

5 RW to JG, 12 July 1961, Tulsa.

6 *Sunflower*, p. 248.

7 RW to Evelyn and Margaret Hutchison, 28 January 1962, Beinecke.

8 RW to EA, 4 April 1962, Beinecke.

9 RW to EA, 17 March 1963, Beinecke.

10 RW to EA, 10 July 1962, Beinecke.

11 2/S1/4, typed MS, Tulsa.

12 RW to EA, 8 July 1963, Beinecke.

13 RW to EA, November 1963, Beinecke.

14 RW to EA, 28 December 1963, Beinecke.

15 RW to EA, 2 February 1964, Beinecke.

16 RW to Norman Macleod, 13 November 1964, Beinecke.

17 RW to EA, 6 February 1964, Beinecke.

18 RW to EA, 28 March 1964, Beinecke.
19 *The Archers* is the world's longest running radio drama and is still broadcast on BBC Radio 4.
20 RW to EA, 16 July 1964, Beinecke.
21 These were compiled and published posthumously in 2003. See West, Rebecca, *Survivors in Mexico* (Yale University Press, 2003).
22 RW to LF, 31 July 1965, Lilly.
23 RW to LF, 24 September 1966, Lilly.
24 From a note by RW, in series 2, box 50, folder 4, Tulsa.
25 RW to EA, 24 July 1968, Beinecke.
26 EA to RW, undated, Beinecke.
27 Memoirs D 2/51/7, p. 14, Tulsa.
28 Memoirs D 2/51/7, p. 12, Tulsa.
29 2/45/19, notebook, Tulsa.
30 RW to EA, 1 January 1969, Beinecke.
31 Memoirs D 2/51/7m, p. 17, Tulsa.
32 MH to RW, 8 November 1968, Tulsa.
33 AW to RW, undated, Tulsa.
34 RW to EA, 1 January 1969, Tulsa.
35 RW to EA, 15 December 1968, Tulsa.

Chapter Thirteen

1 RW to Lovat Dickson, 26 January 1969. See Scott, pp. 419–420.
2 RW to AW, 31 May 1969. See Scott, pp. 422–423.
3 Agnes George de Mille to RW, 16 June 1970, Tulsa.
4 RW to EA, 10 October 1969, Tulsa.
5 Ibid.
6 Ibid.
7 RW to EA, 2 December 1969, Tulsa.
8 RW to Vita and Edmund West, 14 December, undated, Tulsa.
9 RW to EA, March 1970, Tulsa.
10 Diary entry, 14 July 1971, Tulsa.
11 RW to EA, 15 January 1971, Tulsa.
12 Diary entry, 21 January, 1971, Tulsa.
13 Notes on Lebanon, Tulsa.
14 Diary entry, 7 April 1971.

15 Dairy entry, 22 June 1953, Tulsa.

16 RW to EA, 7 October 1953, Tulsa.

17 Ibid.

18 Ibid

19 RW to EA, 22 April 1972.Tulsa

20 RW to Gip Wells, 16 May 1973, Tulsa.

21 RW to EA, 22 February 1973, Tulsa.

22 RW to EA, 18 April 1973, Tulsa.

23 RW to Gip Wells, 21 May 1973, Tulsa.

24 *Times Literary Supplement*, 21 December 1973.

25 See Ray, pp. xi–xii.

26 West, Anthony, 'The Mystery of My Birth', *Harper's Magazine*, January 1975.

27 Ibid.

28 RW to the Editor, *Harper's Magazine*, 11 January 1975. See Scott, p. 447.

29 EA to RW, 16 February 1974, Beinecke.

30 RW to EA, 11 February 1975, Tulsa.

31 RW to Emily Hahn, 11 February 1975, Tulsa.

32 *The Paris Review Interviews: 1*, p. 256.

33 RW to Gordon Ray, 24 February 1977, Gordon Ray Collection, Pierpont Morgan Library. See also Rollyson (1995), p. 350.

34 Gip Wells to RW, 17 February 1976, Tulsa.

35 Ibid.

36 Much of the material from the period between 1976 and 1979 comes from my conversations with Elizabeth Leyshon about her memories of working for Rebecca. She also very kindly gave me access to the diaries she kept in those years. Some of Elizabeth's recollections have been published in *Women's History Review* (2011) as 'Dame Rebecca West and the Sliding Boundary'.

37 Elizabeth Leyshon, personal communication, 4 March 2011.

38 Elizabeth Leyshon's diary entry, 9 September 1976.

39 RW to EA, 21 May 1975, Tulsa.

40 See Leyshon, 'Rebecca West and the Sliding Boundaries'.

41 RW to Tony Redd, December 1976. See Scott, p. 459.

42 All quotes taken from note dated 3 January 1977, Tulsa (catalogued with Emanie letters).

43 Memoir D 2/51/7, Tulsa.

44 Merlin Holland, personal communication.
45 Alison Selford, personal communication.
46 RW to Kitty West, 15 November 1978, Tulsa.
47 Liz Leyshon, personal communication.
48 Alison Selford, personal communication.
49 Caro West to RW, 28 October 1978, Tulsa.
50 Kitty West to RW, 20 Nov 1978, Tulsa.
51 Undated letter from Kitty West to RW, 1/58/2, Tulsa.
52 Journal entry, 17 March 1979, Tulsa.
53 RW to KW, 22 March 1979, Tulsa.
54 RW to Norman Macleod, 16 August 1977, private collection.
55 'Memories of Working for Rebecca West', 22 February 1987, Rollyson Archive, Tulsa.
56 *Reds*, 1981. Film directed by Warren Beaty special features, DVD 2: 'The Testimonials'.
57 Alison Selford, personal communication.
58 Much of the material in this section comes from 'For Victoria Glendinning: Dame Rebecca: The Last Six Months', a manuscript by Diana Stainforth kept in Tulsa (Rollyson Archive).
59 Ibid. and Diana Stainforth, personal communication.
60 Philippa Thorp to S. and I. Barclay, 26 March 1983, Rollyson Archive, Tulsa.
61 'The Memorial Service for Dame Rebecca West – 21 April 1983', document, Tulsa.

Epilogue

1 *Time*, 14 May 1984.
2 See Introduction, Anthony West, *H.G. Wells: Aspects of a Life*.

Acknowledgements

1 'Dame Rebecca West at 80', BBC Radio interview with Anthony Curtiss, 21 December 1972.

Select Bibliography

Baird, Nancy Disher, 'Rebel with a Cause: Emanie Nahm Sachs Arling Philips', in *Library Presentations, Lectures, Research Guides Paper 4* (Kentucky: Western Kentucky University, 2008).

Barker, Ernest (ed.), *The Character of England* (Oxford: Clarendon Press, 1947).

Blythe, Ronald (ed), *Private Words:Letters and Diaries from the Second World War* (London: Viking, 1991).

Brittain, Vera, *Selected Letters of Winifred Holtby and Vera Brittain* (Pittsburg: Caliban Books, 1970).

———— *Testament of Youth* (London: Virago, 1978).

———— *Chronicle of Friendship* (London: Gollancz, 1986).

Brome, Vincent, *H.G. Wells: A Biography* (London: Longmans, Green and Co., 1951).

Chamberlain, Lesley, 'Rebecca West in Yugoslavia', *Contemporary Review* 248 (1986), 262–266.

Clark, Victoria, *Why Angels Fall: A Journey through Orthodox Europe from Byzantium to Kosovo* (London: Macmillan, 2000).

Cole, Margaret (ed.), *Beatrice Webb's Diaries 1912–1924* (London: Longmans, 1952).

Conklin, Groff, *The New Republic Anthology* (New York: Dodge Publishing Company, 1936).

Deakin, Motley F., *Rebecca West* (Boston: Twayne, 1980).

Drabble, Margaret, *Arnold Bennett: A Biography* (New York: Knopf, 1974).

Fitzgerald, Scott and Fitzgerald, Zelda, *Dearest Scott, Dearest Zelda: The Love Letters of F.Scott and Zelda Fitzgerald* (London: Bloomsbury, 2003).

Ford, Ford Madox, *The Good Soldier* (Oxford: Oxford World Classics, 1999).

Fremantle, Anne, *This Little Band of Prophets* (London: George Allen and Unwin, 1960).

Garner, Les, *A Brave and Beautiful Spirit: Dora Marsden* (Aldershot: Avebury, 1990).

Gavrilovic, Kosara, *Rebecca West and the Gavs* (Belgrade: 500 copies printed by Solaris Kragujevac, 2008).

Glendinning, Victoria, *Rebecca West* (London: Weidenfeld & Nicolson, 1987).

Glenny, Misha, *The Balkans 1804–1999: Nationalism, War and the Great Powers* (London: Granta, 2000).

―――― *The Fall of Yugoslavia* (Harmondsworth: Penguin, 1996).

Goldman, Emma, *My Disillusionment in Russia* (London: the C.W. Daniel Company, 1925).

Goldring, Douglas, *South Lodge* (London: Constable, 1943).

Gourevitch, Philip (ed.), *The Paris Review Interviews: 1* (Edinburgh: Canongate, 2007).

Graves, Robert and Hodge, Alan, *The Long Weekend: A Social History of Britain 1918–1939* (London: Hutchinson and Co., 1985).

Hammond, J.R., *H.G. Wells and Rebecca West* (Hemel Hempstead: Harvester Wheatsheaf, 1991).

Hardwick, Joan, *The Immodest Violet* (London: Andre Deutsch, 1990).

Hastings, Selina, *The Secret Lives of Somerset Maugham* (London: John Murray, 2009).

Hayman, Ronald, 'Rebecca West', in *Books and Bookman* (March 1982).

Hertog, Susan, *Dangerous Ambition* (New York: Ballantyne, 2011).

Hunt, Violet, *Sooner or Later* (London: Chapman and Hall, 1904).

―――― *The Flurried Years* (London: Hurst and Blackett, 1922).

―――― *I Have This To Say* (New York: Boni and Liveright, 1926).

Hutchinson, G. Evelyn, *A Preliminary List of the Writings of Rebecca West 1912–1951* (New Haven: Yale, 1957).

Judd, Alan, *Ford Madox Ford* (Cambridge: Harvard University Press, 1991).

Kennard, Jean E., *Vera Brittain and Winifred Holtby* (Hanover: University Press of New England, 1989).

Knightley, Philip and Kennedy, Caroline, *An Affair of State* (London: Jonathan Cape, 1987).

Kyvig, David E., *Daily Life in the United States 1920–1940* (Chicago: Ivan R. Dee, 2002).

Leneman, Leah, *A Guid Cause: The Women's Suffrage Movement in Scotland* (Aberdeen: Aberdeen University Press, 1995).

Levin, Bernard, 'Rebecca West: The Light that Never Failed', *The Times*, 21 December 1972.

Leyshon, Elizabeth, 'Rebecca West and the Sliding Boundaries', in *Women's History Review* 20:3 (2011).

Lewis, C.S., *That Hideous Strength* (Basingstoke: Pan Macmillan, 1971).

Lidderdale, Jane and Nicholson, Mary, *Dear Miss Weaver* (London: Faber and Faber, 1970).

Low and Lynx, *Lions and Lambs* (London: Jonathan Cape, 1928).

Lucas, C.P., *History of South Africa to the Jameson Raid* (London: Clarendon Press).

Mackenzie, Jeanne, *A Victorian Courtship* (London: Weidenfeld & Nicolson, 1979).

Mackenzie, Norman and Mackenzie, Jeanne, *The Fabians* (New York: Simon and Schuster, 1977).

Marcus, Jane, *The Young Rebecca* (New York: Viking, 1982).

Marsden, Dora, 'The Work of Miss Rebecca West', *The Egoist* (October 1918).

Marwick, Arthur, *The Deluge: British Society and the First World War* (London: Macmillan, 1965).

Meyer, M.M., *H.G. Wells and His Family* (Edinburgh: International Publishing Company, 1955).

Milford, Nancy, *Zelda: A Biography* (New York: Harper and Row, 1970).

Moore, Julian, 'The Damned Precursors: Rebecca West and her Fairfield Inheritance' (unpublished manuscript, 2010).

Newton, Michael, *The Age of Assassins* (London: Faber and Faber, 2012).

Nicolson, Nigel and Trautmann, Joanne (eds.), *The Letters of Virginia Woolf*, 6 vols. (London: Harcourt Brace Jovanovich, 1978).

Nin, Anaïs, *Incest: From A Journal of Love* (London: Peter Owen, 1992).

——— *Fire: From A Journal of Love* (London: Peter Owen, 1996).

Norton, Ann V., *Paradoxical Feminism: The Novels of Rebecca West* (International Scholars Publications, 2000).

Orel, Harold, *The Literary Achievement of Rebecca West* (London: Macmillan, 1986).

Packer, Joan Garrett, *Rebecca West: An Annotated Bibliography* (New York: Garland, 1991).

Penrose, Barrie and Freeman, Simon, *Conspiracy of Silence: The Secret Life of Anthony Blunt* (London: Grafton Books, 1986).

Ray, Gordon N., *H.G. Wells and Rebecca West* (London: Macmillan, 1974).

Rollyson, Carl, *Rebecca West, A Saga of the Century* (London: Sceptre, 1995).

——— *The Literary Legacy of Rebecca West* (San Francsico: International Scholar Publications, 1998).

——— *Rebecca West and the God that Failed* (www.iuniverse.com, e-book, 2005).

Russell, Leonard, *Parody Party* (London: Hutchinson, 1936).

Sachs, Emanie, *The Octangle* (London: Eyre and Spottiswood, 1932).

Saint Augustine, *Confessions* (London: Penguin, 1961).

Scott, Bonnie Kime, *Selected Letters of Rebecca West* (New Haven: Yale University Press, 2000).

Sebba, Anne, *That Woman: The Life of Wallis Simpson, Duchess of Windsor* (London: Weidenfeld and Nicolson, 2011).

Sherbourne, Michael, *H.G. Wells: Another Kind of Life* (London: Peter Owen, 2010).

Sladen, Douglas (ed.), *In Ruhleben* (London: Hurst and Blackett, 1917).

Smith, David C., *H.G. Wells, Desperately Mortal* (New Haven: Yale University Press, 1986).

——— *The Correspondence of H.G. Wells*, vols. 1–4 (London: Pickering and Chatto, 1998).

Stern, G.B., *And did He Stop and Speak to You?* (London: Coram Ltd, 1960).

Tillinghast, Richard, 'Rebecca West and the Tragedy of Yugoslavia', *New Criterion* (June 1992).

Usborne, Karen, *Elizabeth* (London: The Bodley Head, 1986).

Vassall, John, *Vassall: The Autobiography of a Spy* (London: Sidgwick & Jackson, 1975).

West, Anthony, *H.G. Wells in Love* (London: Faber and Faber, 1984).

——— 'Life with Aunty Panther and H.G. Wells', *Observer*, 4 January 1976.

——— 'My Father's Unpaid Debts of Love', *Observer*, 11 January 1976.

——— *Heritage* (London: Coronet Books, 1984).

——— *H.G. Wells: Aspects of a Life* (Harmondsworth: Penguin, 1985).

West, Rebecca, *The Return of the Soldier* (London: Virago, 1918).

——— *The Judge* (New York: George H. Doran, 1922).

——— *War Nurse: The True Story of a Woman Who Lived, Loved and Suffered on the Western Front* (New York: Cosmopolitan Book Corporation, 1930).

——— *Ending in Earnest: A Literary Log* (New York: Doubleday Doran, 1931).

——— *St Augustine* (London: Peter Davies, 1933).

——— 'The Necessity and Grandeur of the International Ideal' by Storm Jameson, in *Challenge to Death* (London: Constable, 1934).

——— *The Harsh Voice* (London: Jonathan Cape, 1935).

——— 'Mind and Materialism', in *The University of Books*, ed. Frank Swinnerton (London: Newnes, 1936).

——— *Black Lamb and Grey Falcon* (London: Macmillan, 1941).

——— *The Meaning of Treason* (London: Macmillan, 1949).

——— *A Train of Powder* (London: Macmillan, 1955).

——— *The Court and the Castle* (London: Macmillan, 1958).

——— *The Meaning of Treason* (revised edn.) (London: Macmillan, 1965).

——— *Harriet Hume* (London: Virago, 1980).

——— *1900* (London: Weidenfeld & Nicolson, 1982).

——— *The Essential Rebecca West* (London: Penguin Books, 1983).

——— *This Real Night* (London: Macmillan, 1984).

——— *The Birds Fall Down* (London: Virago, 1986).

——— *Cousin Rosamund* (London: Macmillan, 1986).

——— *Sunflower* (London: Virago, 1987).

——— *Family Memories* (London: Virago, 1987).

——— *The Only Poet* (London: Virago, 1992).

White, Tony, *Another Fool in the Balkans* (London: Cadogan, 2006).

Wiesenfarth, Joseph, *Ford Madox Ford and the Regiment of Women* (Wisconsin: University of Wisconsin Press, 2005).

Wolfe, Peter, *Rebecca West: Artist and Thinker* (Illinois: Southern Illinois University Press, 1969).

Woolfe, Virginia, *The Diary of Virginia Woolfe*, vols. 3 and 4 (London: The Hogarth Press, 1980).

Index

PICTURE ACKNOWLEDGEMENTS

1, 2, 3, 4, 5, 7, 16, by courtesy of Norman Macleod; 6 © Wellcome Collection; 8, 9, 21, 25, 31 © Getty Images; 10, 11, 12, 18, 19, 27, 32 © The Rebecca West papers, Collection. No. 1986.002, Department of Special Collections and University Archives, McFarlin Library, University of Tulsa, Tulsa, Oklahoma; 14 © Corbis; 15 © Gamma-Keystone via Getty Images; 17 © Popperfoto/Getty Images; 20 © Alamy; 21 © Getty Images, 22,23 © Time & Life Pictures/Getty Images; 24 by courtesy of the author; 26 © Press Association Images; 28 © Royal Academy of Dance/ArenaPAL; 30 © Gamma-Rapho via Getty Images.